The Best *Places*
To Kiss
In New England

Other Books in *THE BEST PLACES TO KISS*...Series

The Best Places To Kiss In The Northwest $12.95

The Best Places To Kiss In Southern California $10.95

The Best Places To Kiss In Northern California $10.95

The Best Places To Kiss In And Around New York City . $10.95

The Best Places To Kiss In Hawaii $12.95

The Best Places To Kiss In New England $13.95

Any of these books can be ordered directly from the publisher.

Please send a check or money order for the total amount of the books, plus $1.50 for shipping and handling per book ordered, to:

Beginning Press
5418 South Brandon
Seattle, Washington 98118

Or call (800) 831-4088 for charge card orders.

The Best Places
To Kiss
In New England

by Pamela P. Hegarty

Beginning Press

Art Direction and Production: Lasergraphics
Cover Design: Patrick Howe
Typography: Lasergraphics
Editor: Miriam Bulmer
Printing: Bookcrafters
Contributors: Shirley Moskow, Valerie Tamis

First Edition: May 1993
1 2 3 4 5 6 7 8 9 10

Best Places To Kiss(tm) is a registered trademark of Beginning Press
ISBN 1-877988-05-7

This book is distributed to the U.S. book trade by:
Publisher's Group West
4065 Hollis Street
Emeryville, California 94608
(800) 788-3123

This book is distributed to the Canadian book trade by:
Raincoast Books
112 East Third Avenue
Vancouver, British Columbia V5T 1C8
Canada
(604) 873-6581

TABLE OF CONTENTS

THE FINE ART OF KISSING

THE BEST KISSING PLACES

Special Acknowledgment

To Avis Begoun, for her extremely creative and romantic original idea for this book and to our significant others, who helped us hone our craft.

Publisher's Note

Travel books have many different formats and criteria for the places they include. We would like the reader to know that this book is not an advertising vehicle. As is true in all the *Best Places To Kiss* books, none of the businesses included here were charged fees, nor did they pay us for their review. This book is a sincere effort to highlight those special parts of the region that are filled with romance and splendor. Sometimes these places were created by people, e.g. restaurants, inns, lounges, lodges, hotels, and bed and breakfasts. Sometimes those places are untouched by people and simply created by G-d for us to enjoy. Wherever you go, be gentle with each other and gentle with the earth.

We Would Love to Hear From You

The recommendations in this collection were the final decision of the publisher, but we would love to hear what you think of our suggestions. It is our desire to be a reliable source for your amorous outings, and, in this quest for blissful sojourns, your romantic feedback assists greatly in increasing our accuracy and resources for information. Please feel free to write Beginning Press if you have any additional comments, criticisms, or cherished memories of your own of a place we directed you to or of a place you discovered on your own.

Beginning Press
5418 South Brandon
Seattle, Washington 98118

THE FINE ART OF KISSING

Why It's Best To Kiss In New England

New England is a sensational, truly unique part of the world, filled with all the things you might require for a romantic encounter. There is nothing like the drama of fall in Vermont, New Hampshire, and the Berkshires, when torrents of amber leaves cast their magic over the land. From late September through October, particularly in Vermont, *leaf peepers* (that's the term used for those who come here to watch nature change out of her velvet green summer coat) come in droves. It is essential to book autumn visits to this region far in advance to assure your participation in this annual miracle.

In winter snow covers New England with sweeping blankets of white, turning Vermont, New Hampshire, and Massachusetts into a wonderland for skiers, skaters, and snugglers alike. After too much winter has exhausted even the most die-hard enthusiast, spring is welcomed like a long lost love. Both wildflowers and people emerge gently but joyously from their frosty hibernation. Hiking through woods alive with green once again is a joy for all who come here. The Connecticut River Valley, Boston Public Gardens, the Green Mountains of Vermont, and the White Mountains of New Hampshire are the best for those who love solitude and each other.

Summer is a major event up and down the New England coast, from Mystic, Connecticut, to Block Island off the coast of Rhode Island, to the Cape Cod peninsula and the islands of Martha's Vineyard and Nantucket in Massachusetts. The sultry, white sand beaches and cool blue surf draw affectionate couples who want to escape the heat and spend cherished, lingering time together. Of course, Maine is the quintessential New England summer getaway. Its exquisite, near flawless blend of rugged land and infinite water is more than heart-stirring—it is spectacular.

If historical significance lights your fire, you will appreciate the rich Colonial heritage so abundant in New England. Although a circa-1775 home or restaurant may not have romantic flair just because it is old, if it has been restored and refurbished by owners who respect the past, you can wander calmly through a piece of history with all the pleasures of today. Couples born too late to live in the Gilded Age can experience it nevertheless: opulent turn-of-the-century mansions converted to beguiling inns in the Berkshires; Newport, Rhode Island; Arcadia, Maine; and northern Vermont offer dazzling retreats with an emphasis on intimacy and passion.

For those who want both cosmopolitan pleasures and more than just a taste of this country's history, Boston provides the best of both. The hotels, museums, ballet, symphony, theater, and restaurants here are world class, while the Freedom Trail, which takes you back through the centuries, is a singularly American ramble for hand-holding couples of all ages.

In short, regardless of the season, there probably is not a more diverse place in the world in which to pucker up than New England. It gets fairly crowded during summer and fall, but the beauty and the potential for cherished moments are waiting year-round.

◆ **Romantic Note:** Many of the country inns and bed and breakfasts on the Maine coast, Martha's Vineyard, Nantucket, and Block Island are closed most of the winter. Always call ahead.

You Call This Research?

This book was undertaken primarily as a journalistic effort. It is the product of earnest interviews, travel, and careful investigation and observation. Although it would have been nice, even preferable, kissing was not the major research method used to select the locations listed in this book. If smooching had been the determining factor, several inescapable problems would have developed. First, we would still be researching, and this book would be just a good idea, some breathless moments, random notes, and nothing more. Second, depending on the mood of the moment, many kisses might have occurred in places that do not meet the requirements of this travel guide. Therefore, for both practical and physical reasons, more objective criteria had to be established.

You may be wondering, if we did not kiss at every location during our research, how we could be certain that a particular place was good for such an activity? The answer is that we employed our reporters' instincts to evaluate the heartfelt, magnetic pull of each place visited. If, upon examining a place, we felt a longing inside for our special someone to share what we had discovered, we considered this to be as reliable as a kissing analysis. In the final evaluation, I can guarantee that once you choose where to go from among any of the places listed, you will be assured of some degree of privacy, a beautiful setting, heart-stirring ambience, and first-rate accommodations. When you get there, what you do romantically is up to you and your partner.

What Isn't Romantic

You may be skeptical about the idea that one location is more romantic than another. You may think, "Well, it isn't the setting, it's who you're with that makes a place special." And you'd be right. But aside from the chemistry that exists between the two of you without any help from us, there are some locations that can facilitate and enhance that chemistry, just as there are some that discourage and frustrate the magic in the moment.

For example, holding hands over a hamburger and fries at McDonald's, might be, for some, a blissful interlude. But the french-fry fight in full swing near your heads and the preoccupied employee who took a year and a day to get your order will put a damper on heart-throb stuff for most of us, even the most adoring. No, location isn't everything; but when a certain type of place combines with all the right atmospheric details, including the right person, the odds are better for achieving unhindered and uninterrupted romance.

With that in mind, here is a list of things that were never considered to be even remotely romantic: olive green or orange carpeting (especially if it is mildewed or dirty); older properties that are more dilapidated than rustic; anything overly plastic or overly veneered; an abundance of neon (even if it is very art deco or very neo-modern); most tourist traps; restaurants with no-smoking sections that ignore their own policy; overpriced hotels with impressive names and motel-style accommodations; discos; the latest need-to-be-seen-in nightspot; restaurants with officious, sneering waiters; and, last but not least, a roomful of people discussing the stock market or the hottest and latest business acquisition in town.

Above and beyond these unromantic location details, unromantic *behavior* can negate the affection potential of even the most majestic surroundings. These are mood killers every time: any amount of moaning over the weather; creating a scene over the quality of food or service, no matter how justified; worrying about work; getting angry about traffic; incessant backseat driving, no matter how warranted; groaning about heartburn and other related symptoms, no matter how painful or justified.

Rating Romance

The three major factors that determined whether or not we included a place were:

1. Surrounding splendor
2. Privacy
3. Tug-at-your-heartstrings ambience

Of the three determining factors, "surrounding splendor" and "privacy" are fairly self-explanatory; "heart-tugging ambience" can probably use some clarification. Wonderful, loving environments are not just four-poster beds covered with down quilts and lace pillows, or tables decorated with white tablecloths and nicely folded linen napkins. Instead, there must be more plush or other engaging features that encourage intimacy and allow for uninterrupted affectionate discussions. For the most part, ambience was rated according to degree of comfort and number of gracious appointments, as opposed to image and frills.

If a place had all three factors going for it, inclusion was automatic. But if one or two of those of the criteria were weak or nonexistent, the other feature(s) had to be superior before the location would be included. For example, if a breathtakingly beautiful panoramic vista was in a spot that was inundated with tourists and children on field trips, the place was not included. If a fabulous bed and breakfast was set in a less-than-desirable location, it would be included if, and only if, its interior was so wonderfully inviting and cozy that the outside world no longer mattered.

Kiss Ratings

If you've flipped through this book and noticed the miniature lips that follow each entry, you're probably curious about what they mean. The rating system notwithstanding, all the places listed in this book are wonderfully special places to be, and all of them have heart-pleasing details and are worthwhile, enticing places to visit. The tiny lips indicate only our personal preferences and nothing more. They are a way of indicating just how delightfully romantic a place is and how pleased we were with our experience during our visit. The number of lips awarded each location indicates:

> ◆ *Romantic Possibilities*
> ◆◆ *Very Romantic*
> ◆◆◆ *Irresistible*
> ◆◆◆◆ *Sublime*

Cost Ratings

We have included additional ratings to help you determine whether your lips can afford to kiss in a particular restaurant, hotel, or bed and breakfast (almost all of the outdoor places are free; some charge a small fee). The price for overnight accommodations is always based on double occupancy; otherwise there wouldn't be anyone to kiss. Eating establishment prices are based on a full dinner for two, excluding liquor, unless otherwise indicated. Because prices and business hours change, it is always advisable to call each place you consider visiting, so your lips will not end up disappointed.

◆ **Romantic Note:** All rates listed in this book are bed-and-breakfast rates, unless otherwise noted. Unique to New England are meal plans that include multicourse dinners in the cost of the room and breakfast. These dinners frequently are some of the best in the region. If you are staying at a bed-and-breakfast that offers this Modified American Plan (**MAP**—rates that include both breakfast and dinner) take advantage of this: it is often a great kissing bargain in spite of the Very Expensive rating. A few inns have a European Plan (**EP**), which means breakfast is not included in the room rate.

◆ **One More Romantic Note:** The rates for lodging quoted in this book are all high-season rates. Off-season rates are often drastically reduced. Be sure to ask for special packages and seasonal discounts.

Restaurant Rating

Inexpensive	Under $25
Moderate	$25 to $50
Expensive	$50 to $80
Very Expensive	$80 to $110
Unbelievably Expensive	$110 and up

Lodging Rating

Inexpensive	$75 to $90
Moderate	$90 to $125
Expensive	$125 to $185
Very Expensive	$185 to $250
Unbelievably Expensive	$250 and up

What If You Don't Want To Kiss?

For most couples, romance isn't easy. Some people I interviewed resisted the idea of best kissing locales. Their resistance stemmed from expectation worries. They were apprehensive that once they arrived at the place of their dreams, they'd never get the feeling they thought they were supposed to have. They imagined spending time setting up itineraries, taking extra time to get ready, making the journey to the promised land, and, once they were there, not being swept away in a flourish of romance. Their understandable fear was, What happens if nothing happens? Because in spite of the best intentions, even with this book in hand, romance is not easy.

Having experienced situations like this more than once in my life, I empathize, but I'm prepared with solutions. To prevent this anticlimactic scenario from becoming a reality, and to help you survive a romantic outing, consider these suggestions. When you make decisions about where and when to go, pay close attention to details; talk over your preferences and discuss your feelings about them. For some people there is no passion associated with fast pre-theater dinners that are all but inhaled, or with walking farther than expected in overly high, high heels, or with finding a place closed because its hours have changed. Keep in mind the difficulties of second-guessing traffic patterns in the city. My strong recommendation, although I know this is difficult, is not to schedule a romantic outing too tightly or you will be more assured of a headache then an affectionate interlude.

Do not discuss money, family, or the kids. If you have a headache, take some aspirin now and not later. Regardless of how good-looking the person at the next table is, remember that such distractions are never considered to be in good romantic taste. How different factors might affect your lips, not to mention your mood, is something to agree on before you head out the door, not after—or during.

Remember that part of the whole experience of an intimate time together is to allow whatever happens to be an opportunity to let affection reign. Regardless of what takes place, that is what is romantic. For example, remember the incredibly intense scene in the film *Body Heat* where Kathleen Turner is standing in the hall and William Hurt smashes through the door (even though it appears to be unlocked) and rushes into her waiting arms, tumbling them both to the floor? Well, how romantic would it have been if Kathleen had started fretting about having to clean up the broken glass, getting the door fixed, and repairing her torn underwear? Or remember the scene between Kevin Costner and Susan Sarandon in *Bull Durham* where he throws his full cereal bowl against the wall, cleans the kitchen table with a sweep of his arm, then picks Susan up and throws her passionately on the table? How romantic would that have been if Kevin had started complaining about the broken china in his hair and the spilled milk running down his arms? Get the idea?

So, if the car breaks down, the waiter is rude to you, your reservations get screwed up, or both of you tire out and want to call it a day, you can still be endearing and charming. Really, it only takes an attitude change to turn any dilemma into a delight.

"Lips only sing when they cannot kiss."
James Thomson

"The naked promise in a glance, the electricity in a touch, the delicious heat in a kiss ..."
Trudy Culross

CONNECTICUT

Southwestern Connecticut

Norwalk

Restaurant Kissing

SILVERMINE TAVERN, Norwalk
194 Perry Avenue, (203) 847-4558
Expensive (dining), Moderate (inn)

Call for directions.

On warm summer evenings, when tables are set on a deck embraced by motherly trees near the old mill pond, a splashing waterfall plays its happy melody for diners. Ringed by forest, the still blue waters below are rippled only by a pair of snow white swans, and the occasional mallard and his mate. Surely New Yorkers love this casual restaurant not only for its sylvan setting but also for its determined unpretentiousness. The service is country friendly, the food generous and homespun. Rough wooden tables crowd the tavern's array of capacious rooms, their walls replete with antique farm tools and folk art that ranges from quaint to intriguing. In the colder months, be sure to ask for one of the rooms with a fireplace. I found the porch's wall of windows and brick floor a particularly appealing setting for such New England delicacies as chicken pie, seafood stew, prime rib, and four different lobster dishes, with pie, Indian pudding, or a traditional sundae for dessert. And be sure to partake in one of their delectable honeybuns with your own honeybun.

◆ **Romantic Note:** Guest rooms, above the restaurant and in the building across the street, are decorated in simple Colonial style with painted floors, hand-hooked rugs, and petite writing desks. One has the kind of white-eyelet-trimmed canopy bed little girls dream of. Some rooms are tiny, and they could use sprucing up and some fresh paint here and there, but these are reasonably affordable accommodations in this country setting shadowed by New York's pricey influence.

Westport

Hotel/Bed and Breakfast Kissing

THE COTSWOLD INN, Westport   ◆◆◆
76 Myrtle Avenue, (203) 226-3766
Very Expensive

Call for directions.

The Cotswold Inn is a beautiful bed and breakfast that is both authentic and charming. It is a plush place to immerse yourself for the weekend. The house is extemely comfortable, with exquisite antique furniture and four-poster beds. One room even has a working fireplace. The bedrooms are quite private and are decorated with fine prints and fabrics. Breakfast is a deluxe continental presentation of fresh muffins and pastries, and complimentary wine and snacks are available in the early evening. Although more expensive than most bed and breakfasts in the area, the Cotswold provides a romantic ambience that the others lack.

Restaurant Kissing

AMADEO'S RISTORANTE, Westport
1431 Post Road East, (203) 254-9482
Expensive

From Interstate 95, take Exit 18 and turn left at the top of the ramp. Then turn right onto Post Road East; the restaurant is about two miles down, on the left side.

The small, unobtrusive brown house is easy to miss on this busy road lined with modern businesses, but if you're in the mood for conviviality with an Italian flair, search it out. Once over the threshold, you leave the bustling traffic behind and enter a tiny slice of the old country. Theatrical trompe l'oeil murals transform the Lilliputian-size porch into a stone villa, with potted plants flowering in windows that reveal a hint of flawless countryside. A second, petite dining room is squeezed into the house, this one more traditionally formal with peach-toned wall coverings, impressionist paintings, and miniature glass lamps on each table. Bruschetta, scampi, carpaccio, fettuccine al salmone, saltimbocca, sole Florentine, and calamari are a few of the remarkable dishes that make this restaurant very popular. Not surprisingly, the room is somewhat noisy on a busy evening.

◆ **Romantic Alternative:** If French cuisine is your raison d'etre, **LE CHAMBORD,** 1572 Post Road East, Westport, (203) 255-2654, (Expensive), is a jewel. In deference to its older, loyal customers who dine here routinely, the restaurant retains its dated but dignified decor of trellis arches over mirrors, gilt-framed oils of still lifes and Parisian scenes, and candles, potted plants, and pink linens on each table. For dessert, try the crêpes Suzette made for two.

THE INN AT LONGSHORE DINING ROOM, Westport
260 South Compo Road, (203) 226-3316
Expensive

Call for directions.

The restaurant here, surrounded by a premier golf course, is a refreshing place to enjoy a drink or dinner together, regardless of your handicap. The dining room faces a beautiful vantage point overlooking the Connecticut shoreline, where boaters and windsurfers whisk by in the summer and the quiet is all about in the winter. You can eat on the terrace just inches above the water. There is a fine selection of seafood and pasta. Though not exceptional, the food is good and consistent.

◆ **Romantic Note:** The inn has live jazz every Friday and Saturday night, but it attracts quite a crowd. If you are looking for quiet, intimate dining, perhaps earlier in the week is your best bet. But for the view, this spot is perfect at any time.

Outdoor Kissing

SHERWOOD ISLAND STATE PARK

From Interstate 95, take Exit 18 and follow signs to the park.

If you want to picnic by the water but detest sand in your sandwiches, plan on a day in the sun at this popular park. Picnic tables are set on the grass—some on the rocky point, others shaded by trees—overlooking Long Island Sound. A small strip of sand curves around a series of coves, with serene, safe waters for swimming. Although summer can be busy, the off-season is delightfully quiet, especially in late afternoon, when migrating Canada geese outnumber people. Bring a blanket and share a warm hug.

Western Connecticut

Greenwich

Hotel/Bed and Breakfast Kissing

THE HOMESTEAD INN, Greenwich   ❖
20 Field Point Road, (203) 869-7500
Moderate

Call for directions.

The Homestead is a traditional Connecticut farmhouse built in 1799. With its setting of trees and tranquil sloping lawns it would be hard to ignore the seclusion this place has to offer. The rooms in the main house were not our favorites: the furnishings in several of them seem a bit second-hand instead of antique, and the televisions seem out of place in all of them. The most charming rooms by far are in the wing called the Independent House. Each suite is outfitted with a canopy bed, bright fabrics, and large windows that open onto a deck with white wicker furniture where you can enjoy the view in the peace of a summer evening. All the rooms have private baths, and a delightful breakfast is served in an elegant dining room.

The inn's appeal is greatly enhanced by **LA GRANGE,** the restaurant located in the main house. The chef here will dazzle you with his classic French cuisine while you indulge yourself in the relaxed, elegant country setting.

◆ **Romantic Alternative: THE STANTON HOUSE INN,** 76 Maple Avenue, Greenwich, (203) 869-2110, (Inexpensive), is a white farmhouse built in 1840 and now a part of a bustling Greenwich neighborhood. Although the hallways are plain and a bit rundown, the rooms are actually rather bright and inviting. Each room has a wet bar and most have private baths. The service is extremely friendly and welcoming. Breakfast is a complimentary continental buffet. Although the Stanton House is located in town and does not offer the seclusion of the Homestead, its simple warmth can provide a great stay.

◆ **Romantic Option: BRETT'S RESTAURANT AND BAR,** 21 Field Point Road, Greenwich, (203) 629-1114, (Inexpensive), is an option for dinner if you are in the mood for a more casual dining experience. It has a friendly, warm atmosphere that is stylish and potentially romantic, as well as good Italian cuisine (pasta, interesting pizzas, etc.) that is more than reasonably priced. Most evenings they have live music. It changes nightly; expect anything from country to jazz.

Restaurant Kissing

BERTRAND'S RESTAURANT FRANCAIS, Greenwich
253 Greenwich Avenue, (203) 661-4618
Expensive to Very Expensive

The restaurant is in the center of town, but call for directions to be safe.

As you pass through the door of Bertrand's coral stucco exterior you will immediately be taken by the elegance and grandeur of this three-level restaurant, glowing beneath a unique tile-and-glass dome ceiling. The peach brick walls and the light radiating from above add to the bright, chic atmosphere. The tables overlooking the front windows are particularly romantic spots where you can enjoy the atmosphere but keep your privacy as well.

Bertrand's prides itself on its feats of culinary excellence. The aromas emanating from the kitchen add a certain panache to your entire evening. If you are looking for truly authentic, four-star French cuisine, Bertrand's is surely the place. On Thursdays, a prix fixe menu highlights a particular region of France.

◆   **Romantic Option:** JEAN LOUIS, 61 Lewis Street, Greenwich, (203) 622-8450, (Moderate), is a cozy French restaurant just around the corner from Bertrand's. The coral stucco motif of the exterior continues inside with coral wallpaper. There are only a handful of tables, and there is a decidedly less impressive atmosphere here than at the neighboring Bertrand's, but the menu more than makes up for any stylistic gaps.

Ridgefield

Hotel/Bed and Breakfast Kissing

STONEHENGE, Ridgefield
Route 7, (203) 438-6511
Moderate to Very Expensive (inn), Very Expensive (dining)

From Route 7, just south of its intersection with Route 35, take the fork to the right onto Stonehenge Drive.

The setting is ideal. Ducks and snow white geese paddle across a pond hemmed by a path and benches; hiking trails radiate into the forested hills beyond. On the shore, three Colonial buildings comprise a small estate. Come early for dinner when the days are long and you'll discover there's no need for artwork on one wall of the elegant dining room, where a grand picture window frames a living impressionist scene of the picture-perfect waters and woods. The extravagant menu features appetizers such as a terrine of lobster, shrimp, and new potatoes enclosed in Scottish smoked salmon, and escargots in a spinach nest with a merlot and caramelized garlic sauce. Deluxe entrées include grouper in a poppy-seed crust, chicken filled with wild mushrooms and wrapped in puff pastry with champagne sauce, and Idaho trout with toasted pecans and lime-parsley butter sauce.

Guest rooms are equally inviting, decked out in Early American furnishings, lavish wall coverings, and modern white-tiled baths, with the requisite television for the many midweek business travelers. Rooms in the Guest House, in back of the main inn, are secluded and spacious. Cottage rooms aren't as spacious and grand as the main inn and are closer to the traffic noise of Route 7; they are best avoided.

◆ **Romantic Warning:** Not surprisingly, weddings are popular here, and are held almost every weekend in summer.

WEST LANE INN, Ridgefield
22 West Lane (Route 35), (203) 438-7323
Expensive

From Interstate 84, take Exit 3 and head south on Route 35. Just south of Ridgefield center, bear right at a fork near a fountain onto West Lane. The inn is 100 yards down, on the right.

Built in the early 1800s and refurbished as an inn in 1978, this home bridges the gap between past and present. Reproductions lend many of the rooms— some with ceramic tile hearths—a nostalgic flair. All rooms have televisions tucked away in cabinets, phones, and bedside reading lamps. In many rooms, colorful florals blanket the walls; they are sometimes mirrored in the curtains and upholstery, which may be a little overwhelming to some, perfectly blended to others. In the breakfast room, adjacent to the dark, oak-paneled lobby, a Danish, juice, and coffee will take the edge off your appetites. More continental-type items are available à la carte.

Restaurant Kissing

THE ELMS, Ridgefield
500 Main Street, (203) 438-2541
Expensive

From Interstate 84, take Exit 3, which is Route 7. At the intersection of Routes 7 and 35, bear right onto Route 35 and follow it approximately three miles. The restaurant is on the left side before you enter the town center.

Two centuries ago, fireplaces were not a luxury but a necessity. Today, you can have a firelit dinner in this 1760 inn and dream of days of yore. Four of the five dining and tavern rooms are warmed by blazing hearths. From the moment you enter the foyer, with its folk art murals depicting a Revolutionary battle scene on one side and a happier Colonial country day on the other, you know you're in for a fine New England feast. Starched linens, brass chandeliers, sconces, gilt china, fresh flowers, candles, built-in corner cabinets, and Windsor chairs inspire a sentimental journey into history. Continental dishes include homemade pâté, crab-stuffed mushrooms, roast duckling, tournedos au poivre, and chateaubriand prepared tableside. For a sweet ending, the crêpes Suzette and baked Alaska are made especially for two.

◆ **Romantic Note:** Guest rooms, available in the vintage Colonial next door, have standard motel furnishings enhanced by the occasional canopy bed, and a breakfast of pastries and yogurt is brought to your room.

THE INN AT RIDGEFIELD, Ridgefield
20 West Lane (Route 35), (203) 438-8282
Very Expensive

Call for directions.

Fireplaces and a pianist set a heartwarming mood on winter weekends at this rambling home turned high-toned restaurant. A brick hearth is at the entrance to the main dining room, next to the piano bar, with a table for two set toe-toastingly close. On busy nights, a pink marble hearth warms an inner room. In a third room, a mirrored wall reflects the rich fabric wall coverings, upholstered chairs, and brass candle holders. Fresh flowers brighten each table. The cuisine is French-inspired cosmopolitan, with showy tableside service. Terrine of goose liver, wild hare, and artichoke hearts; seviche of bay scallops and poached oysters; steamed Maine lobster in young corn coulis; and veal in a crust with a melange of chanterelles and morels are some of the dishes that will delight citified lovers surrounded by pure Connecticut country.

Kent

Restaurant Kissing

THE CORNUCOPIA OF KENT RESTAURANT, Kent
24 South Main Street (Route 7), (203) 927-3136
Moderate (Closed Wednesdays)

From Interstate 84, take Exit 3, which is Route 7. Follow Route 7 all the way to Kent; the restaurant is on the left side.

While some restaurants are well suited for lingering lunches and others are best for romantic dinners, this charming eatery is ideal for light-hearted lovers any time of day. At lunch, ask for a table in the rear of the enclosed porch room, akin to a greenhouse, where a sloped glass ceiling and a wall of windows overlook a verdant meadow backdropped by playing fields and forested hills. In the evening, a brick hearth warms the cozy inner dining room, once the hayloft of a circa-1800 dairy barn. The contemporary American cuisine updates traditional dishes with fresh new sauces: grilled sea scallops are served with red pepper pesto; steaks come with a confit of hot and sweet pickled red onion; lamb and eggplant are simmered in a maple-curry sauce. Old-fashioned bread pudding or newfangled espresso chocolate swirl cheesecake can be a happy ending to your fling in the hayloft.

FIFE 'N DRUM, Kent   ●●
10 Main Street (Route 7), (203) 927-3509
Expensive (dining), Inexpensive to Moderate (inn)

From Interstate 84, take Route 7 North and head all the way into Kent. The Fife 'n Drum is on the left.

Eating here is like taking a trip back to the days of Colonial taverns, with a sophisticated difference—an extensive, award-winning wine list. Still, the ambience is amiable and relaxed. Exposed brick makes up one wall, barn-wood paneling another, with a brick hearth tucked into one corner. Pink linens, pewter plates, prints of New England, lanterns along the wall, and seasonal decorations (petite pumpkins enlivened each table when I visited in October) blend to create a festive, nostalgic feel. French, Italian, and American dishes spice up the menu, with tantalizing entrées such as grilled duck breast flamed tableside, baked scrod with herb crust in lemon-caper sauce, gnocchi with wild mushrooms, and fillet of sole in papillote.

Guest rooms are available in the adjacent building. Antique beds and patchwork quilts are juxtaposed with such modern amenities as televisions on stands, coffee makers, and hairdryers. Some rooms have twin beds and cots to accommodate families of prep students at Kent School. Nothing fancy here, just good old Yankee hospitality.

Salisbury

Hotel/Bed and Breakfast Kissing

WHITE HART INN, Salisbury
The Village Green, (203) 435-0030
Moderate to Very Expensive (inn),
Expensive (dining), Moderate (Tap Room)

At the junction of Routes 41 and 44.

The veranda alone is enough to win you over, with white and pink wicker gathered about the colorful flower boxes. Even when snow blankets the village green, painted morning glories twirling up the classical columns bring on a summer smile. Inside, elegant comfort prevails. In colder weather, a fireplace warms the lobby, where you can peruse a magazine on the Queen Anne love seat or examine the Oriental vases displayed along the wall. Rose-carpeted stairs lead to the guest rooms, which range in size from cozy to commodious. All are lusciously decorated in a gentlewoman's garden of chintzes and Early American furnishings; televisions are tucked away in cabinets. The beautifully framed botanical prints found throughout the inn make spring feel near even in the dead of winter.

Famous for their cuisine, the three dining rooms will suit any guest's appetite. The award-winning New American Sea Grill is a study in superb taste. Muted deep green and terra-cotta accents, fine sky blue and cloud white linens, cane-back chairs, and gilt-framed still lifes create a serene, elegant ambience. The menu coaxes American fine dining into the '90s with appetizers including corn soup with grilled shrimp, tuna sashimi spring rolls, and beef carpaccio with arugula and Parmesan. Celebrate our country's bounty with entrées such as snapper with basil and baby artichokes, or beef fillet with sweet onions and Armagnac. For more casual dining, with delicious, generous meals, try the Tap Room, a buoyant tavern that's a favorite with the locals. The slate-floored Garden Room, with its bentwood chairs and multipaned windows that overlook the small-town street, is a bright, airy setting for a daylight meal. No matter where you dine, be sure to save room for one of the pastry chef's creations: purely sinful.

◆ **Romantic Alternative:** The **WAKE ROBIN INN**, Route 41, Lakeville, (203) 435-2515, (Expensive to Very Expensive), may not be as inviting as the White Hart Inn, but all the elegant trappings are to be found in the 25 European-style guest rooms, from voluptuous canopy beds to French doors opening onto a balcony. Firelight warms the well-respected restaurant, with its crewel-look drapes, flickering tapers, and soft rose walls adding to the undeniably romantic ambience. In keeping with the traditional language of love, the cuisine is pure French.

Restaurant Kissing

CHAIWALLA TEA ROOM, Salisbury
1 Main Street, (203) 435-9758
Inexpensive

At the junction of Routes 41 and 44.

You will certainly meet a true-blue "chai walla," or tea maker, in the petite, unpretentious tea room of this mustard-colored clapboard house. That Oriental beverage is the only liquid served, and it's some of the best in the world. Rare imports are presented in sleek, contemporary glass teapots, award-winners from the Museum of Modern Art collection. Each teapot is placed on a candle warmer at each table, where you can watch the tea's hue deepen as it steeps. To accompany the tea, "tiffin," or light sandwiches and hors d'oeuvres, constitutes the menu, but the cobblers and cakes displayed on the sideboard are nearly irresistible.

Connecticut River Valley

Higganum

Outdoor Kissing

SUNDIAL HERB GARDEN, Higganum
Braut Hill Road, (203) 345-4290
Moderate (tea for two)

From Route 9, take Exit 9 onto Route 81 South. About three miles down, turn right onto Braut Hill Road (second right after the Gulf station). Head uphill, and bear right at the fork, onto Braut Hill Road; the garden is on the left.

If you've ever wondered why brave men risked lives to open a tea trade with China, why the British are so obsessed with afternoon tea, or why American colonists began a revolution over it, come to tea at this delightful, off-the-beaten-path garden. Seated in a restored 18th-century barn with a wide-planked floor and hand-hewn beams soaring above, you can enjoy a Kusmi tea, once made exclusively for Russian tsars. Or the tea of the day may be a unique blend from China, unavailable in the States but here through the shopkeeper's special European connection. Some teas are so rare that the Chinese regulate how much can leave their country. For China Rose Congou, for instance, each tea leaf is laid between two fresh rose petals so it can absorb the delicate aroma. All of the the teas are custom-selected to blend with the hazelnut scones, ginger-brandy tea cake, linzer torte, and other gourmet delectables created by the shopkeeper's chef husband.

Afterwards, a tour of the garden is in order, and this may be enjoyed even if you can't make it to tea. The backyard has been transformed into three splendid garden rooms: a knot garden with interlocking low hedges, a formal main garden, and the topiary garden with its happily splashing fountain. Benches tucked away in secluded corners invite you to breathe in the beauty of it all and pretend you're in your own Eden.

◆ **Romantic Note:** The gardens and the wonderful gift shop are open on weekends or by appointment, and every day from November 1 through Christmas. Write for the schedule and reserve well in advance for teas, generally offered weekends in February, March, June, July, and September, and on special holidays, including, thank goodness, Valentine's Day.

East Haddam

Hotel/Bed and Breakfast Kissing

BISHOPSGATE INN, **East Haddam**   ◆◆
Goodspeed Landing, (203) 873-1677
Inexpensive to Moderate

After crossing the swing bridge over the Connecticut River via Route 82, you will see the Goodspeed Opera House on the right. Follow Route 82 for a quarter mile to the inn's driveway on the left.

Fireplaces and featherbeds embrace you with warmth in this old-fashioned bed and breakfast. Harbored in an 1818 Colonial crafted by a shipbuilder, the inn is pure New England—nothing fancy, just good old homespun hospitality. In the colder months, soup simmers in a cast-iron pot in the entryway's Colonial brick hearth—a warm, welcome aroma on a chilly day. A plaid sofa and chairs sit before another brick hearth in the parlor. Rooms radiate from this heart of the home. Those off the parlor are less private, but pleasantly decorated in simple Colonial style. Each has a fireplace. Narrow, steep shipbuilder's stairs lead to the second-floor rooms. My favorite, the Jenny Lind, has a lovely ivory and pastel Oriental carpet, fishnet canopy bed, tufted wing chair, and a hearth. The Director's Room is decidedly different, with a private balcony and sauna; its modern bath has bright lights encircling the mirror so you can dream of starring in your own Broadway love story.

◆ **Romantic Note:** You'll notice autographed publicity shots of actors in the entryway and other theater memorabilia throughout the inn. This is inspired by the fabulous **GOODSPEED OPERA HOUSE**, Route 82, East Haddam, (203) 873-8668, a majestic 1876 Victorian theater on the river. The Goodspeed hosts locally produced musicals—a fun idea for a tuneful night.

Chester

Restaurant Kissing

INN AT CHESTER, Chester   ◆◆◆
318 West Main Street (Route 148), (203) 526-9541
Expensive (dining), Moderate to Unbelievably Expensive (inn)

Just over the town line from Killingworth, on Route 148.

In the foyer, a couple, exhausted from strained city life, cuddles before a fire blazing in the fieldstone fireplace. Someone drops a quarter in the antique Polyphon, and the happy, gentle melodies of this old-fashioned music box lull them to sleep. This rambling country inn is made for simple, tranquil getaways.

The aptly named Post and Beam restaurant is an inviting converted barn. Chandeliers add elegance to the original hand-hewn rafters and half timbers; tables are richly laid out with linen, white china, and shining silver. A large fieldstone fireplace highlights one wall, and a cheery greenhouse window overlooks the back lawn and pond. Tables are also arranged in the porch and inner room, but these don't share the charm of the barn. Lamb with celery root and apple puree, sautéed salmon in basil cream sauce, and stuffed game hen are some of the traditional entrées. After dinner, step across the threshold and two centuries forward into the bright, contemporary lounge for a comforting cocktail or coffee.

◆ **Romantic Note:** When I visited, the inn, really a small hotel, had recently reopened, and guest rooms needed some finishing touches to add personality. They are on their way, however, with authentic-looking reproductions, a smattering of folk art, and fishnet canopies over several beds.

Hadlyme

Outdoor Kissing

GILLETTE CASTLE STATE PARK, Hadlyme

From Route 9, take Exit 7 over the East Hadlyme Bridge, then follow the signs.

It looks like a movie set, this storybook castle high on a hill where princes woo princesses (and vice versa) and live happily ever after. After you've shared a heavenly view of the Connecticut River, picture-perfect picnic spots by placid ponds, and hiking trails through the woods, you too may feel you've entered a happy fairy tale here. The best approach is from the Hadlyme ferry, crossing the Connecticut River from west to east, the castle towering above you. Just after you cross, you may want to picnic at the tables along the shore, a lovely site on a sunny day. As you wind uphill and into the state park, more picnic tables await, perched by the stone bridge above a pond or nestled in the woods. You're free to wander around the stone castle above. Its patio offers one of the most panoramic views in the state: the river winding through green or, in fall, brilliant gold and crimson hills.

◆ **Romantic Suggestion:** A picnic site as magical as Gillette Castle State Park deserves a magical meal. Luckily, you can pick up one at **THE WHEAT MARKET**, 4 Water Street, Chester, (203) 526-9347, (Inexpensive). Chinese noodle salad, herbed Brie, beet-garlic chips, meltaway shortbreads—this specialty food market has all the fixin's and more. Pick and choose your own favorites or indulge in their full-fledged "Lovers' Picnic," with orange and passionfruit sodas, Camembert with grapes, pâté, French bread with cornichons, potato salad, sliced turkey with honeycup mustard, and, of course, chocolate kisses. They'll even lend you a picnic basket (there are no table settings here). It's best to order the "Lovers' Picnic" a day ahead so it will be ready when you are.

Centerbrook

Restaurant Kissing

FINE BOUCHE RESTAURANT, Centerbrook
78 Main Street, (203) 767-1277
Expensive

From Interstate 95, take Exit 69, which puts you onto Route 9. Then take Exit 3 and turn left at the end of the ramp. The restaurant is on Main Street, on the left side.

A crackling fire greets you in the foyer of this converted Victorian home, where a series of rooms bathed in soft light and classical music invite you to relax and be pampered for an evening. In the enclosed veranda, white trelliswork around the windows is gently backlit, lending a gazebo-like feeling to the setting. Of the inner rooms, I prefer the first, with just four tables, rich green floral wall coverings, and coordinating valances over lacy sheers. The changing menu may include sweet potato ravioli; warm pear soup; salad with lobster, papaya, and arugula; tournedos of beef; pork medallions with celery root and apple puree; or quail with green grapes and spinach served with tarragon-scented egg pasta. Linger a bit and relax. You deserve dessert, even if it's just a sweet, soft kiss.

Ivoryton

Hotel/Bed and Breakfast Kissing

COPPER BEECH INN, Ivoryton
46 Main Street, (203) 767-0330
Moderate to Expensive (inn), Expensive to Very Expensive (dining)

From Route 95, take Exit 69 onto Route 9 North. From Route 9, take Exit 3 and turn left off the exit ramp. The inn is one and three-quarters miles down on the left side.

If you're looking for the sort of first-class dinner that you thought could be found only in a city, look no further than little Ivoryton's Copper Beech Inn. Cosmopolitan cuisine blends perfectly with elegant Victoriana and very formal service in this 1880s "cottage." French-inspired appetizers include a terrine of duck breast, foie gras, and truffles baked with port wine; and artichoke bottoms and fresh escargots baked with garlic in pastry and served with a white wine and tomato sauce. The entrées are equally Gallic: filet mignon with seared apples and a sauce of Roquefort, white wine, and shallots; rabbit stuffed with vegetables, chestnuts, and dried apricots; plus veal sweetbreads, duck, lobster, and venison. Desserts are special, from the individual raspberry charlotte to a perfect white chocolate mousse.

To complete the getaway, bubble away the outside world in the deep oval whirlpool tub in your Carriage House room. The Carriage House combines the anonymity of a small hotel and the charm of a country inn; rooms here are spacious and elegantly decorated in Early American and Queen Anne reproductions. Several have step-up four-poster and canopy beds; all boast decks embraced by leafy trees. Comfortable sofas and reading chairs invite relaxing. Exposed timbers and Colonial tin candle sconces add a touch of old New England. Main inn rooms share a more antique look. Number 1 is especially spacious, with a sitting area by the hearth, table and chairs below a crystal chandelier, and a canopy bed with pretty print fabric flowing down at each corner.

In the morning, take time to enjoy the grounds, with their terraced lawns, shade trees, and the grand namesake beech. When we visited at the tail end of foliage season, we stepped onto our deck into the golden arms of the trees and embraced in the midst of beautiful New England, a golden moment to share throughout the seasons of life.

Essex

Hotel/Bed and Breakfast Kissing

GRISWOLD INN, Essex   ◆◆
36 Main Street, (203) 767-1776
Inexpensive to Expensive (inn), Expensive (dining)

From Interstate 95, take Exit 69 onto Route 9 North. Then take Exit 3 and go left off the ramp. Turn right at the first light; the inn is on the right side of Main Street.

If you were traveling by stage from Boston to New York in the middle of the American Revolution, chances are you would have stopped at the Griswold Inn. Opened in 1776 and continuously operated as an inn since then, this fair establishment still greets travelers with homespun bed and board. Guest rooms are simple and homespun, showing a little age around the edges.

In the restaurant, wooden tables and chairs crowd a series of dining rooms, several with a fireplace. The hearths, and the candles on each table, seem to provide most of the lighting, as few windows can be found. Nearly every inch of wall is blanketed with marine memorabilia, primarily prints of steamships and ferries, a display case of antique firearms, and antique books on built-in shelves. "Broiled and roasted meats & birds" including homemade sausages, game hen, and traditional steaks, top the menu. In the evenings, the Tap Room hosts jovial, live entertainment, from banjo pickers to sing-alongs to spoon players.

Restaurant Kissing

SHE SELLS SANDWICHES, Essex   ◆◀
35 Pratt Street, Brewers Dauntless Shipyard, (203) 767-3288
Inexpensive

From North Main Street, turn left onto Pratt Street, shortly before the Griswold Inn. Follow Pratt Street around a bend to the shipyard. The restaurant is in the shipyard, past the dry-docked boats; look for the sign.

When the sun shines and you're by the sea, you can't help getting in a nautical mood. Head to the marina and you'll find a casual deli as simple as a sea gull perched above the dry-docked boats. The "comfort food" sandwiches, from a three-layer peanut butter and jelly to Philly cheese steak to a Mexican BLT on a tortilla to your own custom-made deli special, are best enjoyed on the deck. Be sure to get a table on the far end, beyond the dry-dock lot. With this view of the marina, river, and forested hills beyond, you can almost believe that the two of you are on your private yacht, firmly anchored in love.

Westbrook

Hotel/Bed and Breakfast Kissing

CAPTAIN STANNARD HOUSE, Westbrook
138 South Main Street, (203) 399-4634
Inexpensive

From Interstate 95, take Exit 65 and go a quarter mile into the center of town. Turn right onto Route 1, then take a quick left at the light onto South Main Street. The inn is on the left side.

Some work at marriage, others play at it. If you're the play type, check into this recently restored captain's house. In one of the cavernous common rooms, a billiard table challenges guests to grab a cue and laugh when the rain melts away dreams of the beach. On cold days, the wood stove radiates warmth to counteract New England's occasionally contrary weather. The breakfast room is equally expansive, nearly dwarfing the grand piano in its corner. Guest rooms, on the other hand, are cozy in size, with a sloped ceiling along one side. Each features an antique bed and stenciled borders of shells, bows, or flowers along crisply painted walls. Nothing fancy here, just a friendly spot to remind you that sometimes all you need for romance is each other.

WATER'S EDGE INN AND RESORT, Westbrook
1525 Boston Post Road, (203) 399-5901
Moderate to Very Expensive (inn), Expensive (dining)

From Interstate 95, head south at Exit 65 to the junction of Route 1 and turn left. The inn is approximately three-quarters of a mile down, on the right side.

Cast upon the water's edge like shells upon the shore is this sprawling but nicely landscaped complex of buildings. About 75% are time-shares. The main inn harbors pleasant hotel rooms decorated in neutral and pastel tones, featuring nice furnishings with brass hardware and modern baths. What sets this place apart from other resorts is the view—and you must get a room with a view or why bother? Put your feet up on your private deck and just gaze out over calm Long Island Sound with Long Island on the horizon.

The multilevel restaurant shares this panorama. Come for lunch or before sunset and ask for a table in the main room by the two-story-high windows. Spiced calamari with lobster, seafood sausage with sun-dried tomatoes, Cajun tuna steak, and lamb with green peppercorns, blackberries and braised leeks spice up the menu. And don't worry: you can always work off dessert in the hotel's state-of-the-art exercise room and indoor pool.

Southeast Shore

North Stonington

Hotel/Bed and Breakfast Kissing

RANDALL'S ORDINARY, North Stonington
Route 2, (203) 599-4540
Inexpensive to Expensive (inn), Expensive (dining)

From Interstate 95, take Exit 92 and drive north one-third mile on Route 2. The inn's drive is on the left.

Enter the realm of Randall's Ordinary and leave today far behind. The farmstead itself looks like an etching in a history book: the 1685 center-chimney home and its massive 1819 barn have both been restored to perfection. The aromas of stews, breads, and meats cooked on the three-century-old hearth of the chimney home waft through the tiny main-floor rooms of the traditional "Ordinary"'s dining area. There are rooms in this building that are on the small side and feel too much a part of the restaurant domain to be private.

The 12 guest rooms in the amazingly refurbished barn intermingle country rusticity with modern luxury. The decor is sparse, focusing on authentically restored walls, with little artwork to detract from the exposed timbers and beams. Attractive details like fishnet canopy beds or a skylit sleeping loft enhance your journey to the past, while whirlpool tubs and televisions provide contemporary comfort. The most unusual room in the barn, if not the state, is housed in the towering silo. Spiral up the stairs to the Adirondack birch bed set in the circular wall. In the private sitting room, old barn doors form an intriguing backdrop for the gas fireplace, rope love seat, and convenient kitchen area. Spiral upward again and you'll come to the crown jewel: a cloverleaf whirlpool set in the rounded cone top of the silo.

All meals are prepared using authentic recipes and techniques in the Ordinary's hearth. Cross the threshold and you're immersed in the days when colonists spoke of liberty within these very walls. Each of the intimate dining rooms that circle round the chimney glows with its own fireplace. Rough wooden tables, pewter steins on the mantels, sloping wide plank floors, 12-over-12 windows, and cast-iron chandeliers create an authentic atmosphere for your 1600s repast. Before your weekday dinner, you can play period games, enjoy a vintage "spirit," and listen to a classical guitarist or harpist or even a singer of folk songs and sea chanteys. Wait staff and cooks in period dress dish out onion soup warmed in cast-iron pots above the flames, slice a piece of "spider" cornbread baked in the iron cookpot in the coals, and test the roast pork slowly cooking in the reflector oven in front of the massive hearth. The ingredients are basic; the tastes are different and delicious. Savor a meal that any Connecticut Yankee, no matter what the century, would relish.

◆ **Romantic Note:** Dinners are served at one seating, at 7:00 p.m. Reserve in advance.

Mystic

Hotel/Bed and Breakfast Kissing

THE INN AT MYSTIC, Mystic
Junction of Routes 1 and 27, (203) 536-9604
Moderate to Very Expensive (EP)

From Interstate 95, take Exit 90 and drive two miles south on Route 27 to Route 1. The inn is located on the corner to the left.

Humphrey Bogart and Lauren Bacall honeymooned at this grand Colonial Revival mansion on a hill. Today, the Inn at Mystic carries on its heritage of romance, but now it's part of an expansive complex encompassing the mansion, the old-fashioned gatehouse, and a contemporary motor inn. All of the diverse accommodations stand head and shoulders above most of their peers.

Rooms in the motor inn feature graceful Early American furnishings, hairdryers, and coffee makers. Ten rooms have canopied four-poster beds. Those in the east wing have a fireplace, whirlpool, or both; a canopied pencil-post bed; and perhaps private balcony overlooking the tennis courts and waterways beyond.

Head up the inn's drive to the more secluded gatehouse and main inn. In the gatehouse, you'll find richly decorated rooms with old-fashioned charm; one has a fireplace, dark wood paneling, and a canopy bed with plaid ruffles. The inn, a stately home built in 1904, is the complex's crowning glory. Walk up the stone steps, past the massive white columns, and enter a unique world of turn-of-the-century elegance that somehow feels like home. Relax by the Delft-tile hearth in the parlor, with its warm wood walls, Oriental carpets, and comfortable sofas. Swirl up the grand staircase to your bedchamber. Spacious rooms, regal canopy beds, a fireplace, jetted soaking tub, private deck, and vintage furnishings provide an ambience that is impressive but not so glorious that you feel uncomfortable.

No matter which type of room you choose, you're invited to splash in the pool or explore the waterways together in one of the inn's complimentary canoes, rowboats, or paddle boats.

STEAMBOAT INN, Mystic   ◆◆◆◀
73 Steamboat Wharf, (203) 536-8300
Expensive to Unbelievably Expensive

From Interstate 95 southbound, take Exit 90 and turn left onto Route 27. Drive to Route 1 (East Main Street), turn right, and cross the drawbridge. Look for the inn's sign on the left.

Pause by the window of your luxurious room on the river and you'll be entertained by a cavalcade of ships passing slowly out to sea. Just steps away, on the other side of a narrow dock, the two-masted schooner *Argia* stands sentinel to Mystic's past. An even more majestic windjammer occasionally docks in the river outside your bedchamber.

In the heart of bustling Mystic, but facing the serene river, this inn offers a unique voyage to luxury and romance. All of the eight rooms have whirlpool baths; six have working fireplaces. The decor is sophisticated contemporary. The Ariadne Room is stunning, a spacious chamber clothed in ivory, with curtained bed, sitting area by the fireplace, and oval whirlpool tub. The Mystic Room frames a splendid river panorama, its gilt mirror reflecting a four-poster bed, sitting area by the hearth, and beckoning bookshelves. A half-tester rises above the Victoria Room's bed. Downstairs rooms, directly on the dock, are less private, but you'll find such luxuries as a two-room suite with wet bar, refrigerator, microwave, deep oval whirlpool, and luscious decor. In the morning, a continental breakfast, served in the stylish common room, will revive you for a day on land or sea.

Restaurant Kissing

FLOOD TIDE RESTAURANT, Mystic
Junction of Routes 1 and 27, in The Inn at Mystic
(203) 536-8140
Expensive

From Interstate 95, take Exit 90 and drive two miles south on Route 27 to Route 1.
The restaurant is located at the Inn at Mystic, on the corner to the left.

The affectionate couple sighed with delight as the roast chicken was presented to them on a silver platter. A bouquet of vegetables formed a colorful ring, and sweet aromas wafted through the air as the apple, chestnut, and sage dressing was placed on each plate and the meat was flawlessly sliced. This is only one of this remarkable restaurant's select dinners, created just for two and presented tableside. Perhaps you'll enjoy rack of lamb, beef Wellington, or chateaubriand.

Some candlelit tables overlook the waterways that made Mystic famous, others are in a smaller firelit room, where half hulls and tall-ship artifacts whisper of whaling days. Beyond the dinners for two, the extensive menu offers such appetizers as smoked salmon rosettes, carpaccio, vegetable strudel, and seafood cocktail. Entrées include classically prepared seafood, baked stuffed lobster, pork chops with apple-raspberry puree, and veal with lobster, morels, and sun-dried tomatoes. For dessert, what could be better than a sinful sweet for two? We recommend the flaming bananas Foster or the lustful chocolate fondue.

◆   **Romantic Note:** If you come early for dinner, you can enjoy complimentary hors d'oeuvres in the cocktail lounge, a gentleman's club of leather chairs, oil lamps, and multipaned windows overlooking the pool.

Noank

Hotel/Bed and Breakfast Kissing

THE PALMER INN, Noank
25 Church Street, (203) 572-9000
Moderate to Expensive

Call for directions.

There is a touch of the old South in the tiny seaside hamlet of Noank at this grand replica of a plantation house in Knoxville, Tennessee. Inside, you'll be greeted by a blend of Southern hospitality and Yankee effects. On chillier days, a fire crackles in the parlor with its Victorian fringed lamp and colorful stained glass window, one of nine such windows found throughout the home. Carved wood beds highlight the second-floor guest rooms. One has a fireplace, but another, the Oak Room, is more sparse, with little artwork to enliven a stay. High sloping ceilings add a touch of grace to third-floor rooms, one with a white wicker love seat and another with a brass bed blanketed in satin. In the Balcony Room, you can open French doors to an ample deck overlooking a watery horizon that winks from beyond the houses across the street. In the morning, guests gather at the large table at one end of the parlor to munch the inn's homemade granola, a recipe made famous in *Yankee* magazine.

Old Mystic

Hotel/Bed and Breakfast Kissing

THE OLD MYSTIC INN, Old Mystic
58 Main Street, (203) 572-9422
Moderate

From Interstate 95, take Exit 90. Follow Route 27 north one and a half miles to Old Mystic center. Where Route 27 comes to a three-way stop, bear right on a street that becomes Main Street. The inn is on the right.

An antiquarian bookstore turned charming Colonial bed and breakfast is housed in this two-century-old home. Each guest room is named after a great American author, all of whom would feel right at home in this authentically decorated inn. Step o'er the threshold and enter the 1800s.

An immense Colonial hearth warms the common room, with its braided rug on a wide plank floor, stenciled walls, and enticing nut bowl. Fireplaces bring back yesteryear in three of the four bedchambers in the main inn. Downstairs, the firelit Thoreau Room glows with the light from an iron chandelier. A crocheted canopy soars above the turned-post bed in the Melville Room, with its antique writing desk. Firelight warms the Dickinson Room, with its splendid inlaid floors and white wicker chairs nested in a shuttered box window. Each of the rooms holds a selection of titles by its namesake authors.

In the adjacent carriage house, four guest rooms are more modern architecturally as well as more private. These rooms are appointed with four-poster beds with ruffled canopies, wing chairs, cathedral ceilings, and dried floral wreaths, and two have jetted tubs. The rooms in the inn are all the same price on any given night, so reserve early if you prefer a particular room. In the morning, all guests gather in the main house's breakfast room, with its Colonial hearth, brass-based candle lamps, and stenciled walls, for a generous repast of eggs Benedict, omelets, sautéed apples over French toast, or other delectables.

RED BROOK INN, Old Mystic
10 Wells Roads, (203) 572-0349
Moderate to Expensive

Call for directions.

When the chill wind of winter blows, a curl of smoke rises from the chimney of this classic Colonial on a wooded hill. Inside, you'll find the 1700s, complete with a woman in dress and bonnet stirring stew in a cast-iron pot at the immense cooking hearth. On certain Saturday evenings in winter, this savory treat awaits overnight guests, yet any time of year is a delight at this inn that combines our nation's heritage with modern amenities.

In the main house, you can light hearth and heart in three bedchambers. Down comforters, crocheted canopies, quilted patchwork accent pillows, stenciled floors, antique bureaus, and old-fashioned lamps are some of the Colonial-period details. In the firelit Ross Haley Room, step up to a majestic 200-year-old French four-poster with richly quilted valance and tasseled curtain. In the Nancy Crary Room, indulge in modern luxury—a jetted tub for one. In the evening, sip sherry in the gentlemen's parlor or converse with guests in the ladies' parlor.

The inn's second home, the Crary Homestead, offers similarly styled rooms and is a short distance down the hill toward the highway. All guests join in the keeping room for a hearty breakfast that would delight any patriot.

Restaurant Kissing

J.P. DANIELS RESTAURANT, Old Mystic
Route 184, (203) 572-9564
Expensive

Call for directions.

"Sophisticated country" aptly describes this barn turned fine dining establishment, where a high ceiling soars above tables appointed with white linens, faceted glass candle holders, fine crystal, and fresh flowers. A wagon hangs from the rafters, a sleigh decorates the rustic barn-wood wall. Tables on the mezzanine overlook this cavernous room sparkling with candlelight. Seafood-stuffed mushrooms, grilled mussels, and beef teriyaki appetizers tantalize your appetite. Delectable entrées such as duckling stuffed with seasonal fresh fruits and finished with apple brandy, veal Oscar, and tournedos of beef with bordelaise and béarnaise sauces are creatively prepared.

For a more casual and price-conscious meal, try one of the blackboard specials, say shepherd's pie or seafood Newburg, served in the tavern (the lounge part of the restaurant). Although this area doesn't share the grand atmosphere of the main dining room, linens and candles still add a special touch to your evening in the country.

Old Lyme

Hotel/Bed and Breakfast Kissing

OLD LYME INN, Old Lyme
85 Lyme Street, (203) 434-2600
Moderate to Expensive (inn), Expensive (dining)
(Closed first two weeks in January)

Call for directions.

When this timeworn 1870s farmhouse was reborn as an inn and restaurant, it could have been transformed into something either ridiculously opulent or woefully downtrodden. Instead, it is a comfortable, inviting bed and breakfast with Victorian flair and award-winning cuisine. With five rooms in the farmhouse and eight in the north wing, the inn can feel like a small hotel. Step-up four-poster beds with fishnet canopies, old-fashioned bedside lamps, vintage settees, and satin-finish wall coverings add panache to the architecturally plain rooms. Before dinner, a glowing hearth beckons you into the sitting room.

In the main dining room, a single salmon-hued rose, the inn's signature, awaits on each table. Around you is a small palace of a room, with golden wall coverings soaring to high ceilings, golden swags above tall windows, shield-back upholstered chairs, fine linens, and flickering candles. An alcove for special dinners is located off the Champlain Room, decorated with rich blue curtains and Victorian-inspired brass-and-etched-glass chandelier. Escargot in phyllo purses, baked goat cheese encrusted with macadamia nuts, veal and mushroom terrine en croûte, carpaccio of filet mignon, and other exquisite appetizers are uniformly delicious. Entrées such as lobster thermidor, venison Wellington, Connecticut pheasant, and salmon on asparagus with raspberry Hollandaise sauce are equally remarkable. For dessert, chocolate lovers beware! The pastry chef here has won the state's "ultimate chocolate dessert award" three years in a row.

Restaurant Kissing

BEE AND THISTLE INN, Old Lyme
100 Lyme Street, (203) 434-1667, (800) 622-4946
Expensive (dining room), Inexpensive to Moderate (inn, EP)
Call for directions.

Come early for dinner on weekend nights. On Friday, a guitarist sings love ballads as you sip your cocktail by the Colonial hearth in the cultivated but cozy parlor; on Saturday, a harpist soothes tired souls. Locals consistently choose this as the state's most romantic place to dine. A fire glows in the Colonial dining room, too, with its framed posters of impressionist paintings from the nearby museum. More dining areas fill the enclosed wraparound porch. One area, with a terra-cotta floor and white brick hearth, overlooks the garden; in another, baskets hanging from the rafters create a country look. Candles in hurricane globes and fresh flowers inspire romance.

Luscious appetizers, including wild mushroom lasagne, oysters on the half shell, and shrimp in parchment, will whet your appetite for entrées such as crab ravioli, sole poached in apple cider and finished with tarragon cream, pork on a port and pear coulis, and Idaho trout in a pecan crust. For a special treat, locals and visitors alike flock to the afternoon high teas, served on Monday, Wednesday, and Thursday from November through April. The inn is also renowned for breakfast and lunch.

The focus here is on the restaurant, but in keeping with its heritage as a Colonial inn, this 1756 house also offers overnight lodging upstairs. The ambience is comfortable Early American, with a fishnet canopy arching over the beds, white woven spreads, Oriental or braided rugs, antique washstands, and creaky floors just to remind you of the history here. With three meals a day, plus tea in the cooler months, being served downstairs, there's little common space left for overnight guests, so be prepared to join in or lock yourself away for a close night in your cozy bedchamber if you can. In the morning, an à la carte menu of omelets, waffles, popovers, and hash will entice you back to the warmth of the sunlit porch.

RHODE ISLAND

Block Island

Twelve miles south of the Rhode Island coast, 12 miles east of Long Island, and far far away from everyday cares, Block Island is a refreshingly unspoiled getaway, the Martha's Vineyard and Nantucket of 30 years ago. Only 800 residents live here year-round, in a tight-knit community where children attend school in classes of a dozen or so and people zealously safeguard the natural beauty of their home. On sunny summer days, tourists burst from the ferry—call (401) 783-4613 for reservations and information—infusing Old Harbor, the island's only village, with a loud, lively buzz. Many head for the near reaches of Crescent Beach. For more seclusion, continue north along the sandy strip where the crowds peter out. If you prefer quieter pursuits, bicycles, which can be rented in town, provide the best mode of transportation on this 11-square-mile island. A ride up Spring Street will bring you to **THE BLUFFS,** a dramatic landscape of 150-foot cliffs fronting the relentless Atlantic. A little farther away, **RODMAN'S HOLLOW** is one of the island's five wildlife refuges, where hiking trails wind through an overgrown ravine. On the northernmost tip of the island, at the end of Corn Neck Road, you'll discover pastoral **CHAQUM POND,** whose placid waters nearly touch the moody ocean. Although it's most popular on summer weekends, Block Island is even more of a getaway in the colder, windier months, but lodging and dining choices can be very limited. In any season, be sure to make advance reservations.

Block Island

Hotel/Bed and Breakfast Kissing

THE BLUE DORY INN, Block Island
Dodge Street, (401) 466-5891, (800) 992-7290
Moderate to Expensive

From the ferry terminal, turn right on Water Street. The inn is about two blocks down on the right.

Almost as close to the beach as a dory pulled onto the sand, this 10-room inn and adjacent cottages are in the heart of summer activity on Block Island.

The center of town is just steps away and popular Crescent Beach waits beyond the back fence. The main inn, with its Victorian-inspired decor, is anything but a sandy seaside cottage. The parlor could double as a period room, with its wood-frame chairs and sofa, marble-topped tables, lace curtains, and bay window. The non-Victorian television and VCR are tucked away in a cabinet. A downstairs guest room showcases Waverly fabrics, with rich white, green, and rose florals covering the carved wood bed and swagged over the window. More vintage beds, toss pillows, and pleasing hues highlight the cozy upstairs rooms. Numbers 5 and 7 have splendid views, the latter through a skylight in the eave ceiling. The five cottages in back of the property have a more timeworn, beachy feel. Two are efficiencies, one has a full kitchen, and three are better for larger groups. In the petite Doll House, you can fall asleep to the sounds of the ocean and awaken to the happy cries of children splashing in the waves. In the morning, the inn's special chocolate-raspberry coffee will help you welcome the sunshine.

HOTEL MANISSES, Block Island
Spring Street, (401) 466-2421, (401) 466-2063
Expensive to Very Expensive

From the ferry terminal, take a left on Water Street. At the Rebecca statue, head uphill on Spring Street. The inn is on the right, about a five-minute walk.

The Nicholas Ball Cottage, the 1661 Inn, and this richly refurbished hotel are all run by the same family, well known for their discriminating taste. The Manisses is their homage to the island's Victorian era. The gracious 1870 building with gabled third floor and crowning square tower has been completely restored. In the sun room, stained glass windows and a garden of hanging plants surround a parade of games while a Victrola cranks out nostalgic melodies. Upstairs, in the 17 guest rooms, you'll find grand wooden beds that whisper of dreams from long ago, antique vanities, and Victorian-inspired wall coverings. Several bedchambers, including the Princess Augusta, have whirlpool baths. The Pocahontas Room has a private deck overlooking the courtyard, its three-tier fountain, and the rolling lawn beyond. Four-legged visitors from the hotel's menagerie sometimes amble down this way. For a closer look at the friendly collection, stroll up the road to say hello to llamas, fainting goats, ducks that walk like penguins, and other oddities.

Inn guests walk up to the 1661 Inn for the breakfast buffet of scrambled eggs, pancakes, fresh fruit, cereal, muffins, baked beans, homemade hash, bluefish, and other gustatory delights, but dinner belongs to the Manisses. Downstairs, an enclosed glass porch overlooks the backyard, inviting the summer inside. In a second cozy area, appropriately called the Library, a raw bar features fish and eel from the inn's smokehouse. Stretching along one wall of the larger dining area, a vintage tavern bar of carved wood and stained glass adds a jovial touch. A fireplace warms another dining section, while Victorian table lamps glow on delicately patterned china. Creative dishes blend fresh ingredients with local delicacies in a stunning array of entrées; try the lobster stuffed with oysters and walnuts, or the flounder topped with tropical fruits. No meal is complete without their famous bourbon pecan brownies.

NICHOLAS BALL COTTAGE, Block Island
Spring Street
(401) 466-2421, (401) 466-2063
Very Expensive

From the ferry terminal, take a left on Water Street. At the Rebecca statue, head uphill on Spring Street. The inn is on the left, next to the 1661 House, about a five-minute walk.

Housed in a unique replica of an 1888 Episcopal church are three decadent guest rooms, all with fireplaces and Jacuzzis. The open, airy Cassius Room boasts a grand two-level room, white wicker furnishings, and a marble-topped dresser in the sleeping chamber downstairs. In the loft, the Jacuzzi is sensually placed in front of the crackling fire. In the contemporary Shuyler Colfax Room, climb closer to heaven as you sip sherry in the loft's firelit Jacuzzi or watch the moon rise from the outdoor sitting area. The Nicholas Room is absolutely stunning. A canopy bed faces the fireplace and in one corner a stained glass window glows above a Jacuzzi so immense you can nearly swim in it. In all the tastefully appointed rooms, oil paintings, perfectly balanced mood lighting, comfortable reading chairs, fresh fruits, brandy, and candy tempt you to stay forever. Mornings are accentuated with a bountiful breakfast served next door at the 1661 Inn. This impeccable property, located above a resplendent ocean panorama on unspoiled Block Island, is truly the ultimate getaway.

THE ROSE FARM INN, Block Island
Off High Street, (401) 466-2021
Moderate to Expensive (Open May through October)

Call for directions.

Geraniums bloom in window boxes along the porch railing. Perennials shower a rock wall with color. Inside, blossoms find their way into vases in the breakfast and guest rooms. This 10-room inn is as sweet and fresh as the flowers around it. Guest rooms gather just enough extras to be charming without being cluttered. The soft hues echo the serene ocean views in some rooms. In the larger second-floor rooms, fishnet canopies arch over four-poster beds, enhanced by touches such as an antique marble-topped bureau, reading chair, wooden rocking horse, or sailing ship print. In Room 9, you barely need to lift your head from the pillow to watch the sun rise over the water. Even the less expensive rooms, without a view, are welcoming and crisp. The breakfast room is as graceful as a rose petal, with a rounded wall of windows overlooking the Victorian Spring House Hotel and the ocean beyond. Hanging plants, stemware, Windsor chairs, and sky blue cloths invite lingering over the light buffet breakfast while the sun rises higher above Block Island.

SEA BREEZE INN, Block Island
Spring Street, (401) 466-2275
Inexpensive to Expensive

From the ferry terminal, take a left on Water Street. At the Rebecca statue, head uphill on Spring Street. The inn is almost to the crest of the hill, just past the 1661 Inn and Nicholas Ball Cottage. About a five-minute walk.

As fresh as its namesake and just as unpresuming, this old-fashioned bed and breakfast offers a quiet getaway. Garden flowers bloom in the compact courtyard between the petite cottages (each with several rooms) overlooking the water. Inside, the decor is simple and blithe, with shuttered windows and a few understated antiques. Room 8's high-peaked ceiling soars over a Shaker-inspired four-poster bed. Room 10's highlight is the splendid view over the grasslands to the blue ocean horizon. In Room 6, a Jenny Lind bed is blanketed in a blue and gold spread. Only half of the 10 rooms have a private bath, but the ocean vista from the property nicely balances this inconvenience. In the morning, a continental breakfast is delivered in a basket to your room. If it's sunny outside, spread it out at the inn's outdoor picnic table and enjoy a view of the ocean.

THE 1661 INN, Block Island
Spring Street, (401) 466-2421, (401) 466-2063
Very Expensive to Unbelievably Expensive

From the ferry terminal, take a left on Water Street. At the Rebecca statue, head uphill on Spring Street. The inn is on the left, about a five-minute walk.

From high on a hill, grasslands tumble below you to a small, marshy pond where ducks and white swan serenely float, and in the distance the ocean stretches out before you like blue velvet to the horizon. Gaze at this view from your deck, pillow, or Jacuzzi, depending on the room, when you stay at the 1661 Inn, built in 1661. Each of the nine guest rooms holds something special. Five have whirlpools; eight have private sun decks. Antique beds, vintage armoires, marble-topped bureaus, stained glass lamps, velvet reading chairs, and canopy beds set an indulgent yet charming tone. Several rooms contain unobtrusive kitchenettes, for couples who want the convenience and seclusion of dinner for two. In one room, you can dream of faraway lands on a canopy bed, then climb the stairs to an immense oval whirlpool set in the loft. Even rooms without a view are still ample and welcoming. In all the rooms, fresh flowers, brandy, and candy ensure sweet dreams. In the warmer months, a bountiful buffet breakfast is served in the country Colonial dining room or on the deck, both with the stunning seaside panorama.

◆ **Romantic Note:** If you're visiting Block Island for just the day, come here for a buffet lunch or a cooling drink, served during the summer only in the dining room, on the deck, or at umbrella-topped tables set on the lawn above the Atlantic.

◆ **Second Romantic Note: The 1661 GUEST HOUSE,** managed by the inn, is next door and offers less expensive, simply furnished rooms with access to ocean-view decks that overlook one of the most splendid panoramas this side of the island. Of the nine guest rooms, four share baths.

SPRING HOUSE HOTEL, Block Island ◆◆
Spring Street, (401) 466-5844, (800) 234-9263
Expensive to Very Expensive (inn), Expensive (dining)
(Open mid-April through October)

From the ferry terminal, take a left on Water Street. At the Rebecca statue, head uphill on Spring Street. The inn is at the crest of the hill. About a five-minute walk.

You can almost hear the melodies of an old Victrola playing or the swishing of ballroom dresses as you climb up the hill to this movie set of a Victorian resort hotel, with its wraparound veranda, multigabled third floor, and crowning cupola. Although restored, it still has the air of a venerable old dame, not quite as wealthy as she once was but determined to keep up appearances. Forty-nine rooms in two buildings accommodate today's guests. The most romantic are the suites, with four-posters blanketed in white woven spreads, Victorian or Early American sitting areas, wet bars, and wall-to-wall carpeting. Many rooms frame ocean views that are splendid no matter what the century.

The main dining room boasts the same view, through tall multipaned windows at one end. In warmer weather, tables are set on a 150-foot-tall deck that surveys grasslands, a pond, and the ocean. Tabletop candle lamps on pink cloths, soft rose walls, white lacquer Windsor chairs, and brass chandeliers create a refined but summery ambience. Seafood is truly fresh, in dishes such as native lobster sautéed in a cognac sauce, baked scrod, stuffed shrimp, sea scallops Dijon, and Block Island swordfish. Traditional steaks, chicken with tarragon or pecans, and a selection of pastas round out the menu. After dinner, try to find a table for two by the window in the spacious Victoria's lounge, and warm a chilly seaside night with their special raspberry-hazelnut coffee.

◆ **Romantic Note:** If you're in the mood for an extra-special splurge, you can enjoy a private catered dinner for two ($200 per couple) in the cupola, with its 360-degree panorama of island and ocean, especially stunning at sunset.

Restaurant Kissing

WINFIELD'S RESTAURANT, Block Island
Corn Neck Road, (401) 466-5856
Expensive (Open mid-May through November)

From the ferry terminal, turn right on Water Street, turn left on Dodge Street, and turn right on Corn Neck Road. The restaurant is on the right.

Shuck off your sandy beach clothes and treat yourself to a night on the town, Block Island style, at this popular eatery near the center and the shore. Wicker furnishings and a rose granite bar lend a breezy feel to the lounge. The dining room, with wooden chairs, beamed ceiling, and white walls with exposed timbers, is decked out in linens, candles, and flowers. Mussels steamed in white wine with tomatoes, onions, and fennel seed are an island favorite. Superior entrées include local swordfish, veal saltimbocca, rack of lamb, and black pepper fettuccine tossed with native lobster sautéed with snow peas, pine nuts, and brandy.

◆ **Romantic Note:** If a festive after-dinner fling is in order, **MCGOVERN'S YELLOW KITTENS TAVERN,** right next door, is one of tiny Block Island's liveliest nightspots.

Westerly

Hotel/Bed and Breakfast Kissing

SHELTER HARBOR INN, Westerly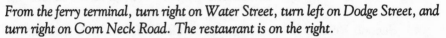
10 Wagner Road (Route 1), (401) 322-8883
Inexpensive to Moderate

Four miles north of Route 1's junction with Route 78, on the right side of Route 1.

While other historic inns strive to emulate sleek yachts or millionaires' mansions, this 1911 former music colony is quite content to provide comfortable lodging and simple relaxation. The barn, though it doesn't resemble one now, has been converted to 10 guest rooms. Each is uncluttered and simply furnished with Early American-style furnishings, white woven spreads, modern baths, and, perhaps, a television on the bureau for families and business travelers. In the more romantic rooms, private decks and brick fireplaces provide all the inspiration you'll need.

Downstairs, you can relax with a good read in the cozy library or sip a cocktail at the etched glass tables on the enclosed porch that doubles as a lounge. A series of hearth-warmed dining rooms feature post-and-beam architecture. The refined country cuisine includes seafood in puff pastry, scrod with walnuts and bacon, smoked haddock, pot roast, and tournedos of beef with a shiitake demi-glaze. In the morning, linger over gingerbread-apple pancakes and orange French toast, then enjoy a stroll along the inn's nearby beach, which stretches for two miles beside pond and ocean.

Narragansett

Hotel/Bed and Breakfast Kissing

THE RICHARDS, Narragansett
144 Gibson Avenue, (401) 789-7746
Very Inexpensive to Inexpensive

Call for directions.

You'll feel like guests at a friend's elegant country home when you visit the Richards, because, well, you are. No gilded sign hangs outside declaring that this is an inn, no hint at all until you're welcomed inside. Then you'll discover that this home is perfect for couples seeking a secluded getaway. In all four bedchambers, the Atlantic chill is countered with fireplaces and sherry. In one, intricately restored brasswork forms a crown canopy above a black iron-and-brass bed. In another, you'll find a white wicker rocker, lavender walls, and a pleated floral canopy over the bed. A third room boasts a half-poster snug beneath a down comforter and shares a hall bath with a guest room featuring a fishnet canopy bed. Flowers blossom in all the rooms, enhancing their rich hues. Downstairs, settle by the hearth in the elegant sitting room or, in nicer weather, head outside to the inn's spacious lawn and colorful gardens. Start your day with a generous breakfast, served at a large wooden table.

STONE LEA, Narragansett
40 Newton Avenue, (401) 783-9546
Inexpensive to Moderate

Call for directions.

The ocean battled with the wind that evening, a tempest of thunder and fury crashing upon the rocky shore, sending fountains of spray skyward like so many fireworks. Yet at dawn, peace prevailed. The blue Atlantic shimmered in the morning sun, as if happy to be lapping at the grassy point upon which this inn stands. No matter the mood of the relentless sea, the location of this 1884 mansion, just a few yards from the rugged coast, is spectacular. Inside, the billiards room, with its magnificent table and glass-encased model ships, looks over this mesmerizing panorama. Unbelievably, the view may be even better from the window seat on the landing of the graceful "harp" staircase that leads up to your quiet seaside sanctuary.

Easygoing comfort prevails here. You may find a brass bed blanketed with a floral quilted spread, antique tables, patchwork quilts, an old-fashioned bath, or dormer window. Rooms 1 and 7, on the corner, frame a view on two sides. Some of the commodious rooms accommodate two or even three beds, although the inn is only appropriate for families with children over the age of 10. In the morning, stuffed French toast and apple puff pancakes are enticing entrées served in the breakfast room, with its collection of candlesticks and depression glass highlighting inset shelves. Eat hearty: you have a full day of ocean gazing ahead of you.

Restaurant Kissing

BASIL'S RESTAURANT, Narragansett
22 Kingstown Road, (401) 789-3743
Expensive

About one and a half blocks inland from the village pier and Coast Guard House, in the small strip shopping center on the left.

Don't be put off by this restaurant's lackluster location in a strip shopping center. Inside, you'll discover one of the city's most intimate restaurants. Candles flicker in stylish holders with black bases and fluted glass shades. Black-rimmed china with gold trim punctuates the white linen. A banquette and upholstered chairs invite lingering beneath gilt-framed still lifes. Downstairs isn't as special, but is still nicely decked out in bold colors and a striped banquette along one wall. French cuisine will entice you in either room. Appetizers of escargots bourguignonne, oysters Rockefeller, frog legs fines herbes, and seviche are excellent. Veal dishes, especially medallions topped with a light cream and mushroom sauce, are superb. Other favorites include the succulent duck à l'orange, soft-shell crab almondine, beef Stroganoff, and shrimp and scallops in a white wine sauce. Delectable parfaits, a perfect crème caramel, chocolate mousse, and the Coupe Basil—vanilla ice cream with fresh fruit, apricots, strawberry sauce, and coconut, finished with a pirouette cookie—are too sweet for words.

SPAIN RESTAURANT, Narragansett
1 Beach Street, (401) 783-9770
Moderate to Expensive

About one block inland from the village pier and Coast Guard House, on the bottom floor of the Village Inn.

Say *"Hola"* to the impassioned cuisine of sunny Spain. Guitar music fills the air, along with the scent of pungent spices. Candles flicker in stunning glass holders on tables cloaked in white linens and pink napkins. Hanging plants and art posters from the owners' homeland add a cheerful touch to the polished decor of this large dining room. A casserole of mussels in a green sauce, grilled chorizos, clams in a picant tomato sauce, garlic soup, and gazpacho are some of the tempting *entradas* on the extensive, authentic menu. Main dishes include tenderloin for two with artichoke hearts and mushroom caps in a wine-Dijon sauce; shellfish casseroles; chicken sautéed with mushrooms and pimento in a tomato-cognac sauce; and veal in a mushroom, sherry, and brandy sauce. These Spanish dishes are a rare treat in Yankee Rhode Island. Two dozen Spanish wines highlight the wine list.

Newport

As extraordinary as the mansions that grace its shores, Newport is one of Rhode Island's premier getaways, where reminders of the golden ages of sailing and the super wealthy still shine. The opulent summer "cottages" built by the Vanderbilts and their peers were fashioned after northern Italian palaces and magnificent French chateaus. Today, the restored homes rival any European royal castle and will set you to dreaming as you walk their gilded halls.

But Newport offers more than these turn-of-the-century icons of indulgence. The **HISTORIC POINT** area, in the Washington Street neighborhood near Goat Island, is perfect for an evening stroll, as the sunset washes the Colonial homes in gold and lanterns flicker along the narrow streets. A drive along **OCEAN AVENUE** offers hypnotizing views of the Atlantic's rocky shore. And the wharf area, especially the restored Colonial **BOWEN'S WHARF,** is a delightful place to window shop, sustained by a quick cup of chowder. In fact, Newport's maritime history could be its most enduring romance, exemplified in yesterday's masted merchant ships and today's graceful yachts.

Hotel/Bed and Breakfast Kissing

CLIFFSIDE INN, Newport
2 Seaview Avenue, (401) 847-1811, (800) 845-1811
Moderate to Very Expensive

Head toward the water on Memorial Boulevard and turn right onto Cliff Avenue, shortly before Easton's Beach. The inn is on the left, at the corner of Cliff and Seaview avenues.

The Victorian era was more than frills, flounces, and cluttered tabletops. It celebrated polite hospitality, honored skillful workmanship, demanded propriety in every aspect of life. This splendidly restored 1880 home epitomizes the best of the Victorian era, updated with today's luxuries. In the evening, hors d'oeuvres are served by the hearth in the parlor where period settees echo the room's graceful architectural lines. On one wall, a haunting self-portrait of a reclusive former owner oversees today's hosts. An authentic Australian phone booth is tucked in one corner, one of the many unusual pieces that blend perfectly with the tasteful decor of this 12-room inn.

In Miss Beatrice's Room, the gilt-framed mirror above the black marble hearth reflects a magnificent wooden bed, a bay window seat smothered with toss pillows, and a marble-topped table. A deep oval Jacuzzi is set in the bathroom's bay window, while two heads offer more clean fun in the separate marble shower. A white eyelet canopy crowns the antique bed in the firelit Victorian Room, one of four bedchambers with fireplaces. The Maryland Room is like a library, with its crown canopy bed hemmed in by bookshelves. In the topmost chamber, the Turner Suite, an immense whirlpool bubbles beneath a skylight, next to a cozy sitting room. Each rooms holds something special, whether it's French doors that open to a stunning whirlpool in the Attic or the private entrance and simple summery feel of the Veranda Room. In the morning, indulge in a sumptuous breakfast. The Cliff Walk (see "Outdoor Kissing" for Newport) is only one block away.

ELM TREE COTTAGE, Newport
336 Gibbs Avenue, (401) 849-1610, (800) 882-3ELM
Expensive to Unbelievably Expensive

Call for directions.

Five of the six guest rooms are warmed by fireplaces in this 110-year-old "cottage," but that's just one highlight. The beautifully decorated common rooms are as generous and gracious as the hosts. In the morning room, sunlight dances through stained glass windows depicting the four seasons as you settle into the cheerfully decked out wicker furniture. In the sweeping living room, a baby grand and upright piano have plenty of room to make beautiful music together. You will, too, as you snuggle on the camelback sofa, gaze out the multipaned windows to the shimmering water, or embrace before the immense ballroom mirror.

Louis XIV beds, more than 200 years old, grace all of the bedchambers, inspiring dreams of courtly French romances. Upstairs, the Windsor Suite (named after the duke and duchess, the original owner's friends) holds a magnificent king-size bed crowned with a half-tester, a love seat by a fireplace, a second sitting area accented by a stained glass lamp, and a bathroom sparkling with a crystal chandelier. Firelit Room 2 will please any gentleman, with sporting prints and a paisley comforter. Sunny yellows, botanical prints, and a carved wood bed lend a cheery welcome to Room 3. Whichever room you choose, you'll find lovely antiques, set off by elegant but understated details such as gilt-framed mirrors, stained glass work, or paintings of tall ships.

Stellar breakfasts—perhaps pumpkin waffles or spinach and cheddar omelets—are served in the firelit dining room, where crochet and cutwork overlays and pots of dried roses embellish your visit to Newport's gilded age.

THE FRANCIS MALBONE HOUSE, Newport
392 Thames Street, (401) 846-0392
Moderate to Very Expensive

From Memorial Boulevard, turn left onto Thames Street. The inn is three blocks down on the left. To reach the guest parking area, turn left onto Brewer Street (the third left off Thames Street) into the first driveway on the right.

When the winter fog rolls in, a fireplace banishes the Atlantic chill in the front parlor of this stately Colonial inn, with its wing chairs, muted green paneled walls, and swagged valances. Two other tastefully appointed sitting rooms assure privacy, if that's what you seek, as you sweeten your afternoon with the tempting cookies served each day. Fireplaces also warm several guest rooms. There you can slip beneath the monogrammed comforter on a four-poster bed or dream of ages past in a wing chair by the hearth. The sophisticated, elegant rooms are done up in burgundy and green, with Turkish carpets, Early American highboys, and Oriental vases. The private Counting House Suite is long and roomy, with a four-poster bed and ample sitting area. In the morning, a full breakfast is served in the dining room near the immense, nonworking Colonial fireplace. This luscious repast would lure any sailor home from the sea.

IVY LODGE, Newport
12 Clay Street
(401) 849-6865
Moderate to Expensive

Call for directions.

The entry of this turreted clapboard Victorian may remind you of a
miniature Gothic cathedral, ensconced in the rich patina of oak, from the
spindle balusters to the high-peaked ceiling soaring above two flights of stairs.
The firelit sitting room has a summery air, with salmon-colored walls and white
wicker, while the spacious parlor is more formal, with its overstuffed sofa and
love seat, a grand piano, and draperies swagged above windows that overlook
the wraparound veranda.

Guest rooms carry on the theme of easy elegance, but are not so grand that
you feel bridled. A sleigh bed, a hearth trimmed in Delft tile, and a double
whirlpool highlight the Library. In the Ivy Room, named for its ivy-motif wall
coverings, piles of white pillows top the white comforter on the four-poster bed
and bleached wood furnishings lend a French country ambience. Some of the
rooms can be rented as a family suite, and celebrities have been known to
indulge themselves and their children here. In the dining room, a candle
chandelier alive with a rich floral arrangement hangs above the 16-seat dining
table. The full buffet breakfast will make you feel like royalty before you tour
America's palaces just down the street.

NEWPORT ISLANDER DOUBLETREE HOTEL, Newport
Goat Island, (401) 849-2600, (800) 528-0444
Expensive to Unbelievably Expensive

Drive across the causeway (abutting Newport Harbor) to Goat Island. This resort
is the only hotel on the tiny island.

Although most large hotels are too businesslike to qualify as kissing places,
the splendid location of this well-run hotel places it above its peers. The
towering skyscraper dominates tiny Goat Island, and guest rooms overlook the
harbor on one side, the bay on the other. Bold navies and reds add an
understated nautical touch to the pleasant but standard hotel furnishings.
Suites are decked out in softer tones of ivory, rose, and pickled wood, and some
have private balconies. From the windows of the Windward Restaurant, you
can gaze over the sailboats moored at this famous yachting town. Rattan and
boldly hued upholstered chairs in the sunken porch room create a breezy,
contemporary feel. An exercise room, indoor and outdoor pools, and two
racquetball courts help you work off an indulgent meal. On weekends, a local

singer, Saucy Sylvia, entertains in the lounge, a fun nightspot no matter where you choose to sleep in Newport.

◆ **Romantic Note:** For the best prices, be sure to ask about their packages when you call to make a reservation.

SANFORD-COVELL VILLA MARINA, Newport
72 Washington Street, (401) 847-0206
Moderate to Very Expensive

Along the shore, between the causeway to Goat Island and the Newport Bridge.

In 1870, when this home was new, the *Boston Journal* proclaimed it "the most elegantly finished house ever built in Newport." Although this venerable Victorian has since been overshadowed by more recently built mansions, it is still impressive. The 35-foot-tall foyer is inspirational, crowned with intricate carved and painted wood. This home has been in the same family since 1895, so staying here is like visiting an eccentric old aunt who has saved heirlooms and furnishings through the years, placing them wherever they'd fit. The entry hall feels downright medieval, with its tapestry on the wall and throne-like chairs. At one end, the window overlooking the saltwater pool and Jacuzzi, private dock, Goat Island, and the shimmering water allows a shaft of sunlight to penetrate this inner sanctum. In the dining room, a gilt, painted ceiling soars above a table that belonged to the founder of the Annapolis Naval Academy. Two grand pianos are tucked into the firelit parlor. Guest rooms are typical of a lived-in but distinguished home; yours may have a slipcovered chair, a marble sink, prints of sailing ships, or rich wood paneling. Water views and perhaps a working fireplace highlight the best rooms. Throughout the house, a collection of tick-tocking vintage clocks reminds you it's time for another kiss.

VICTORIAN LADIES, Newport
63 Memorial Boulevard, (401) 849-9960
Moderate to Expensive

Between Bellevue and Annandale avenues.

Toss pillows and soft feminine colors lend a cheerful air to this attractive Victorian inn. In the parlor, a glowing hearth and sparkling crystal chandelier are enhanced by pink-and-white-striped wall coverings and swagged drapes. Guest rooms display the same panache, with such touches as a love seat nested in a bay window, a four-poster bed crowned with a Battenburg-style canopy, a writing desk, balloon valances, and subtle shades of blue, dusty rose, or mauve. Sadly, the street outside now bustles with automobiles rather than clip-clopping horses, but the noise is somewhat dulled in the rear building of the two homes that comprise this 11-room inn. In the morning, a full buffet breakfast welcomes you into the country-style dining room to celebrate the dawn of your new day in Newport.

THE WILLOWS, Newport
8 Willow Street, (401) 846-5486
Moderate to Expensive

In the Historic Point district near Goat Island. Willow Street is off Washington Street between the Goat Island Causeway and the Newport Bridge. The inn is at the end of Willow Street, on the right.

Long before the local millionaires built their opulent mansions, Newport was a bustling seaport of narrow streets and stalwart Colonials. This five-room inn, housed in an 18th-century home, is in the midst of a historic neighborhood of 200-year-old houses and lantern-lit lanes that brings back the 1700s. (It's an extraordinary place for an evening stroll.) Yet the interior reflects a feminine, Victorian flair. Six shades of pink color the petite parlor, with its tufted settee and antique photos. The guest rooms are on the small side, perhaps too small, but are nicely filled with fresh roses and dimmer lights to set the mood. In one, a teddy bear and bunny bride and groom add whimsy to the brass four-poster canopy bed swathed in lace. Another brass canopy bed fills the French Quarter Room. A carved wooden bed is tucked into the third-floor Captain's Loft. In the morning, softly ringing bells piped over the intercom awaken you. As strange as this seems, following the bells, over the intercom, the innkeeper gives a morning talk telling of Newport's best sites and historical tidbits to inspire you for a day of touring. Depending on your viewpoint this is a bit intrusive, exceptionally cute, or extremely helpful. After the presentation, breakfast is brought to your bed and served on bone china and sterling; your privacy is definitely assured.

Restaurant Kissing

LE BISTRO NEWPORT, Newport
Bowen's Wharf, (401) 849-7778
Moderate

Call for directions.

Climb the open staircase to the third floor and you'll find a cozy bar with a high-peaked ceiling and tables along a banquette to accommodate walk-ins at this popular restaurant. On the two lower floors, golden walls, Windsor chairs, white linens on the tables, and baskets in the beams define French country flair, appropriate for such appetizers as mussels marinière, escargots à la bourguignonne, and platter of charcuterie. The well-prepared seven-hour leg of lamb, bouillabaisse, grilled sirloin, and Burgundy-style sausage with hot potato salad are amazing. And can you resist the vanilla ice cream with chocolate-walnut sauce or Creole bread pudding with bourbon sauce before returning to your home port?

THE MOORING, Newport
Sayer's Wharf, (401) 846-2260
Moderate

Call for directions.

Sailing yachts are moored just outside the picture windows of this aptly named restaurant. You can dream of crossing the sea in these sleek ships as you banish the Atlantic chill with a cup of award-winning chowder. Seafood is the hallmark here, with oysters and littlenecks on the half shell, shrimp cocktail, calamari, and other salty appetizers. Exceptionally fresh fish and seafood entrées include lobster, Newport's catch of the day, sautéed scallops, and sailor's stew. The landlubber is not forsaken, however: filet mignon, asparagus ravioli, chicken Alfredo, sandwiches, and burgers round out the menu. Soft lighting and classical music set a romantic mood, along with burgundy cloths, black lacquer chairs, and smoky glass table lamps. Tables with a view are best, but an inner room, warmed by a large brick hearth with copper flashing, is also a cozy place to contemplate the history surrounding you, inspired by the vintage photographs lining the walls.

THE PLACE AT YESTERDAY'S, Newport
28 Washington Square, (401) 847-0116
Expensive

From Memorial Boulevard, coming from the wharf area, turn left onto Spring Street (one block up from the wharves). Washington Square (where Broadway joins Spring Street) is one block past Touro, about nine short blocks down. Turn left and park.

The cuisine is superb and the service friendly at this upbeat bistro. Brass railings along the mezzanine, candle lamps in brass bases, fresh flowers on white linen, upholstered booths, art deco-inspired lamps, and black-and-white photographs of old Newport decorate the refreshingly cosmopolitan interior. The food is the talk of the town, with such appetizers as Thai beef salad, gratin of wild mushrooms, shrimp and corn tamales with lobster sauce, and Maine crab cakes in Creole sauce. The lamb in a pecan crust with sweet potato hay, stuffed veal chop with a roasted red pepper sauce, and pan-seared red snapper with lobster and guava are all enviably delicious. More casual meals can be enjoyed in the sunken tavern room, where wooden booths, etched glass partitions, piano lamps, hanging plants, and jazzy music lend a festive ambience. Burgers and sandwiches satisfy hearty appetites, and the New York-style cheesecake is as sinfully rich as the builders of Newport's vintage mansions.

THE WHITE HORSE TAVERN, Newport
Marlborough and Farewell Streets, (401) 849-3600
Expensive

Call for directions.

Journey together to the days of yore in this ancient hostelry. It claims to be our nation's oldest, dating to before 1673, and to dramatize its age you are told it was originally run by a pirate. The dark beamed ceiling and well-worn floor, in ages past, heard talks of liberty and a new nation, welcomed home whalers and sea captains. A fire blazes in the cozy bar while another cavernous hearth warms a small dining room. In the formal dining areas, tapers flicker inside hurricane globes and bud vases top white linens. The kitchen turns out what may be the best meals in town. Appetizers include iced shellfish, gravlax, broiled oysters, escargots en croûte, and mushroom ratatouille. The entrées would tempt patriot and pirate alike: baked sea scallops in an almond crust; lobster sautéed with tomatoes, basil, brandy and cream; honey and cinnamon roast duckling; and sautéed veal and sweetbreads in a green peppercorn sauce are all savory delights. After your sumptuous repast, close your eyes and raise a toast to the distant past and near future.

Outdoor Kissing

BRENTON POINT PARK, Newport
Ocean Avenue

At the end of Bellevue Avenue (where many of the mansions are), turn right onto Ocean Avenue. Follow it along the Atlantic shore to the southernmost tip, known as Brenton Point.

For some, the wealth of Newport is expressed in the extravagant palaces created by America's "royalty." But to experience the area's natural riches, pack a picnic lunch and drive along stunning Ocean Avenue to this seaside park. Though it is just a short distance from the mansions, it feels far away. Benches are perched along the Atlantic shore, where the surf crashes upon the rocks, fishing boats bob on the waves, and sea gulls soar overhead. Just to remind you of what's lasting in life, peer across the grassy field to the inland woods. The stone ruins of a once-grand building are now being overcome by forest.

CLIFF WALK

This scenic walk begins just off Memorial Boulevard, near Easton's Beach, and winds along the shore to Ocean Avenue.

Join hands and stroll along one of the most magnificent walkways in New England. On one side, waves pound upon the rocks and the ocean blue stretches to the horizons of your imagination, as timeless as love. On the other side, you can see just what imagination, love, and vast quantities of money can create in the gilded turn-of-the-century "summer cottages" of America's ridiculously wealthy upper class. The magnificent Breakers, built in 1895 by Cornelius Vanderbilt, was modeled after a 16th-century northern Italian palace. In short order, you'll pass Rosecliff, based on the Grand Trianon at Versailles, then the Astors' Beechwood and Marble House. Each one is unbelievably grand.

After the mansions, the trail can get rough, and even dangerous in stormy weather. No matter what the weather or season, be sure to wear comfortable walking shoes and dress appropriately.

> *"People who throw kisses are mighty hopelessly lazy."*
>
> Bob Hope

MASSACHUSETTS

Cape Cod
North Shore to Provincetown

Sandwich

Hotel/Bed and Breakfast Kissing

THE CAPTAIN EZRA NYE HOUSE, Sandwich   ◆◆
152 Main Street, (508) 888-2940, (800) 388-CAPT
Very Inexpensive to Inexpensive

Call for directions.

I half-expected the captain himself to greet me at the door of this no-nonsense, 1829 Federal-style house. He must have been away on his clipper ship, for inside I discovered a much more feminine, easygoing ambience than the battened-down exterior suggests. Perhaps the captain would have spent more time dry-docked if he could have soaked in a clawfoot tub beneath a skylight, stretched his sea legs beneath an arched eyelet-trim canopy, or toasted his toes by the brick fireplace in the Blue Room, with its four-poster bed. Two of the cozy guest rooms share a bath, which usually doesn't appeal to those long at sea or lovers on a romantic getaway.

In the morning, hearty breakfasts consisting of home-baked breads, fried apples, and an entrée such as German puff pancakes are served in the dining room, which features a collection of china reminiscent of dishes that the captain may have brought home from the far-off Orient.

DANIEL WEBSTER INN, Sandwich   ◆◆◆
149 Main Street, (508) 888-3622
Moderate to Expensive (EP), Moderate (dining)

Call for directions.

Steeped in history and nearly as old as Sandwich itself, the Daniel Webster Inn is known far and wide for its Yankee hospitality, hearty fare, and good cheer. Begun as a parsonage in 1692, the inn has grown like the nation around it, which seems only fitting since legend claims local patriots headquartered here during the revolution. Today, the guest rooms in the main inn are invitingly decorated in Hitchcock reproductions of step-up beds and highboys. The guest rooms in motel-like wings along the flowered courtyard behind the main inn are too numerous to be charming. My favorites are those in the Quince Tree House, down the street. Here, you may find an arched canopy bed in your room, a fireplace or a whirlpool. One suite boasts a sitting room with its own grand piano.

Known for their award-winning cuisine, the dining rooms in the main inn will suit nearly any fancy. In the large Heritage Room, the ample hearth adds a cozy glow to the dark, wood-paneled walls embracing tables topped with burgundy cloths and flickering oil lamps. The Conservatory is a favorite for Sunday brunch, lunch, or an early dinner, with glass all around, immense hanging plants, and brass chandeliers. The 18th-century Webster Room is more traditionally formal, with its fireplace, smoky rose walls and white woodwork, and the inn's collection of sparkling, colored glassware showcased on inset shelves. Baked scrod, veal Oscar, rack of lamb, and prime rib are some of the highlights on the classic American menu in this classic American setting.

ISAIAH JONES HOMESTEAD, Sandwich   ◆◆◆
165 Old Main Street, (508) 888-9115
Inexpensive to Moderate

Call for directions.

This graceful 1849 home beautifully blends designer decor, splendid antiques, and modern luxury with a touch of playfulness. In the Deming Jarves Room, with its oversized whirlpool tub and plush half-tester bed, a top hat and a lace-brimmed lady's bonnet balance on an antique cheval mirror. At this inn, it's easy to take a tumble together into the past. Even on a mild, early-autumn evening, you won't be able to resist lighting a flame in the hearth of the Dr. Samuel Beale Room, climbing onto the high four-poster bed, and dousing the Victorian fringed lamps just to see the firelight flicker. Chintz and wicker highlight the Lombard Jones Room, with its fabulous bed floating in a cloud of sheer canopy and curtains. Each luxurious room is full of details from both days gone by and the present. Happy faces gather around the dining table in the morning, to be coaxed slowly into today with a candlelit breakfast fit for any century.

THE SUMMER HOUSE, Sandwich   ◆◀
158 Main Street, (508) 888-4991
Very Inexpensive

Take Interstate 93 to Route 3 to Cape Cod. Cross the Sagamore Bridge, where Route 3 becomes Route 6. Take Exit 2, turn left, and follow to a fork in the road. Turn right onto Main Street.

Many so-called "country inns" can be more plush than a palace. If you're looking for a simple, sentimental example of a true country bed and breakfast, try the Summer House. Housed in a classic Greek Revival Colonial, the guest rooms are clean, welcoming, affordable, and pleasantly decorated with patchwork quilts and a smattering of antiques. A pencil-post bed gleams in the light of a fireplace in the downstairs room. Upstairs, four rooms share two baths. Candles in the rooms evoke a simpler past. In keeping with tradition, a hearty morning meal is served in the sunny breakfast room, with its warm hearth, checkerboard floor, and bright and cheery floral cloths. Seasonal herbs, berries, and vegetables enhance your fresh start to an old-fashioned day on the Cape.

VILLAGE INN, Sandwich
4 Jarves Street, (508) 833-0363, (800) 922-9989
Inexpensive (Closed mid-December through March)

Jarves Street runs between Main Street and Route 6A, just east of the Daniel Webster Inn. The Village Inn is near the corner of Jarves and Main Street.

If you stop to smell the roses at this 1830s Federal-style home, it may take all day. More than 270 rosebushes blossom in the garden, embracing the inn with their sweet perfume in the warmer months. You may be beguiled into lazing away the afternoon on the wraparound porch, watching the comings and goings of this historic town. Inside, you'll discover a Victorian with a twist. Vintage pieces, swag drapes, and dainty floral prints are offset by unique wood furnishings crafted by the innkeeper. Some bedroom sets are hand-painted with flowers that echo the bountiful bushes blooming beneath your window. Fireplaces and brass candle sconces are splendid touches that set an elegant mood.

West Barnstable

Outdoor Kissing

SANDY NECK BEACH, West Barnstable

About four miles east of Sandwich. From Route 6A, turn left onto Sandy Neck Road, across from Michael's at Sandy Neck restaurant. Follow this road to the ocean.

Acres of sand dunes undulate toward the sea; tufted with golden grass and wildflowers, they are a soft, warm contrast to the cold waves ceaselessly crashing upon the shore. On the beach, round smooth pebbles, the kind you love to caress in your palm, are strewn like confetti from the ocean. Come at sunset to walk arm-in-arm beneath a sky brushed with brilliant roses and purples. A secluded spot awaits you on this stretch of sand where you can huddle close against the night breeze while dreaming of far-off lands that sleep in the dark beyond the cobalt sea.

Barnstable

Hotel/Bed and Breakfast Kissing

ASHLEY MANOR, Barnstable
3660 Olde Kings Highway (Route 6A), (508) 362-8044
Moderate to Expensive

Call for directions.

With its little white lights glimmering like stars brought down from the heavens, you can hardly help sneaking out to the isolated gazebo for a late-night smooch. On a cold night, when Jack Frost starts nipping at your nose, you can always retire gleefully inside to warm your love by the fire. All but one of the guest rooms glow with working hearths, and all boast romantic bed treatments. Wide-plank floors with hand-hooked rugs and the unusual speckled "Nantucket" floors add to the sophisticated country feel. Fireplaces, one a large Colonial brick affair with built-in bake oven, blaze in the parlors, too. Decanters are filled with sherry and port, and fruit, crackers, or cookies are served in the afternoon. You'll enjoy breakfast by the firelight in the dining room, served in true country style with a multitude of courses to make sure everyone goes away satisfied.

BEECHWOOD, Barnstable
2839 Main Street, (508) 362-6618
Moderate to Expensive

Take Exit 6 off Route 6 and turn left at the end of the ramp. At Route 6A, turn right. The inn is about two miles up on the right, exactly one-half mile past the railroad overpass.

A magnificent beech tree reigns over this gabled Victorian, its woody arms arching down over the wide veranda as if yearning to swing in the hammock built for two or while away the afternoon in the rocking chair. Inside, too, you're in this stately tree's embrace, especially in the delicate Cottage Room, with its windows that overlook the graceful branches and its feminine bedroom set hand-painted with bouquets of roses. You can swoon on the fainting couch by the hearth in the Rose Room, or recover on the lace canopy bed, two of the many fine antiques found throughout the inn. The Garret Room is akin to your grandmother's attic. A private stairway leads to this whimsical, sloped-ceiling room, complete with a vintage trunk, toys, and two cane chairs perched by the window. In the morning, a full breakfast is served by candlelight and accompanied by classical music in the gleaming, wood-paneled dining room, as the beech tree flutters in the breeze outside, happy to see the Victorian era so graciously revived.

Restaurant Kissing

BARNSTABLE TAVERN, Barnstable
Route 6A, (508) 362-2355
Moderate

Take Route 6 to Exit 6. Turn left off the ramp and go one mile to Route 6A. Turn right and go two miles into Barnstable Village.

In days of yore, travelers stopped by this humble hostelry for a mug and a hearty meal. Today, you can almost see the marks left behind from their riding boots scuffing the hardwood floors. Forest green beams, posts, and shutters; folk art; an antique wall clock; paisley cloths; and votive candles in faceted glass holders add to the casual Colonial charm. Some specials most likely have been enjoyed here since the tavern opened in 1799, including classic clam chowder, lobster bisque, and fish stew. Creative sandwiches and burgers will satisfy your appetite in the tavern. The formal dinner menu features hickory-grilled sirloin; pork with apple, pear, and almond stuffing; pheasant; lamb; and traditional fresh seafood dishes.

Yarmouth Port

Hotel/Bed and Breakfast Kissing

WEDGEWOOD INN, Yarmouth Port
83 Main Street, (508) 362-5157
Moderate to Expensive

Take Route 3 South over Sagamore Bridge, where it becomes Route 6. Take Exit 7 (Willow Street) and turn right. Go to the stop sign and turn right onto Route 6A.

As graceful and precious as its namesake, this stately 1812 Federal-style Colonial is a classic blend of sophisticated charm and country hospitality. A welcome tea tray was brought to my room as I checked in, and the wonderful antique prints meshed perfectly with the decor, but I think my favorite touch was the candles that almost yearn to be lit in every room, even those with fireplaces. Pencil-post beds, fishnet canopies, wing chairs, stenciled floors, exceptional patchwork quilts, and hand-hooked rugs are just the foundation for a decorating flair that whispers elegance without sacrificing Colonial ambience. You may find a ship in a bottle on your fireplace mantel, a hunting print above, an antique vase, or a basket of yarn by the rocking chair by the window. In two fireplace rooms, French doors open to a private screened porch where you can light the candles as the sun sets, then move inside to cuddle by the fire. In the morning, a full breakfast is served in a cheery room highlighted with a bright bay window and majestic prints of sailing ships. The breakfast china, although not Wedgwood, is, literally, poetic.

Restaurant Kissing

ABBICCI, Yarmouth Port
43 Main Street, (508) 362-3501
Expensive

Call for directions.

A Mediterranean whisper wafted west from the sea, sailed across the Atlantic, and breezed into this refreshing restaurant. Any thought of Colonialism is banished beneath boldly colored, Mondrian-inspired walls of white, primary blue, jet black, and pure yellow, highlighted with a stylized map of Italy and contemporary collages and art prints. Traditional Italian fare has been revamped with the '90s in mind, using lighter, fresher ingredients or a demi-glacé rather than heavy sauce. Carpaccio, an exotic mushroom salad, and heartwarming soups are the prelude to pastas with seafood and nearly half a dozen veal dishes. Those who seek lusty foods will find rich, cheesy pasta dishes. With all the hoopla about this restaurant, the promising chocolate torte was disappointingly dry, but other desserts are worth the calories.

Dennis

Restaurant Kissing

GINA'S BY THE SEA, Dennis
134 Taunton Avenue, (508) 385-3213
Moderate (Open April through November)

Call for directions.

One of the best reasons to lunch here is the "dessert": a sunny stroll along the beach, which begins nearly across the street. This tiny café, low-key and a little funky, has been a favorite for many years both with locals and with tourists who are in on its secret. Booths, tables, and an assortment of chairs fill the wood-paneled porch and low-overhead dining room. The unusual vases on each table are crafted by a local potter. In nice weather, you can dine al fresco on the patio. On colder days, a fireplace warms the inner dining room. The delicious Italian cuisine includes cannelloni filled with spinach and ground veal, linguine with clam sauce, veal scaloppine, and traditional pasta and chicken dishes that will make you feel as though the Mediterranean, not the Atlantic, awaits outside.

THE RED PHEASANT INN, Dennis Village
Route 6A, (508) 385-2133
Expensive

Take Exit 9 from Route 6 and turn left onto Route 6A. Drive two and half miles to the inn, on the left.

Tucked inside a 200-year-old, rooster red barn, this restaurant takes its inspiration from the farms of yore—low-key atmosphere and fresh, first-rate food. Pheasant prints are prominent but not overwhelming in the series of adjacent rooms. Whimsical painted sunflowers and trailing vines climb the walls of the porch, with its fruit-motif stained-glass lamps. In the main room, a large white brick hearth and folk art add flair and warmth. Smoked homemade game sausage, wild mushroom strudel, and lobster and scallop lasagne are just some of the seasonal starters. Entrées range from veal Wellington to Portuguese seafood stew to catfish Beaujolais, plus, of course, braised pheasant with Savoy cabbage, red wine, and caramelized leeks.

SCARGO CAFÉ, Dennis
Route 6A, (508) 385-8200
Moderate

Take Exit 8 from Route 6. At the end of the ramp, turn left onto Union Street. Go one mile to Route 6A and turn right. Drive three and a half miles to the café, on the right.

As fresh, clean, and unassuming as a sea breeze, this casual café is a delightful choice for a fun lunch or dinner. Pottery lamps light each table. In one room, skylights invite the sun to shine upon the exposed beams and white walls. In another room, firelight is reflected on the warm, wood panels. Popcorn shrimp, chilled scallop cocktail, and the house's special fettuccine Alfredo lead the way to chicken, artichoke hearts, and cheese in pastry; Italian-style pastas and veal; or, my favorite, chicken flamed in apricot brandy with sweet sausage, mushrooms, and raisins. If you want something lighter, creative sandwiches include

Cajun chicken, fried sole, lamb, or a classic hamburger, just right for a quick bite before a moonlit walk on the beach, where you can enjoy the cool ocean breezes.

Outdoor Kissing

SCARGO TOWER, Dennis

From Route 6A heading east, turn right onto Old Bass River Road. Follow signs to Scargo Hill.

Women may feel like Rapunzel in this singular stone tower cresting a knoll, but once their prince climbs up, they may just want to stay here forever. A spiral staircase leads up the circular edifice to one of the best panoramic views on the Cape. From here you can see Scargo Lake below, a smattering of houses, and the vast expanse of Cape Cod Bay. Kissing here is a tradition, carried on by generations of visitors who first come as mischievous teens and return as old marrieds. Sunsets are especially sublime.

Brewster

Restaurant Kissing

BRAMBLE INN, Brewster
Route 6A, (508) 896-7644
Expensive to Very Expensive (dining), Inexpensive to Moderate (inn)
(Open April through New Year's Day)

Call for directions.

The flickering candles in the windows draw attention in this 1861 inn. At each table, a twosome sits, leaning forward as if aching for a kiss, toasting each other's love or holding hands tenderly as the soft light caresses them. Candles and love are the sole source of light on the porch of this restaurant. Inside, brass chandeliers, antique china, gentle classical music, bouquets of flowers, and more candles in sterling and brass sticks bespeak a subdued romance. Multicourse prix fixe dinners begin with such seasonal appetizers as duck sausage, country pâté, or chilled Moroccan seafood tapas, followed by veal medallions with Vermont cheddar and cranberry apple coulis, chicken with grilled lobster, or Spanish paella.

If you just can't bear to leave, the inn has rooms upstairs and in two other vintage buildings. The decor is sophisticated country, with a wicker bed, perhaps, or an Arts and Crafts-style bureau. A bright, contemporary common room upstairs accommodates guests when the restaurant is operating downstairs. A full buffet breakfast is served in the morning.

◆ **Romantic Alternative:** Why one small town harbors so many first-class restaurants is a mystery, but **HIGH BREWSTER**, 964 Satucket Road, Brewster, (508) 896-3636, (Moderate), is another favorite. Hardwood floors, Oriental-motif china, glass oil lamps, crewel-patterned wall coverings, and a patriotic gilded eagle above the hearth all contribute to the authentic Colonial feel. Prix fixe dinners may include quail with butternut squash demi-glaze or codfish cakes on cilantro crème fraîche, followed by creative pheasant, salmon, lamb, or veal entrées. The homemade desserts provide a sweet ending that spans the centuries.

CHILLINGSWORTH, Brewster
Route 6A, (508) 896-3640
Very Expensive

Call for directions.

The two of them sighed with delight as the waiter closed the curtain behind him. They toasted, surrounded by the beauty of their own private dining room, with its trompe l'oeil wall coverings, shelves showcasing antique books, candles flickering in sterling holders, and a velvet divan, that, I was told discreetly, does get used. Yet this is only one of the magnificent rooms at Chillingsworth, which is brimming with peerless antiques. It's almost as though a well-to-do collector is hosting a dinner party at his home, squeezing tables for fascinating, worldly guests into each room. Hand-painted murals, crystal wall sconces, Second Empire furnishings, priceless shadow boxes, and blazing hearths are just some of the highlights.

The cuisine consistently wins top awards. Prix fixe dinners may include foie gras; French bean, arugula, and jicama salad; or smoked salmon and Vermont chèvre terrine with saffron potato salad, all followed by soup, green salad, and sorbet to clean your palate for salmon with tomatoes, leeks, fennel, basil, and orzo, or veal with saffron risotto, garlic custard, wild mushrooms, and asparagus. Half a dozen dessert choices include chocolate nemesis with English cream, a berry pyramid with an exotic sauce, and others that will pique your curiosity as much as your sweet tooth. Reserve ahead, especially for the private room, and remember to allow plenty of time for your all-night affair.

Outdoor Kissing

CAPE COD RAIL TRAIL

Runs from South Dennis to the Salt Pond Visitor Center at Cape Cod National Seashore.

If you visited the Cape in years past, you may have come by rail, seeing the sights in style as you chugged through woodland, past harbors, to the stunning seashore. Today, you can enjoy the 20-mile trip even more along the paved bike path that leads where rails once glistened. One of my favorite starting points is in Brewster; you'll travel through the best scenery without feeling you've entered a marathon. If you need to rent a bike, try **RAIL TRAIL BIKE RENTALS**, 302 Underpass Road, Brewster, (508) 896-8200, (Inexpensive). They're located right on the trail, next to **MANOS PIZZA AND MORE**, (508) 896-8600, (Moderate), where you can buy a grinder for a picnic. The trail wends through a state park, woodland, past small harbor towns, to the National Seashore, where the energetic can connect with yet another set of trails that lead to the Atlantic.

◆ **Romantic Note:** As the trail winds through **NICKERSON STATE PARK,** you may want to detour onto the roller-coaster trails that curve through the forest to the quiet sandy beach of a woodland lake. The possibilities for enjoying the Cape on two wheels seem endless.

East Orleans

Hotel/Bed and Breakfast Kissing

THE NAUSET HOUSE INN, East Orleans
141 Beach Road, (508) 255-2195
Very Inexpensive to Moderate (Open April through October)

Call for directions.

You may feel like Adam and Eve in the lush conservatory of this country inn. Ivy weaves its verdant lace around the windows and comfortable white wicker furnishings allow you to sit and enjoy your surroundings. In fall, the aroma of the grape arbor is intoxicating. In spring, the weeping cherry tree celebrates with an explosion of blossoms. Inside the inn, an air of homespun fun prevails. Fanciful trompe l'oeil paintings of cats, geese, and even a dresser brimming with toys and quilts peek at you from niches and walls. Guest rooms are cozy and simply furnished in an eclectic blend of old and new: a cross-stitched spread on white wicker, a worn rug, a patchwork quilt, a four-poster bed. Some rooms share a bath. In the afternoon, juice and snacks are served by the hearth in the homey living room. On cold mornings, a Colonial-style fireplace banishes the chill in the low-slung breakfast room, just across the threshold from the greenhouse.

Eastham

Hotel/Bed and Breakfast Kissing

THE OVER LOOK INN, Eastham
3085 Route 6, (508) 255-1886, (800) 356-1121
Moderate

On the left side of Route 6, just north of the entrance to the Cape Cod National Seashore Salt Pond Visitor Center.

A wee bit of Scotland awaits those who don't overlook the Over Look Inn. This lemon yellow and candy pink mansion looks like gingerbread from the outside, but inside you'll discover a decidedly Scotch air. One of the first things you'll notice are the innkeeper's bagpipes. Afternoon tea and scones are served by the hearth in the library, where a collection of Winston Churchill portraits, steins, and other memorabilia fills the walls and shelves. Prints of Edward Hopper's Cape Cod scenes set a more tranquil tone in the breakfast room, while a portrait of Ernest Hemingway challenges you in the billiards room. Or you may simply want to cozy up to the fire in the Victorian parlor brimming with vintage pieces.

Ten guest rooms share the five common rooms. Antiques look right at home in the bedchambers, with their unusual faceted and sloping ceilings highlighted by lilac, green, rose, and other deep hues. In the morning, a proper breakfast will set you up for a day at the Cape Cod National Seashore, its visitor center, and the bike paths just across the street. Some of the seashore's best beaches are a short drive away.

THE WHALEWALK INN, Eastham
220 Bridge Road, (508) 255-0617
Moderate to Expensive (Open April 1 through December 1)

Take Route 6 to the Orleans Rotary. Go three-quarters of the way around, to the Rock Harbor Road exit, and turn left. Take the first right onto Bridge Road. The inn is about a quarter mile up on the right.

If a classic saltbox on the Cape is your vision of the ultimate summer getaway, here's one that's built just for two. Set back from the main inn, your private storybook home awaits, complete with gray shingles and black shutters. Inside you'll feel as though you've slipped into a serene sea as you light a fire in the tiled hearth and watch it glow on the quilt on your white lacquer bed.

The saltbox is just one of a variety of accommodations at this expansive inn. Each is pleasantly decorated in soft tones and coordinated fabrics, much like a country manor home. One follows a fanciful garden motif, with ivy-patterned wall coverings, violets blooming on the dust ruffle and shams, and windows all around. Several accommodations have sitting rooms and kitchenettes. The high-peaked, fireplace Guest House rooms, although spacious, are less charming. When you're not sequestered in your saltbox or suite, the living room and den with their glowing hearths can warm you on a cool Cape evening.

Outdoor Kissing

CAPE COD NATIONAL SEASHORE ◆◆◆◆
(508) 255-3421 (Salt Pond Visitor Center)
(508) 487-1256 (Provincelands Visitor Center)

The Salt Pond Visitor Center is located on Route 6 in Eastham. The Provincelands Visitor Center is located in the Provincelands section of Cape Cod, off Route 6 on Race Point Road.

Stretching as far as the love you'll feel when you embrace here, this unparalleled seashore runs the entire length of the outer Cape. The eternity of thundering waves, the whistle of wind as it sculpts and molds, the whisper of sands shifting—it is like emotion itself, in all its powerful fury, softened by everlasting tenderness. Let your toes sink in the sun-warmed sand, brave the cold waters, or build a castle for your dreams and you'll be experiencing the best of Cape Cod.

The **SALT POND VISITOR CENTER** is a good starting point. You'll learn more about the fragile environment around you and discover the best bike trails, picnic spots, and beaches for your plans. A little-visited area near the southernmost part of the parkland, **FORT HILL** offers a different view of the shore, with its wetlands, woodlands, and grassy meadows—rather than endless sand—along the shore. To the north, don't miss the **PROVINCELANDS VISITOR CENTER**. Its observation tower affords an unbeatable view of the voluptuous sand dunes surrounding you.

Provincetown

Set on the outermost tip of Cape Cod, Provincetown has long been known for its open-minded welcome to persons of all bents, from stalwart fishermen to bohemian writers and artists. With ferries from Boston bringing people by sea and automobiles bringing them by land, the town fairly bustles with activity, especially in the warmer months. Droves of tourists, many of them party-minded, crowd the maze of narrow one-way streets littered with "NO PARKING" signs. Scads of restaurants, guest houses, museums, and shops, selling everything from candy to T-shirts to fine art, are found here. Festivals range from the blessing of the fleet to a dance for transvestites and their wives. In summer, about 70% of the people visiting and staying at the inns are gay and lesbian. Off-season, straight couples are in the majority. Anyone seeking solitude will find it nearby, at the northernmost stretch of the Cape Cod National Seashore, just across Route 6. You'll see some of the most beautiful and extensive sand dunes on the Cape, a sandy sea-swept beach, and an ocean view that takes you from here to eternity.

Hotel/Bed and Breakfast Kissing

BRADFORD GARDENS INN, Provincetown
178 Bradford Street, (508) 487-1616
Moderate to Expensive

Take the Conwell Street exit from Route 6. Follow to the end of the street and make a left on Bradford Street. Go two-tenths of a mile; the inn is on the left side of Bradford, parking is on the right.

Stoke the Franklin stove in the Honeymoon Suite and you're sure to feel your love heat up. Billows of white eyelet seem to swathe the entire room in a mist, arching over the bed, flowing down on each corner. Or put match to tinder in the Alcove Room, with its white brick hearth and antique washstand adding a touch of nostalgia. Vintage furnishings, hardwood floors, swagged drapes, patchwork or lace bedcoverings, and fresh flowers from the garden lend a charm to each room. Beyond the immaculate yard are private, contemporary cottages and townhouses with fireplaces and kitchens. Generous breakfasts are served in the main inn's morning room, with sunlight and firelight glowing on the golden walls, assuring warm memories of your stay.

◆ **Romantic Alternative:** Ten of the 13 rooms at **THE FAIRBANKS INN**, 90 Bradford Street, Provincetown, (508) 487-0386, (Inexpensive to Moderate), are warmed by fireplaces. I found the rooms in the main inn more elegantly decorated and charming than those in the East Wing and Carriage

House, but make sure you request a private bath, as access to the shared baths is too public. The courtyard, with its brick patio, colorful flowers, and splashing fountain, is a delightful afternoon retreat.

THE MASTHEAD, Provincetown
31-41 Commercial Street, (508) 487-0523, (800) 395-5095
Very Inexpensive to Expensive

Take any Commercial Street exit from Route 6 (there are three of them). Commercial Street is one-way; the Masthead is at the very end on the left side.

Accommodations in this compact cluster of buildings are as varied as the visitors to Provincetown. Motel rooms, suites, cottages, efficiencies, and apartments all share two things in common: a location on the quiet end of town and a deck stretching across their 300 feet of private beach. Many of the furnishings are standard motel fare, but all rooms are clean and bright. Some, especially the Porthole Studio and the waterfront units, overlook splendid harbor views. Many suites are large enough for two couples or a family, have kitchenettes, and are available by the week. If you want to stay in Provincetown but prefer a low-key atmosphere and water view, this is a good bet.

WATERMARK INN, Provincetown
603 Commercial Street, (508) 487-0165
Moderate to Very Expensive

Turn left onto the first Provincetown exit (East End/Snail Road) off Route 6. At the dead end, turn right. Bear left at the next fork. The inn is one and a half blocks up on the left.

Imagine peering into a diamond and seeing a luminous seascape awash in the light of a full moon. Small boats bob at their moorings. To the north, a village hugs the shore, punctuated by a lighthouse on the point. This is what you'll experience as you snuggle on the sofa in your second-floor suite with its high-peaked, triangular windows above the water. On a warm afternoon or evening, the decks are irresistible. Inside, the look is fresh, contemporary, and bright. The feel is that of a deluxe condominium rather than an inn. White walls and ceiling fans, light gray overstuffed sofas, white tile coffee tables, Marimekko quilts, and the beachscapes hung on the wall enhance the setting. If it's privacy you seek, you'll find it here. There's little to no interaction with the innkeeper or other guests. Since each suite is equipped with a kitchen, you decide when and what to have for breakfast, perhaps inspired by the Portuguese bakeries in town. The location is on the quiet end of the village, removed from late-night frolickers, but just a short drive, or long walk, away from the center. Although all units are spacious and welcoming, those with a water view are jewels.

◆ **Romantic Alternative: THE ANCHOR INN**, 175 Commercial Street, Provincetown, (508) 487-0432 or (800) 858-ANKR (outside Massachusetts), (Inexpensive to Moderate), is cheek-to-cheek with the bustling town center. Almost all of the modest guest rooms have access to a deck. Harbor views, especially on the lower floor, would be splendid if not for the parking lot in the rear.

Restaurant Kissing

FRANCO'S BY THE SEA, Provincetown
133 Bradford Street, (508) 487-3178
Moderate to Expensive

Follow Route 6A, which turns into Bradford, and follow the right fork, past the corner of Standish Street. Franco's is on the left at the foot of the monument.

Black walls and pink woodwork, black cloths set with white napkins, pink bread plates and red Fiestaware, voluptuously rounded booth backs and Erte-inspired prints create an art deco look without being campy. The menu too reflects the chef/owner's creative tastes. Polly and Don's Favorite Brochette combines shrimp, scallops, and chicken in garlic butter. Veal Franco is served with asparagus, crabmeat, and béarnaise sauce. The signature Hideaway Pasta is liberally sprinkled with raisins, pine nuts, garlic, olive oil, and cheese.

◆ **Romantic Note:** Upstairs, **LUIGI'S**, (Moderate), is a festive Italian eatery, crammed with tables covered in classic red-checked cloths; exposed pipes contribute to a fun atmosphere as low-key as the ceiling.

GLORIA'S, Provincetown
269 Commercial Street, (508) 487-0015
Moderate

From Route 6, take the first Provincetown exit. Follow it to Route 6A. The restaurant is across from the town hall.

Surprisingly few eateries in this seaside town offer a water view. Gloria's does. For lunch or a pre-sunset dinner, ask for a table in the back room. Long and narrow, a wall of windows on one end frames nothing but sand and sea. Above, skylights allow sunbeams through to play amongst the exposed pink rafters and walls and dance across the coordinating pink and gray tile floor. Green plants climb between tables, adding privacy to this airy design. Portuguese and Italian specials fill the extensive menu. Deep-dish pizzas for one, calzone, pastas, and such seafood entrées as calamari, lobster, dried codfish, and traditional fish and chips are a few of Gloria's specialties. The atmosphere is as casual and relaxed as a beachside picnic.

Cape Cod - South Shore

West Falmouth

Hotel/Bed and Breakfast Kissing

INN AT WEST FALMOUTH, West Falmouth   ◆◆◆◀
66 Fraser, (508) 540-7696
Moderate to Very Expensive

Call for directions.

This inn isn't a page out of *Metropolitan Life*, it's the whole issue and then some. One of the Cape's most enviable properties, this secluded site enjoys an extraordinary view west over the forest to Buzzards Bay and the sunset. Each room is a designer's showcase of contemporary style and singular flair. The spacious parlor harbors several sitting areas, highlighted by the ample brick hearth, voluptuous bouquets of flowers, and Oriental-motif vases and lamps. The compact conservatory opens onto a large sun deck and graceful pool overlooking the water. French Provincial with a contemporary twist reigns in one guest room, while the Far East is the inspiration in another. A third room is dressed in soft mocha tones, and simple seashells replace the usual clutter of knickknacks. Many rooms have jetted tubs, and private balconies where you can view the sunset. But the best view is found at the apex of this large Victorian, a crowning cupola that allows you to kiss a little closer to the top of the world.

Restaurant Kissing

DOMINGO'S OLDE RESTAURANT, West Falmouth
856 Main Street (Route 28A), (508) 540-0575
Moderate

Take Route 28 South across the Bourne Bridge, following signs to Falmouth. Exit at Tos. B. Landers Road and make a left. The restaurant is 100 yards down the ramp.

The gifts of the sea are yours to savor in this cozy shingle-style home turned restaurant, where only three or four tables can squeeze into each of the small dining rooms. The atmosphere is as unpretentious as the food is delicious and generous. Glass tops the blue and green linen overlays on each table. Candles flicker in smoked glass next to dainty bud vases. Bright white walls are highlighted with an emerald-hued chair rail, a few hanging plants, and little else. Swing and light jazz set the mood for Domingo's fresh, creative cuisine. Like many of this area's early settlers, the chef/owner is of Cape Verdian descent, and his menu focuses on seafood and Portuguese spices. The mussel appetizer would be considered a meal at any other restaurant; the bouillabaisse, scrod Creole, haddock Portuguese, and unusual lobster creations are remarkable.

◆   **Romantic Alternative: THE QUARTERDECK RESTAURANT,** 164 Main Street, Falmouth, (508) 548-9900, (Moderate), is a favorite with locals for its Portuguese-inspired cuisine. The interior is casually nautical, with rough-hewn wood walls and lacquered place mats depicting sailing ships. Unfortunately, it can be overwhelmingly smoky.

Falmouth

Hotel/Bed and Breakfast Kissing

THE COONAMESSETT INN, Falmouth   ◆◆◀
Jones Road and Gifford Street, (508) 548-2300
Moderate to Expensive

Call for directions.

Bordered by a busy intersection on one side and an emerald lawn and sapphire blue Jones Pond on the other, the Coonamessett is at the crossroads of contemporary convenience and Colonial charm. Several buildings make up this compact estate, which is especially popular with seasoned romantics. Wood paneling, stenciled draperies, televisions tucked into Colonial cabinets, and modern sofas and chairs lend the guest rooms a cozy, modest comfort. In the formal dining room, copper pots shimmer in the glow of the brick hearth. Tiny white lights sparkle in a bronzed grape arbor above tall, ladder-back chairs clustered around tables with white and pink linens. In the more casual Eli's Tavern, traditional Colonial decor, with deep greens, duck prints, and tufted booth seats, prevails. A pianist plays nightly in summer. Try a Cape Codder (cranberry juice and vodka) and make an appropriate toast to your stay.

MOSTLY HALL, Falmouth   ◆◆◆◀
27 Main Street, (508) 548-3786, (800) 682-0565
Moderate (Closed from January through mid-February)

Cross the Bourne Bridge on Route 28 South, and follow signs for Falmouth into the town center. The inn is across from the village green, about 20 minutes from the Bourne Bridge.

Imagine the new Mrs. Albert Nye's amazement in 1849 when her groom presented his wedding gift to her: a stately plantation-style home equal to any in her native New Orleans. Today, the home still radiates love and gracious living. Once across the threshold, even busy lives slow to a languid Southern pace. Antique wall clocks tick-tock on Georgia peach walls. White shutters frame windows that soar toward the high ceiling. Pour yourself a glass of sherry or enjoy a mug of the inn's gourmet cocoa and set a spell in the tufted chairs or peruse a coffee-table book by the black marble hearth. In the hall, a magnificent staircase rises to your guest room. Soft hues, delicate florals, fishnet or ruffled canopy beds, airy ceilings, and gracious reading chairs make each room feel serene. In the morning, guests gather about the table for a gourmet breakfast of fruit, muffins, and stuffed French toast or eggs Benedict soufflé, recipes so popular the innkeepers put together their own cookbook. Just one last suggestion before you leave Mostly Hall and return to today: stroll across the back lawn to the octagonal gazebo for a lasting embrace.

◆   **Romantic Note:** Southern hospitality doesn't end at breakfast. These congenial innkeepers go to extraordinary lengths to please their guests, introducing each by name to neighbors who may be in the parlor (which can be uncomfortable for shy visitors), providing maps and excellent directions, and selling ferry tickets. Complimentary top-notch bikes are available if you would like to enjoy the Shining Sea Bike Path (see "Outdoor Kissing"), which begins just down the street.

PALMER HOUSE INN, Falmouth
81 Palmer Avenue, (508) 548-1230, (800) 472-2632
Inexpensive to Moderate

Route 28 South, from the Bourne Bridge, turns left onto Palmer Avenue as it enters Falmouth center. The inn is the first house on the left past the shops.

"Breakfast and bed" may be a better description of this cozy Victorian inn. The morning repast is billed as the "highlight of your stay," and even *Gourmet* magazine has been after the innkeepers for their recipes. Served with candle-light and classical music, the meal may begin with an orange frappe, followed by poached pears in raspberry sauce, and a main course of *pain perdue* with orange cream or chocolate-stuffed French toast with vanilla cream. The parlor is an inviting spot to sigh with postprandial delight, with its wing chairs and doily-topped sofa by the brick hearth. Guest rooms are on the cozy side (some baths were squeezed into former closets), but all are richly decorated in florals and flounces. The inn offers complimentary use of their bicycles, and the splendid Shining Sea Bike Path is just around the corner.

PEACOCK'S INN ON THE SOUND, Falmouth
313 Grand Avenue, (508) 457-9666
Inexpensive to Moderate

Call for directions.

This country inn stands as proudly as a peacock on the shores of Vineyard Sound. Its feathers have been recently refurbished in quaint cottage style, from Priscilla curtains to muted blue silk flowers. The location is superb, just across the street from the deep blue sea, with Martha's Vineyard on the horizon. The view is best from the upstairs rooms, done up mostly in blues and peaches: one room has a love seat in front of the window where the two of you can listen to the waves caress the shore. Even in the nonview room, you can find romance by the hearth. A stone hearth warms the homey living room, too, with its panorama of the water.

♦ **Romantic Alternative: THE GRAFTON INN**, 261 Grand Avenue, Falmouth, (508) 540-8688 or (800) 642-4069, (Inexpensive to Moderate), shares the same marvelous Martha's Vineyard view and is equally enchanting, with swagged drapes, vintage furnishings, turret rooms with four-poster or white brass beds, and elaborate breakfasts for a hearty start to a day on the beach, located diagonally across the street.

VILLAGE GREEN INN, Falmouth
40 West Main Street, (508) 548-5621
Moderate

Take Route 28 from the Cape Cod Canal to the Falmouth village green and turn right onto Hewins Street. The inn is on the corner of Hewins and Main streets.

Sipping lemonade on the porch, feeling the light caress of a breeze dancing through the garden flowers, watching the twilight cast its golden shawl over a hazy summer day—these are the simple pursuits you can enjoy at this graciously restored Victorian inn on the green. Fresh and clean, decorated in soft, summery hues, different guest rooms feature amenities such as a pencil-post bed, an overstuffed sofa tucked into a box window, or candles in hurricane globes. All the rooms have fireplaces, giving you an additional way to heat up your romance. In the morning, join the other guests for a hearty Yankee breakfast before heading out to explore the sights of the Cape that so many other loving couples have enjoyed for generations.

Outdoor Kissing

THE NOB, Quissett Harbor

At the west end of Falmouth's Main Street, where it bends north to join Route 28, bear left onto Locust towards Woods Hole. Turn right onto Quissett Harbor Road, drive to the end, and park.

Veer off the well-beaten tourist path to find this quiet, picture-postcard harbor. First, just sit a spell and drink it in, then look for the gate to the nature trail. You'll wind through woodland along the harbor's shore, taking a quiet stroll back to the old Cape of sailing and fishing vessels snug in a cozy cove. Sailors take delight in a red sky at night, and so will you when you share the beauty of the Cape during a magic sunset here.

SHINING SEA BIKE PATH, Falmouth

At the west end of Main Street, where it bends north to join Route 28, bear left onto Locust. Ride past the anchor and look for the opening from the sidewalk to the bike path on the left.

This is one of the world's most leisurely bike paths. It's easy, level, and short enough to complete, even at a relaxed pace, before you start your day of touring. Best of all, you glide by the kind of lovely scenery that brings people back to the Cape year after year: grapevines and woodland, sparkling ocean vistas and sandy beaches, and serene ponds where snowy egrets roost. The path ends at Woods Hole, the authentic Cape Cod fishing and ferry harbor. If your inn doesn't have bikes available, one place to rent just about any kind of wheeled human-powered vehicle, including a bicycle built for two, is **HOLI-DAY CYCLES**, 465 Grand Avenue, Falmouth, (508) 540-3549. From here, it's an easy ride along a scenic shoreline road to the bikeway.

Cotuit

Restaurant Kissing

THE REGATTA OF COTUIT, Cotuit
Route 28, (508) 428-5715
Expensive

Take Route 3 across the Sagamore Bridge. Take Exit 2, which is Route 130 South, and go 10 miles south to Cotuit. When you reach the traffic light at Route 28, turn left.

You can return to dine at the Regatta every day for a week, yet experience a new setting each time. Housed in a 202-year-old Federal mansion, its eight intimate rooms attract diners with their sophisticated charm. Although each is different, all are elegantly decorated in the style of a country manor, with swags above the windows, glass oil lamps, candle wall sconces, and fine linens and china. No wonder locals voted it the Cape's most romantic restaurant.

The food, of course, is top-notch, the menu à la carte rather than prix fixe. Nearly a dozen soups, chowders, and bisques celebrate the seasons, in combinations such as native plum tomato and basil, scallop bisque, or fresh corn and crab chowder. Steak tartare, tuna carpaccio, grilled calamari, and wild mushroom strudel are some of the tempting appetizers. Entrées, often made with vegetables and herbs grown exclusively for the restaurant, include fresh seafood, venison, rabbit, quail, and pheasant, plus traditional beef, veal, and chicken dishes. The Thai lobster is out of this world. If you really want to win your lover over, suggest the chocolate seduction for dessert.

◆   **Romantic Note:** Perched at the entrance to Falmouth Harbor, **THE REGATTA OF FALMOUTH BY-THE-SEA,** Scranton Avenue, Falmouth, (508) 548-5400, (Expensive), is equally delectable and looks over a splendid panorama. It is open from May through September.

Centerville

Hotel/Bed and Breakfast Kissing

THE INN AT FERNBROOK, Centerville   ◆◆◆◆
481 Main Street, (508) 775-4334
Moderate to Very Expensive

From Route 6, take Exit 6 onto Route 132. At the traffic light, turn right onto Phinney's Lane. Cross Route 28 (carefully: it's a dangerous intersection). Phinney's Lane turns into Main Street. The inn is on the left.

Near a splashing fountain, surrounded by trees imported from around the world, roses bloom in a heart-shaped garden, a valentine to the guests of this gracious manor and the love that blossoms within its walls. The garden is small but special, the legacy of Frederick Law Olmsted, designer of the Boston Public Garden and New York's Central Park. The turn-of-the-century mansion is grand but not overwhelming; each room offers a classic evening of romance. The Spellman Room, with its 17-foot pyramid ceiling, stained glass windows, radiant corner hearth, and angelic canopy bed, is enchanting. Peek through the lace curtains of the Cardinal Suite, with its king-size canopy bed and graceful antiques, to see the well-tended sweetheart garden below. The third floor is one suite encompassing two bedrooms, a living room with fireplace, contemporary furnishings, and a built-in bookcase. A balcony complete with telescope is perched above, and stairs lead to a widow's walk-inspired sun deck. The common room is gracious, but you may prefer watching the evening come from the two porches overlooking the delightful grounds. In the dining room, extravagant breakfasts are served at a black walnut table where the likes of John F. Kennedy, Richard Nixon, Gloria Swanson, Walt Disney, and Cecil B. DeMille have been entertained.

Hyannis

Restaurant Kissing

CAPE COD DINNER TRAIN, Hyannis   ◆◆◆
Hyannis Depot: Wednesdays and Saturdays
Buzzards Bay Railroad Station: Fridays
(508) 771-3788, (800) 872-4508 (in Massachusetts)
Expensive (Closed for the winter)

Call for directions.

Romance rides the rails in this Victorian-style dining car. On a recent evening, as the maitre d' reminisced about one man who got down on his knees and proposed in front of everyone, another, more discreet diner reached across a table, took the hand of his beloved, and quietly popped the question. Of course, she couldn't resist.

Gently rotating ceiling fans, soft classical music, elegant linens, candles, and one perfect red rose on every table recreate the luxurious ambience of the fabled Orient Express. Conspire amorously as waiters in black ties and white ruffled shirts serve the prix-fixe, five-course dinner.

The three-hour excursion begins with cocktails and crudités while the train rolls alongside the Cape Cod Canal. Your window frames picture-postcard views that change with each course: soup and salad by sand dunes; a main course of, say, grilled swordfish or rack of lamb when the train stops at the Great Salt Marsh of Barnstable. Enjoy dessert on the return trip as lights come on one by one in tiny hamlets clinging to the spit of land that has inspired poets, writers, and painters. This is truly a sentimental journey.

◆ **Romantic Warning:** Tables seat four. For an additional $25, however, you may reserve a table for two.

Harwichport

Hotel/Bed and Breakfast Kissing

AUGUSTUS SNOW HOUSE, Harwichport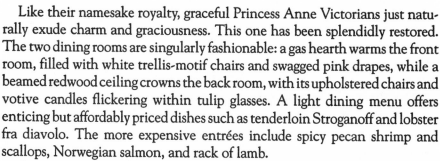
528 Main Street, (508) 430-0528
Expensive

Call for directions

Like their namesake royalty, graceful Princess Anne Victorians just naturally exude charm and graciousness. This one has been splendidly restored. The two dining rooms are singularly fashionable: a gas hearth warms the front room, filled with white trellis-motif chairs and swagged pink drapes, while a beamed redwood ceiling crowns the back room, with its upholstered chairs and votive candles flickering within tulip glasses. A light dining menu offers enticing but affordably priced dishes such as tenderloin Stroganoff and lobster fra diavolo. The more expensive entrées include spicy pecan shrimp and scallops, Norwegian salmon, and rack of lamb.

Guest rooms are decorated in period furnishings, with some canopy and four-poster beds, plush wall treatments, and whirlpool baths. Unfortunately, the inn tries to be all things to all people. Smoking is not restricted, so nonsmokers may end up with a beautifully decorated room permeated with a stale smell. Also, the restaurant takes up the charming parlors, leaving no common area for overnight guests to enjoy.

Chatham

Perched on the pointy elbow of Cape Cod is Chatham, one of my favorite beachside towns. Its prize catch is a bounty of boutiques hemming a genuine example of Main Street America. From crafts to clothing, even the nonshopper will find intriguing window browsing. Where else can you peek through a century-old telescope from a sailing ship of yore, nibble on a scone, and buy a touristy seashell souvenir? Take a stroll along the shoreline drive that hems the town. You'll see handsome seaside mansions and graceful schooners. The village's famous lighthouse stands sentinel over the vast blue waters; stop to snap a picture and enjoy a salty kiss.

Hotel/Bed and Breakfast Kissing

THE CAPTAIN'S HOUSE INN, Chatham
369-377 Old Harbor Road, (508) 945-0127
Moderate to Very Expensive (Closed mid-November through mid-February)

From Chatham center, follow the rotary out of town on Route 28 toward Orleans. The driveway to the inn is on the left in one-half mile.

You may find yourself leaving the beach early so you won't miss tea time at this elegant inn. Served in high style from an intricate sterling urn and tray, delectables range from simple scones to elaborate cakes, depending on the mood of the chef. Enjoy it all in the conservatory-inspired breakfast room, with its slate floor and windows overlooking lush landscaping. In keeping with the elegance of yesteryear, guest rooms have a Colonial Williamsburg flavor. Beautiful antiques and crewelwork chairs fill the common rooms. In the bedchambers, fishnet canopies arch over white woven spreads. The velvet wing chairs and swag drapes would delight any well-to-do colonist, while Oriental carpets and braided throw rugs bring out the warm patina of pumpkin pine floors. Fireplaces glow in five of the 16 guest rooms. A cathedral ceiling adds contemporary flair to the spacious and private Carriage House room, with its high canopy bed and balcony overlooking the lawn. With a house this inviting, it's a wonder the captain ever returned to sea.

CHATHAM BARS INN, Chatham
Shore Road, (508) 945-0096, (800) 527-4884
Expensive to Unbelievably Expensive (EP)

Follow Main Street through the town of Chatham, past the hardware store, to Seaview Road, and take a left. The inn is on the right, on the corner of Seaview and Shore Streets.

If you're not the type to enjoy socializing with innkeepers or showering in closet-sized baths but you are still seeking a small-town stay, this sprawling resort offers anonymous comfort with all the modern amenities just a short distance from Chatham center. A complex of shingled gray Cape-style buildings harbors a variety of accommodations, from traditional rooms to secluded oceanfront cottages. Early American reproductions and chintz spreads and drapes jazz up the neutral hotel rooms. Some cottages feel sunny no matter what the season with blond wood or white wicker furnishings, light walls, and perhaps a fireplace in the living room. All guests have access to tennis courts, an exercise room, the pool, a beachside grill and bar, and private beach.

The common rooms of this grand old dame are majestically poised above the sea. You can relax before a maritime panorama while chasing away the Atlantic chill by the fire in the cavernous South Lounge or, if you're lucky, get a window seat in the immense formal dining room. The more casual Tavern Room is extremely cozy and rich, with deep maroon paisley walls and dark woods on the octagonal ceiling, but has no view.

◆ **Romantic Warning:** During the shoulder months of May, June, September, and October, large conventions overwhelm this classic resort's beauty, crowding into the formal dining room, sometimes overflowing with their slide projectors into the South Lounge. You may want to ask if you'll be sharing your getaway with conventioneers when you call to reserve your room.

CYRUS KENT HOUSE, Chatham
63 Cross Street, (508) 945-9104, (800) 338-5368
Moderate to Expensive

From Main Street, bear right on Cross Street at the Town Offices. The inn is about one block up on the left.

Just as a weekend getaway can make any married couple feel like newlyweds again, so can a masterful restoration pump bright, new life into a stalwart captain's home. The 1877 architectural details, high ceilings, marble hearth, and plasterwork are enhanced by pencil-post and brass beds, wing chairs, voluminous dried flower arrangements, Cape Cod curtains, and braided rugs on hardwood floors. You'll find seclusion and a more contemporary country look in the two Carriage House suites. The second floor feels especially airy, with its high-peaked ceiling and canopy bed. Both have sitting rooms warmed by fireplaces. All rooms have the requisite television and phone. A generous continental breakfast served in the Colonial-style dining room lends a warm start to your special time together.

◆ **Romantic Alternative: THE CRANBERRY INN AT CHATHAM,** 359 Main Street, Chatham, (508) 945-9232 or (800) 332-4667, (Moderate to Expensive), is smack in the middle of charming Chatham center. Its personality is more that of a dignified small Colonial hotel than a bed and breakfast. Rooms are classically furnished with pencil-post beds and wing chairs; some have fireplaces, and televisions are tucked away in wardrobes.

MOSES NICKERSON HOUSE, Chatham
364 Old Harbor Road, (508) 945-5859, (800) 628-6972
Moderate to Expensive

From Chatham center, take Route 28 (Old Harbor Road) a half mile up from the Chatham rotary.

A crackling fire greeted us as we entered the gracious parlor of this stately captain's home. With a glass of wine and our own tray of snacks, we began to relax, cherishing the late-afternoon sun pouring through the cranberry glass windows, flipping through the piles of picture and poetry books, and admiring the vases of prize-winning flowers that seem to bloom everywhere in the inn. The guest rooms are even more alluring. Once you've closed the door behind you, you barely can pull yourself away for dinner. Just off the parlor, the Emily Dickinson Room is sublime: painted roses twine and spiral up the four-poster bed and coordinating dresser, a gas fireplace glows before the velvet bowtie settee, and lace-trimmed French doors open to a private front porch. Another room is inspired by Ralph Lauren, with a maroon paisley spread and shams on a fluted four-poster bed, knotty pine paneling, and a leather easy chair standing before the hearth. In the garden-view rooms, the soft melody of a fountain lulls you to sleep. Details set this inn above its competitors. Here, touches such as top hats, an antique hunting horn, and pheasant feathers tucked bouquet-style in a pottery vase add a special flair. Each room brims with an intimate warmth. The aroma of a fresh-baked breakfast rouses you in the morning. Served in the bright conservatory, fruit topped with garden flowers and such select offerings as fresh strudel will see you off to a day by the sea.

Restaurant Kissing

CHATHAM COOKWARE
524 Main Street, (508) 945-1550
Inexpensive

Betweeen Chatham Jewelers and Wayside Inn on Main Street.

Can you find romance in a cookware store? The aroma of gourmet coffee brewing will lure you into this boutique. Follow your nose to the back and you'll find a gratifying surprise: café tables tucked into a bright, cozy room with a high-peaked, skylit ceiling. Ivy-motif wall coverings, mint green floors, and windows laced with vines lend a cheery greenhouse ambience. Bright florals bloom on plates and dishes displayed in the cabinet. A sliding glass door opens onto a redwood deck with a motherly shade tree for its canopy. Coffees, cheeses, and freshly baked muffins and scones make this a perfect place for a moment's pause together in your exploration of Chatham.

CHATHAM WAYSIDE INN, Chatham
512 Main Street, (508) 945-1800, (800) 545-INNS
Moderate

Located in the middle of the village, next to Kate Gould Park.

In summer, every small-town bandstand on the Cape seems to come alive with the sound of music. Fancier restaurants may have grand pianists, but the casual outdoor patio here is just a drumbeat away from Chatham's concerts. Cheery green- or red-and-white-striped umbrellas shade diners as they enjoy continental dishes such as grilled tuna, salmon, and sirloin steaks, or home-made pastas with seafood. Even when the bandstand is silent, this is still a wonderful place to enjoy lunch or an early dinner as you watch happy sightseers walk along Main Street, soaking in Chatham's sunshine. Inside, a more formal garden-inspired room, open only in summer, celebrates the outdoors with ivy-motif cloths, lemon yellow walls, a slate floor, and plenty of windows for gazing across the green lawn when you're not gazing into each other's eyes.

Martha's Vineyard and Nantucket

Looking like emeralds set in a blue velvet sea, the verdant islands of Martha's Vineyard and Nantucket are places where you can dig your toes into the warm beach sand, bike tandem through tangled woodland, and watch moonbeams dance on the ocean waves. Excursions to the islands are either by ferry, **STEAMSHIP AUTHORITY,** (508) 540-2022, or on an eight-passen-ger Cessna, **CAPE AIR,** (800) 352-0714. Martha's Vineyard, the island nearest to Cape Cod and Nantucket, booms with tourists in summer and whispers in the off-season. Day-trippers to Nantucket tend to cluster in the bustling village, with its gray shingled, rose-trellised cottages and exclusive boutiques that epitomize the island. The islands' true riches, however, are their moors and beaches. Each island is best seen on foot, by bicycle, or, for cross-island exploring, by moped. Transporting an automobile to the islands, especially to Nantucket, is prohibitively expensive.

Edgartown

Hotel/Bed and Breakfast Kissing

THE CHARLOTTE INN, Edgartown
27 South Summer Street, (508) 627-4751
Expensive to Unbelievably Expensive (inn), Very Expensive (dining)
Restaurant open nightly in season, weekends off-season

Follow signs to Edgartown. Head down Main Street and turn right on South Summer Street. The inn is a block and a half down on the right.

Exquisite English antiques, elegant decor, and fine art are present in every room of this inn. The parlor doubles as an art gallery, where you can sip sherry and peruse paintings, hung museum-style, that are available for purchase. In a second sitting room, relax by the fire and browse through magazines that advertise European castles for sale. The art collection spills over to the hallways and guest rooms, where early flashlights, silver-topped perfume bottles, sterling dresser sets, and antique luggage provide interest. The private Coach House has its own wood-paneled antique car parked on the lower level, while another room boasts a white, baby grand piano. Other highlights include Battenburg lace comforters, silk-tasseled draperies, high ceilings, half-poster beds, needlepoint pillows, flowers in cut crystal vases, and the occasional fireplace. Five vintage buildings, two of them sea captain's homes, cluster around a garden courtyard and quiet side street to accommodate discriminating guests.

In keeping with the establishment's devotion to quality, L'Etoile restaurant serves gourmet, prix fixe dinners in a garden porch setting. Voluptuous green plants hang from a peaked, skylit ceiling; white wooden chairs with green cushions are set on a brick and slate floor. Multipaned windows overlook the garden, while angled walls create intimate dining spaces. On warmer days, you can dine in the garden itself, with its ceiling of tree branches and a splashing fountain.

Dinner may begin with sautéed rock shrimp ravioli or salmon mousselines with a roasted red and yellow pepper coulis. Entrées include native lobster and scallops with vegetable tagliatelle, duck breast with wild rice and dried corn melange, and grilled veal chop with butternut squash and chive pasta; all are served with delectable sauces. Breakfast is served in the same lush atmosphere. A muffin and juice are complimentary; full meals are available at extra cost.

DAGGETT HOUSE, Edgartown   ◆❮
59 North Water Street, (508) 627-4600
Moderate to Unbelievably Expensive (inn), Moderate (dining)
(Closed for the winter)

On Edgartown Harbor, on the corner of Daggett and North Water streets, three blocks from Main Street.

More than a century before the American Revolution, pioneering ladies stirred harvest stews by the fire in this low-slung dining room. Dating back to 1660, the immense hearth is one of the oldest beehive fireplaces in New England. In the evening, firelight is reflected on the exposed brick walls. Linens, candles, and flowers top the rough-hewn wood tables. Lobster is a staple in the summer, and the ever-changing, albeit limited, menu may also include corn chowder, scrod baked in parchment, or roast chicken breast with a vegetable and herbed cream cheese stuffing.

This basement room doubles as a breakfast room for lodgers upstairs and in adjacent buildings. The guest rooms are inviting—some offer a canopy bed, water views, and a hot tub—but the quality is less then desirable, especially at these prices. Still, this inn has an impressive history, and is splendidly located in the midst of this village of regal captain's homes that grew up around it.

THE HARBOR VIEW HOTEL, Edgartown ◆◆◆
131 North Water Street, (508) 627-7000, (800) 225-6005
Very Expensive to Unbelievably Expensive (EP), Expensive (dining)

Call for directions.

Imagine embracing by your window as the stars twinkle above and a lighthouse casts its sweeping beam of hope over a sea of darkness. Standing like a beacon at the edge of Edgartown village, this grand Victorian hotel draws visitors to one of the best locations of any island hostelry. The point, with its lighthouse and strip of shell-strewn beach, is just across the street. Upstairs rooms in the main hotel, especially those on the fourth floor, look over this splendid panorama. Recently renovated to suit a varied clientele, the spacious rooms are finished in sandy tones of beige, mocha, and ivory, with refrigerators tucked away in light wood cabinets. Hairdryers, room service, a heated outdoor pool, and cable television are some of the other amenities offered in this complex of 124 hotel rooms and cottages popular with conventions and tour groups. Ask for a table by the window of the Harbor View's fine dining restaurant and enjoy lobster, king crab legs, flounder, or scrod while watching the lighthouse reach out to sailors and fishermen returning back to hearth and home. Or simply settle into a rocking chair on the wraparound veranda until the cool ocean breezes urge you inside to the firelit lobby, welcoming you in from the dark.

◆ **Romantic Note:** Rates are considerably lower in the off-season. Also, the hotel is popular with conventions and tour groups, so you may want to call ahead to best choose a time to visit or dine here.

THE SHIVERICK INN, Edgartown ◆◆◆◆
Pease's Point Way, (508) 627-3797, (800) 723-4292
Expensive to Very Expensive

On the corner of Pent Lane.

Elegance without pretension describes the ambience at this refined 1840 country manor. You enter through the back door into a conservatory warmed by the afternoon sun, where two walls of windows encircle a black marble hearth and white metal café chairs surround glass-topped tables. Just inside, a formal living room awaits after-dinner conversations as guests relax in the comfortable sofas and wing chairs. Upstairs is another common room, this one for readers and television watchers, and a sunny porch that invites basking in the sun. Guest rooms, aglow with firelight and a flair for romance, feature American and English 18th- and 19th-century antiques, rich fabrics, serene hues, and intriguing collectibles. All of the rooms are magnificent, but those on the top floor have canopy beds and private balconies, some overlooking the lighthouse. Heartwarming breakfasts are served in the conservatory.

THE VICTORIAN INN, Edgartown
24 South Water Street, (508) 627-4784
Moderate to Very Expensive

In the village center, between Main and Davis streets.

While some Victorian inns overwhelm you with florals and frills, this circa-1820 captain's home welcomes you with its unpretentious style, casual charm, and period decor. In your third-floor room, you can dream of the past on ruffled canopy beds, then gaze from your private balcony over Edgartown's rooftops to the harbor across the street. Although some bedchambers are a bit too cozy, details are charming. In all the rooms, sherry in cut-glass decanters will help warm your spirits. Breakfasts, full in season and continental in the slower months, are served in a cheerful room appointed with Windsor chairs and floral cloths.

Restaurant Kissing

ANDREA'S RESTAURANT, Edgartown
Upper Main Street, (508) 627-5850
Expensive (Closed in February)

Several blocks inland from the village center.

Andrea's promises you a rose garden in the warmer months—and delivers. Walk through the arched trellis and you'll reach a delightful brick patio, with a ring of tables circling an old shade tree. There you'll dine, lulled by the sweet scent of blossoming roses and serenaded by the cheerful splash of an intricate triple-tiered fountain. If rain should fall, move to the restaurant's series of dining rooms, which are equally charming and intimate. An enclosed porch wraps around the home, its multipaned windows beckoning the outdoors in, no matter what the weather. In the main dining room, grapevines painted on posts and along beams continue the simple garden theme.

A dozen creative pastas highlight the seasonal menu, dressed with such combinations as creamy garlic sauce, hot cherry peppers, olives, and anchovies, or basil, Parmesan, garlic, walnuts, and olive oil. Entrées include traditional Italian chicken dishes along with scampi, rack of lamb, and fresh fish. If dinner is over but your evening out is just beginning, head downstairs to the bistro to enjoy live jazz on weekend nights.

NAVIGATOR RESTAURANT, Edgartown
2 Main Street, (508) 627-4320
Expensive (Open May through Columbus Day)

In the center of the village, on the waterfront.

On a clear day, navigate your way through the boutiques of Edgartown to this nautical restaurant with one of the best views in town. Downstairs, one side of the dining rooms is literally dockside, a great place to watch the activity of the harbor or just gaze over the water. In summer, fine dining is on the second floor, with its crow's-nest view. Laminated wooden tables and chairs fill the spacious room, with lobster-trap markers, ships' lanterns, and lines and blocks thrown in to remind us this is a seafaring town after all. Seafood, including quahog (a very large clam) chowder, littlenecks on the half shell, and locally harvested lobster, top the American menu, with steaks, roast chicken, and lamb for the landlubber.

THE NEWES FROM AMERICA, Edgartown
23 Kelly Street, (508) 627-7900, (800) 225-6005
Moderate

In the basement of the Kelly House inn, at the corner of North Water and Kelly streets.

Raise a mug to the romance of yesteryear in this happy Colonial tavern. As snug as a captain's cabin, this is one of Edgartown's most popular stops for a casual meal. The original 250-year-old ballast brick walls, rough-hewn beams, low ceiling, and crackling fire add to the old-world charm. Hearty pub meals include traditional clam chowder, a brown bag brimming with fajita fries or onion rings, the popular gyro hero, and other hot sandwiches. Locally brewed ales and stouts and imported lagers top the list of a dozen brews on tap.

WARRINERS RESTAURANT, Edgartown
Old Post Office Square, (508) 627-4488
Expensive

In the center of town, behind the Whaling Church on Main Street near Pease's Point Way.

Surprisingly few fine dining establishments are found in well-heeled Edgartown. This is one of the finest, with top-notch cooking and a pleasant, understated ambience. Tucked away down a quiet side street, it has more the feel of a home than a restaurant, especially in the stylish library room, with its linen-draped tables hemmed by wood paneling and bookshelves. A less formal atmosphere prevails in an adjacent intimate room, where botanical prints and brass sconces decorate golden walls, and woven place mats and brass-based electric lamps top wooden tables. Seasonal dishes range from crab-corn chowder, carpaccio, and gravlax to entrées such as as pastas, roast rack of lamb, linguine and lobster with green onions and whiskey-shallot cream sauce, pork with sausage-apple-mushroom stuffing and gingersnap gravy, and even simple hamburgers.

Oak Bluffs

Hotel/Bed and Breakfast Kissing

OAK HOUSE, Oak Bluffs
Seaview Avenue, (508) 693-4187
Moderate to Very Expensive (Closed for winter)

From the Oak Bluffs ferry terminal, follow Seaview Avenue along the shore toward Edgartown. The inn is on the right, three streets past the green expanse of Ocean Park, between Narragansett and Pequot avenues.

Like an elegant clipper ship, this splendidly restored 1872 Victorian is resplendently decked out in richly rubbed oak walls and ceilings, from the parlor to the stairway to the bedchambers. Add to that leaded glass windows, Oriental carpets, select antiques, and a location about as close to the ocean as you can get here. On sultry summer afternoons, guests gather in the white wicker furnishings of the enclosed sun porch to enjoy high tea while watching the gulls soar over the waves across the street.

The ambience here is like that of a casual beach house. Half of the 10 guest rooms have balconies with put-your-feet-up water views (or pea-soup fog views, depending on the weather). Stained glass accent windows and lamps, lace curtains, brass or oak beds, and wing chairs highlight the oak-paneled guest rooms. At twilight, snuggle on the porch swing as the sea and sky embrace you in deepening hues of blue, and feel your hearts set sail.

West Tisbury

Hotel/Bed and Breakfast Kissing

LAMBERT'S COVE COUNTRY INN, West Tisbury
Lambert's Cove Road, (508) 693-2298
Moderate to Expensive (inn), Expensive (dining)

Call for directions.

As you trundle down one of this remote island's most rural routes, then navigate another half mile down a narrow drive through woodland, you'll know that this inn embodies the true meaning of "getaway." Surrounded by woods, a secluded backyard, and apple trees, this inn offers a retreat with elegant yet understated style. Spacious common rooms harbor several sitting areas where guests can curl up with a favorite book. The firelit Bridal Room has a ruffled canopy bed and just enough antiques to lend charm without clutter.

The inn's dining room draws visitors and islanders alike for its gourmet dinners and Sunday brunch. Meals are served in an intimate room with Hepplewhite-inspired chairs gathered around tables clothed in peach and white, and a new menu is presented each day. The skilled kitchen prepares classic dishes such as filet mignon with béarnaise sauce or pheasant with a bosc pear coulis. Traditional brunch dishes include eggs Benedict and omelets with mushrooms, smoked salmon, and scallions. Although this getaway is well off the beaten path, be sure to call ahead for dinner and brunch reservations.

Vineyard Haven

Hotel/Bed and Breakfast Kissing

CAPTAIN DEXTER HOUSE, Vineyard Haven
100 Main Street, (508) 693-6564
Moderate to Expensive (Closed for winter)

Call for directions.

In the 1840s, after long stretches at sea, captains wanted to come back to a hearth and home that welcomed them, indulged them, but did not over-whelm them. Today, we look for the same thing after long stretches in the office or with the kids, and find it here. The whales and boats stenciled in the entryway pay tribute to the home's beginnings. In the parlor, well-used furnishings are gathered by the fireplace, while venerable period pieces fill the bedchambers. A full canopy bed is warmed by a Colonial blue fireplace, and a love seat is tucked into a bay window in one downstairs room. Upstairs, you can watch the firelight cast its glow on a carved four-poster bed with a fishnet canopy. In other rooms, you'll find antique dressers, half-testers (headboard canopies), more canopies, and softly colored walls. Third-floor rooms are cute but small, and several baths are squeezed into closets. In the morning, you can enjoy a continental breakfast around the family dining table before heading out to discover the island.

THORNCROFT INN, Vineyard Haven
278 Main Street, (508) 693-3333
Expensive to Unbelievably Expensive (inn), Expensive (dining)

Call for directions.

Seclusion is the primary emphasis, but elegance is the encompassing theme. Canopy beds, fireplaces, whirlpool baths, plush furnishings, candlelit dinners, gourmet breakfasts: Thorncroft has it all and more. Although the first impression is a bit too formal—you may have to dial the innkeeper from the outside security phone—the pampering starts the moment you enter the inner sanctum; you even receive a personalized map for discovering the island after breakfast. On chilly afternoons, a fire blazes in the parlor, where brown wicker furnishings are softened with pink floral cushions. Summer days call for lounging on the bright sun porch. Nine of the 13 bedchambers glow with wood-burning fireplaces. The exquisite furnishings include high carved wooden beds, one dating from 1815, an antique camelback love seat, rich floral wall coverings, and a fishnet canopy. Spacious Carriage House rooms are the most private and luxurious. One has a private balcony and snow white wing chairs hemming a corner marble hearth, another has an immense whirlpool tub, while a third features its own private hot tub, big enough for six to soak.

Candlelit dinners are served in two rooms, one warmed by a brick hearth, but both are intimate and subtly lit with electric candles in the windows or Victorian-style wall sconces. The wonderfully prepared prix fixe menu may include an unusual autumn pumpkin fondue with smoked duck sausage; a parsley-crusted veal chop with a ragout of smoked bacon, shiitake mushrooms, and sun-dried tomatoes; and a lavishly rich flourless chocolate torte for dessert. Afterward, you'll discover chocolates on your triple-sheeted, turned-down bed, and stationery and postcards, prestamped of course, so you can share the happiness with your friends at home.

Restaurant Kissing

LE GRENIER RESTAURANT, Vineyard Haven
Main Street, (508) 693-4906
Expensive

In the center of the small village.

Take a gourmet French menu, add a dash of unpretentious charm, and *voila!* You've got a slice of lusty Paris in the heart of Vineyard Haven. Outdoor tables, with plastic patio chairs and green-and-white-checked vinyl cloths, are set on the porch along the sidewalk. Upstairs is more formal, with skylights shining above cheerful floral tablecloths and coordinating napkins, minty green walls hand-painted with white doves, and trompe l'oeil morning glories spiraling up posts. The food is equal to that served in high-brow restaurants, with appetizers such as vichyssoise, mussels steamed in white wine, or escargot in a pastry shell. The extensive selection of traditional entrées lists frog legs, veal Oscar, venison, soft-shell crabs, sweetbreads, and beef Wellington. For tableside pyrotechnics, order quails with cognac, lobster flamed with Calvados, shrimp flamed with Pernod, or scallops flamed with vodka and served with red caviar and cream sauce. Of course, several desserts are flamed as well, including crêpes Suzette and bananas flambé.

Chilmark

Hotel/Bed and Breakfast Kissing

BREAKFAST AT TIASQUAM, Chilmark
Off Middle Road, (508) 645-3685
Moderate to Expensive

Call for directions.

Some 20 skylights let the sunshine in at this sleek, contemporary home in the forest. An open, airy dining room and parlor house graceful, hand-crafted furnishings; the cherry breakfast table and cherry and ash chairs are like works of art in their craftsmanship. In the living room, sink into the overstuffed blue leather sofa or open the glass doors to one of the many decks. Guest rooms are uncluttered, with sleek wood furnishings, contemporary art, and white walls. In the baths, some of which are shared, custom-made hand-thrown pottery sinks continue the inn's devotion to fine craftsmanship. On the second floor, one room has a bed basking in the sun brought in from the skylight above. In another, a two-person whirlpool provides romantic relaxation. Breakfast, not surprisingly, is a special treat here, cooked to order and featuring everything from fresh fish to waffles to their special blueberry-corn pancakes.

◆ **Romantic Note:** Guests at this inn have the unique pleasure of a pass to Lucy Vincent Beach, one of the island's finest.

Menemsha

Restaurant Kissing

BEACH PLUM INN AND RESTAURANT, Menemsha
North Road, (508) 645-9454, (800) 528-6616
Expensive to Very Expensive (dining)
Expensive to Unbelievably Expensive (MAP or EP)(Open May through October)

Call for directions.

Tucked away in a secluded spot surrounded by delightful flower gardens, this is your cottage by the sea, at least for an evening. As the sun sets over the water, its golden rays weave through the dining room. Melodies from a piano, flute, or stand-up bass drift among the diners. Hand-painted Italian china, white linens, candles, and flowers from the inn's garden set the scene for fixed price, three- or five-course dinners. The menu changes daily, but repeat favorites are the Brie en croûte, homemade pâté, gazpacho, clam chowder, lamb Dijonnaise, and sole stuffed with salmon mousse. On certain nights, they offer an authentic New England clam bake.

◆ **Romantic Note:** The inn has a private beach and patio that are perfect for basking in the moonlight. Guest rooms are serenely decorated, and some have private decks where you can embrace the sunset over Menemsha Harbor.

◆ **Romantic Warning:** Reservations are essential, as dinner is planned only for those with reservations.

HOME PORT RESTAURANT, Menemsha
(508) 645-2679
Moderate (Open May through October)

At the harbor of this tiny fishing village.

If you're looking for something casual and fun, the only airs that this seafood restaurant puts on are fresh ocean breezes. In the tiny fishing village of Menemsha, you'll dine with a splendid view of the harbor on one side and a duck pond on the other. This is one of the few places on the East Coast where you can watch the sun set over the sea because of its location on the western shore of Martha's Vineyard. Lacquered wooden tables and models of fish on the walls get you in the mood for broiled Menemsha swordfish, baked stuffed shrimp, scrod, salmon, scallops, seven different lobster dinners, and steak for the landlubbers. The price includes appetizer, salad, and homemade pie. When the Home Port feels as busy as a fishnet bursting with today's catch, you can enjoy your dinner al fresco on the patio.

◆ **Romantic Note:** Even if you're not dining at the Home Port, take a drive or bike ride here to see nearby **DUTCHER DOCK**, a quintessential New England fishing harbor, complete with colorful lobster-pot markers clustered on weatherworn buildings.

Gay Head

Hotel/Bed and Breakfast Kissing

THE OUTERMOST INN, Gay Head
Lighthouse Road, (508) 645-3511
Very Expensive (inn), Expensive (dining)

Call for directions.

Set on the tip of Martha's Vineyard with little more than a lighthouse for company, this inn lives up to its name. The decor, as unaffected as the sand on a beach, focuses on the simple beauty of warm woods and splendid ocean views. In the bright, airy "Bash" (for beech and ash) Room, two white wicker chairs are placed by the window overlooking nothing but trees, grass, chaparral, and ocean. In another of the seven rooms, a hot tub is framed by a sylvan mural of a mermaid gazing into a pond with water lilies and swans, with the added detail of a man painting a picture of it all. You can soak all night here and watch the moon rise over the cobalt sea. The lighthouse flashes through the doors of the Lighthouse Suite, with its separate entrance, sitting room with two twins, and bedroom overlooking the back with a whisper of water on the horizon.

On busier weekends, fixed price dinners are served in the low-key breakfast room, with a choice of two appetizers and four entrées, and a view that stretches to the outermost blue horizon.

Nantucket

Hotel/Bed and Breakfast Kissing

THE BREAKERS, Nantucket ◆◆◆◀
Easton Street, (508) 228-5500, (800) ISLANDS
Unbelievably Expensive (EP) (Open Memorial Day through Labor Day)

From Steamboat Wharf, turn right onto South Beach Street. Then take the third right onto Easton Street. Adjacent to the White Elephant Hotel, along the harbor shore.

Prestige is the watchword at this elegant hotel, just a step away from its sister property, the White Elephant (reviewed elsewhere in this section), and just a step above it in ambience. All of the 26 airy rooms have private decks with spectacular views of the harbor. Third-floor bedchambers are especially regal, and all have king-size beds. Need I mention the bath's double vanity, room service, mini-bars, refrigerators, hairdryers, and televisions tucked away in cabinets? Guests here are welcome to use the White Elephant's heated pool, where you can sip something cool together as you watch sleek yachts sail into the harbor, perhaps heading to one of the hotel's private slips.

CENTERBOARD GUEST HOUSE, Nantucket
8 Chester Street, (508) 228-9696
Expensive to Very Expensive

At the corner of Chester and Centre Streets.

As subtle as a single rose petal, this six-room inn offers a gentle embrace of serenity, from the moment you enter the light, airy parlor. Downstairs, forest green and burgundy color the inn's grand suite. Relax by the fire in the sitting room or luxuriate in the green marble whirlpool bath, then snuggle on the four-poster bed with its soaring fishnet canopy. Light, airy pastels reminiscent of an impressionist painting whisper in the cozy upstairs bedchambers, where a basket of fruit and cheese greets each guest. Room 2 has a white iron-and-brass bed blanketed with a white coverlet quilted with a pink dogwood design, hand-hooked rugs, and pickled wood furniture. In Room 3, a Monet-inspired wall of serene pinks and blues backdrops a white fencepost bed. In Room 4, shades of mocha and sand hues set off a sea blue love seat. All rooms have feather beds, unobtrusive televisions, and refrigerators with complimentary sodas. In the morning, enjoy a continental breakfast of Portuguese bread, granola, fresh fruit, and home-baked muffins.

CLIFF LODGE, Nantucket   ❤❤❤
9 Cliff Road, (508) 228-9480
Moderate to Very Expensive
(Closed in January; open weekends only in February and March)

From the ferry dock, head straight on Broad Street and turn right on North Water. The inn is near the corner of Chester and North Water streets.

Even when rain dampens your spirits and washes away dreams of an afternoon at the beach, you'll feel a little sunshine at this delightful, circa-1771 sea captain's home. A cheerful floral sofa brightens the sitting room, where the hearth offers a warm welcome in winter. Down the hall, in another sitting room, wicker furnishings top a traditional Nantucket speckled floor, one of many in the inn. Entering Room 1, off the foyer, is like diving into the ocean on a sultry summer day: the white floor is splashed with blue speckles; a white wicker bed and white walls perfectly balance the marine hues. The room above, Room 2, is equally spacious and airy, with a bountiful basket of silk tulips filling the nonworking hearth. Third-floor rooms are smaller (some are downright tiny), but still cozy and warm with patchwork quilts. Each room has a television hidden away, some behind a wall mirror, but a few are positioned so you'd have to sit on the floor to watch. Then again, they won't distract you from a true getaway for two. The only scene you'll really want to watch together is from the widow's walk, as sunset paints its roses and blues over the village panorama below.

CORNER HOUSE, Nantucket
49 Centre Street, (508) 228-1530
Inexpensive to Expensive

It's a five-minute walk from the ferry terminal. Walk straight up Main Street and turn right onto Centre Street. The inn is four doors behind the Jared Coffin House and across from the Congregational church.

This home was built shortly after the Colonials won their right to tax-free tea, so it's only fitting that the steaming beverage is served in high style each afternoon. Mango tea is their specialty, laid out on the sideboard with such goodies as scones, smoked kipper pâté, ginger slices, and cucumber sandwiches. You can enjoy your repast by the fire on chilly winter days or on the screened-in porch with its white wicker and hanging ferns in summer. Beyond, a garden blooms with pink and white impatiens.

Your own love will blossom inside this authentic, refreshingly homespun old-fashioned bed and breakfast. In the parlor, you can sink into the overstuffed down sofa by the Colonial blue hearth. You may feel as if you're traveling back in time as you wend your way along the sloping floors of the dimly lit halls. Bedchambers, ranging from spacious to snug, are highlighted with English and American antiques, wide plank floors, down comforters and pillows, prints of sailing ships or botanical etchings, and the occasional canopy bed. Although it's a short walk to the village's posh boutiques, the atmosphere is far removed from their sometimes too obvious pretension.

◆ **Romantic Note:** The inn operates a second home, **THE SWAN'S NEST**, around the corner. Four rooms, two large and two petite, are richly decorated with deep hues and canopy beds. They are more private, but you must walk to the main inn for tea and breakfast or to enjoy the common room.

GREAT HARBOR INN, Nantucket
31 India Street, (508) 228-6609, (800) 377-6609
Moderate to Expensive

From Steamboat Wharf, drive straight onto Broad Street, turn left onto Center Street, and take the third right onto India Street. The inn is on the right.

If you love the charm of an 18th-century sea captain's home, but need the amenities of today, sail into this inviting inn for a night or two. Wide-plank pumpkin pine floors, pencil-post canopy beds, and patchwork quilts harbor the charm of yesteryear while modern baths, color televisions, and perhaps a contemporary love seat keep you well anchored in today. Although some rooms can be as snug as a ship's cabin, all are as fresh and bright as a sea breeze, colored in neutral tones and muted Colonial hues. A wood stove sits in one corner of the modern living room, the only common room, where afternoon cheese and crackers are served and a continental breakfast is laid out in the morning. The pocket courtyard is a tranquil spot to enjoy these light but tasty nibbles.

JARED COFFIN HOUSE, Nantucket
29 Broad Street, (508) 228-2400, (800) 248-2405
Expensive (Inn & Dining)

A complex of six buildings at the corner of Broad and Centre Streets, directly up the street from Steamboat Wharf.

Rising like an exclamation point at the end of Broad Street, this dignified three-story brick whaling mansion, with its black shutters and white cupola, stands dauntless before the passing of the centuries, ensconced as one of Nantucket village's most venerated landmarks. It is the Jared Coffin House, built in the grand tradition of ship owners in 1845. The accommodations have grown to encompass five more vintage buildings, some attuned to families, others offering more privacy.

To be in the midst of it all, stay and dine at the Coffin House. A grand, firelit double parlor, resplendently adorned with black marble hearth, plush tasseled draperies, Oriental rugs, and crystal chandelier, brings back an era of elegance. Guest rooms can be somewhat disappointing given the extravagant parlor, but are pleasantly decorated, some with four-poster beds, Oriental carpets, and shuttered windows. The corner rooms are best, with such highlights as a regal canopy bed and a superb view of the village. Among the other buildings, the Harrison Gray House is the most conducive to kissing, with its more secluded parlor; Early American furnishings adorn the bedchambers, some with private sun rooms and porches.

Dinner at **JARED'S RESTAURANT** is an elegant, indulgent affair that is open to the public. Salmon-colored walls and Colonial green chairs set off the Federal-period sideboards, gilt-framed vintage artwork, and an intricate mural screen of sailing ships gliding into Nantucket Harbor. Rich seasonal appetizers include oysters with champagne vinaigrette and caviar, and honey-glazed quail with risotto and chanterelles. For your entrée, try the sautéed Nantucket Bay scallops with saffron cream on black angel-hair pasta, or baked stuffed lobster with sweet potato hash. Cranberry steamed pudding, crème brûlée, and pear-almond tart ensure a sweet ending to your meal.

Before you leave, ask to see the cupola, where you can climb up together and kiss before a 360-degree panorama of the village and harbor that has endured the centuries as beautifully as everlasting love.

SEVEN SEA STREET, Nantucket
7 Sea Street, (508) 228-3577
Expensive to Very Expensive

From Steamship Wharf, head straight on Broad Street and take the first right onto Beach Street, then take the second left onto Sea Street. The inn is between North Water and South Beach streets.

Built in 1987, this post-and-beam inn was created by skilled craftsmen who used the best woods available and worked them to perfection. Here you'll find time-honored detailing celebrated in a fresh new inn. In the hallway, warm red oak glows with warmth, enhanced by Amish runners and white walls highlighted with stenciling and copper sconces. Bedchambers are equally crisp, with Shaker-style four-posters topped with arched fishnet canopies, a writing desk or rocking chair, and braided rugs enlivening the floors. Modern amenities are present but unobtrusive, including televisions, hairdryers, phones, and refrigerators disguised as antique iceboxes. A Franklin stove and contemporary sofa invite lingering and game-playing in the upstairs common room. For an indulgence that Colonials would not have dreamed possible, reserve time for a private soak in the whirlpool downstairs or, for a setting that spans the centuries, sneak up to the widow's walk for an embrace before a timeless view of Nantucket's gray shingled cottages and the lighthouse radiating its beam deep into the past.

TEN LYON STREET, Nantucket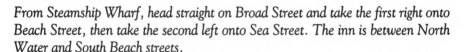
10 Lyon Street, (508) 228-5040
Moderate to Expensive (Closed mid-December through April)

Call for directions.

Pink and peach-colored roses twist up a trellis at this classic gray shingled cottage, promising sweet dreams within its walls. Inside, you'll find little to distract you from dreaming, with nostalgic but simple decor and just enough loving touches to inspire that romantic feeling. White walls and pine wood-work in the seven guest rooms are affectionate foils for the antique beds, patchwork quilts, Persian rugs, and impressionist prints. You'll find a sleigh bed tucked into one bedchamber, a crocheted canopy in another. The largest room is decked out with a splendid 1810 French country half-tester bed with sheer netting falling like snow around your pillows. Common rooms are cozy and country-style, with baskets hanging from the rafters in the entryway parlor. Low-fat but mouthwatering muffins are served at a long table squeezed into the breakfast room.

◆　**Romantic Note:** If you've checked out of your room but want to feel the cool of the ocean one last time before leaving the island, the inn provides a downstairs washroom so you can leave the salt and sand behind and return home with only each other and your memories.

THE WAUWINET, Nantucket　　　　　　　　　　◆◆◆◆
120 Wauwinet Road, (508) 228-0145, (800) 426-8718
Unbelievably Expensive (Open mid-May through October)

Call for directions. Inn provides transportation from Nantucket Village to the inn.

You can expect to find many select activities at this revamped 19th-century resort. Savor gourmet cuisine while overlooking Nantucket's unspoiled shore, explore the hidden natural life of a pristine beach on a customized jeep tour, sail or bike on your own day trip, or simply relax in bed watching the sun set over the waves. Ensconced on its own private spit of land, with the Atlantic on one side and Nantucket Bay on the other, this splendid inn harbors 35 enviable rooms, 25 in the main inn and 10 in cottages. In each, the colors are as serene and subtle as their surroundings, the furnishings elegant and airy. Most rooms have soothing seaside views, although some face away from the water. Throughout, bold modern and primitive objets d'art and accent pieces lend country cosmopolitan flair. In the spacious, breezy library, afternoon port and cheese are served by the hearth in the colder months or taken out to the veranda on sultry days.

Although the view from the patio is intoxicating, you'll be coaxed into the elegant but understated **TOPPER'S RESTAURANT** come dinnertime. Brass lamps top tables along with starched linen napery, mellow silver, and sparkling stemware. Country plaid chairs remind you that this is a beachside resort, after all, a place to feel relaxed, not restricted. "Country inn cuisine" best describes the menu. Begin your meal with lobster and crab cakes with smoked corn, jalapeño olives, and mustard sauce, or grilled shrimp with Italian sausage, buffalo mozzarella, and basil. Beautifully prepared entrées include grilled swordfish with saffron, orange, and black sesame seed butter, and smoked chicken with curried basmati rice and grilled banana.

WESTMOOR INN, Nantucket
Cliff Road, (508) 228-0877
Moderate to Very Expensive (Closed early December through April)

Call for directions.

In generations past, the wealthy voyaged to Nantucket Island for the summer, entertaining friends in their homes on the moors or strolling to the beach to cool warm toes and steal a kiss in the moonlight. So it is today at the Westmoor, a refined country manor that carries on its heritage of gentle hospitality. Removed from, although easily accessible to, town, the early-20th-century home is nestled down a private lane in a quiet residential area, a short walk from the beach. From the spacious third-floor room, with its windows on three sides, all you can see is the blue horizon, cottages, rolling moors, and, more recently, an eccentric neighbor's "field of dreams," his own private baseball field. Bedchambers are both warm and breezy, and always inviting. Some of the rooms have a crown canopy of fine netting or a white eyelet arch canopy, lace-trimmed comforter, and a brass, elaborate wicker, or carved wood bed. Downstairs, a commodious, summery suite boasts windows all around, a deep oval whirlpool, and a porch, but upstairs rooms are more cozy. In the afternoon, wine and hors d'oeuvres are served in the parlor, with its grand piano, sailing ship painting, shield-back chairs, and comfortable sofas. In the morning, sun pours into the greenhouse of a breakfast room, where you can linger over tea and croissants, just as vacationers did generations ago.

THE WHITE ELEPHANT HOTEL, Nantucket
Easton Street, (508) 228-5500, (800) ISLANDS
Very Expensive to Unbelievably Expensive (EP), Expensive (dining)

From Steamboat Wharf, turn right onto South Beach Street, then take the third right onto Easton Street. The hotel is along the harbor shore.

No white elephants here. This is one of the island's classiest resorts and a premier location, *the* place to come for pampering with a view. Stay on the second floor of the 22-room hotel for a quintessential Nantucket panorama. Just below is the hotel's heated swimming pool. Beyond, boats bob at their moorings. A strip of sand hems one side of the harbor, and gray shingled cottages sit shoulder-to-shoulder along the old, crooked streets of the village. Inside, the decor is as light and fresh as the summer breeze, with sandy-hued sponged walls, a salmon-and-gray-striped spread on a brown wicker bed, a comfortable sofa, and the requisite writing desk for their many lucky business travelers or for writing a love poem or two. All but one room opens to the harbor-view deck that stretches the length of the building. Around the grounds, eight Spindrift Cottages form a tiny cluster of rose-trellised, gray shingled homes, more secluded than the main building, but most lack the view.

In keeping with the tradition of pampered but easygoing luxury, the **REGATTA RESTAURANT** offers one of the island's finest dining settings. Chandeliers of amethyst and moss green glass shimmer from a trellis ceiling. Tables clothed in white linen are topped with handcrafted ceramic flowers that echo the amethyst hues above. In fair weather, tables are set on the heated outdoor terrace overlooking Nantucket Harbor. The menu changes nightly, but appetizers may include salmon tartare with caviar, crème fraîche, and capers, or hazelnut-crusted fried oysters and spinach leaves with grain mustard. Equally indulgent entrées are lobster and asparagus in puff pastry, grilled salmon in champagne sauce, and roast beef with a fricassee of wild mushrooms. Afterwards, drink in the view from the lounge overlooking the harbor and toast the beauty of the "gray lady" known as Nantucket.

Restaurant Kissing

THE BROTHERHOOD OF THIEVES, Nantucket
23 Broad Street, no telephone
Inexpensive to Moderate

In the heart of Nantucket village. Just ask any shopkeeper where it is and you will be pointed in the right direction.

This 1840 whaling tavern is so beloved that islanders use it as a landmark, describing a boutique as being just across the street or around the corner from "the Brotherhood." It's a place for casual romance, a fun meal, or one of their hundreds of specialty cocktails from the most extensive drink list in New England, if not the nation. Toast the tavern's old English pub ambience as you toast your toes by the raised brick hearth. Candles glow on the rough wooden tables, lighting the brick walls and low-slung beamed ceiling. Although you may find a table for two, many choose to sit at the long convivial tables in one of the few restaurants where you're actually encouraged to say hello to your neighbor. Hearty pub meals include sandwiches, burgers, and fried fish, often served with a heaping plate of their famous shoestring fries. To round off your meal, try one of the two dozen imported and liqueur-enhanced coffees.

COMPANY OF THE CAULDRON, Nantucket
7 India Street, (508) 228-4016
Expensive to Very Expensive
(Open Memorial Day through Columbus Day; closed Mondays)

Call for directions.

You may feel like an honored guest at a close-knit dinner party rather than a restaurant patron in this intimate Colonial setting. Candles provide the only light, flickering in tin wall sconces and within hurricane globes, highlighting the rough-hewn posts and beams. Spindle-back and Windsor chairs surround tables topped with fresh flowers. On certain summer nights, a harpist complements the setting, ensuring an unforgettable evening. The creative fixed-price menu changes nightly, but always pleases visitors and islanders alike. You may enjoy Nantucket Bay scallops, lobster and shrimp in pastry, a winter salad with roasted red pepper vinaigrette, almond- and hazelnut-crusted salmon with wild rice, and a poached pear with chocolate sauce and framboise crème anglaise for dessert.

◆ **Romantic Note:** Dinner seatings are at 7:00 p.m. and 9:00 p.m. Reservations are essential.

LE LANGUEDOC INN RESTAURANT
AND CAFÉ, Nantucket
3 Housie Street, (508) 228-2552
Very Expensive (restaurant), Moderate (café)

Call for directions.

If your head is in the clouds, but your budget is down to earth, this cozy establishment offers the best of both worlds. Downstairs, the casual café is a breath of old Paris, with its blue-and-white-checked cloths, cheerful modern art on deep gray walls, and wine bottles tucked teasingly into the ceramic tile hearth. Bistro delights, such as a smoked chicken club sandwich with apple bacon and autumn chutney, or seafood and saffron stew, are less expensive but taste just as delicious as the meals served in the more formal diningroom upstairs.

Prices rise when you ascend the staircase. Candlelight, fine linens, swag drapes, and splendid dried floral arrangements set the tone for a tête-à-tête over dishes such as a hearty lobster bisque, foie gras, carpaccio, Black Angus beef, onion-crusted Atlantic salmon, and rack of lamb with garlic bread pudding.

THE WOODBOX INN RESTAURANT, Nantucket
29 Fair Street, (508) 228-0587
Expensive (Open June through January; closed Mondays)

Call for directions.

Love spans generations, and so does the good cheer and warm atmosphere of this circa-1709 tavern. Intimate and snug, warmed by fire and candlelight, you can easily imagine history in the making. Three cozy dining rooms are tucked into the antique building. In one, a rifle is perched above the rough-hewn mantel of the immense brick hearth, a period candelabra hangs from the low-beamed ceiling, and pewter dishes line the plate rail. King's boards, so wide they were destined only for royalty (these somehow "fell" off the ship), make up the walls. In other rooms, Oriental rugs soften hardwood floors and multipaned windows look over Nantucket's old street. Candles provide virtually the only light, just as they did almost three centuries ago.

The chef describes his cuisine as hearty "peasant" food, but it is more elegant than that. The lobster cocktail and foie gras appetizers and such entrées as rack of lamb Provencal, crisp roast duck with three-berry sauce, and jumbo scampi with sherry-mustard-tarragon sauce are excellent. Perhaps if you had met in 1709, you would be just where you are today, dining together in Nantucket village, dreaming of your future together.

Siasconset

Hotel/Bed and Breakfast Kissing

SUMMER HOUSE, Siasconset   ◆◆◆
Ocean Avenue, (508) 257-9976
Unbelievably Expensive (Closed mid-October through mid-May)

From Nantucket town, follow Milestone Road to Siasconset, where it turns into Main Street. Bear right at the town center onto Ocean Avenue. The inn is on the right.

These rose-trellised cottages by the sea are a perfect escape *pas deux*. Tucked down a quiet shoreline road in the petite village of 'Sconset, they feel oceans away from the bustle and boutiques of Nantucket. Eight gray shingled cottages cluster around a grassy courtyard. Each is simply furnished with English pine antiques and the added modern luxury of a whirlpool bath. Across the street, you can while away the day by the outdoor pool or on a private beach where the waves have crashed for eternity. In the main house, where a restaurant serves dinner and a continental breakfast, you can enjoy the melodies of the piano bar, then stroll along the beach in the moonlight, in harmony with the rhythms of nature and love.

Restaurant Kissing

CHANTICLEER RESTAURANT, Siasconset   ◆◆◆◆
9 New Street, (508) 257-6231
Very Expensive

From Nantucket town, follow Milestone Road to Siasconset. New Street is on the left, just before the village.

Ask any islander for Nantucket's most romantic restaurant and many will sigh and whisper, "Chanticleer," with a faraway look in their eyes. You, too, may walk away with that gaze of love and longing after dining at this rose-covered cottage. A delicately painted carousel horse ringed with flowers is the centerpiece of a grassy courtyard hemmed with tables set on arbored brick walkways. Inside, a fire crackles at one end of the main dining room, where candles in sconces glow on golden walls. Beyond, a sunken greenhouse room overlooks the restaurant's herb garden. Every table is a delightful backdrop for a multicourse dinner for two. The menu emphasizes fresh fish with such specials as lobster soufflé and rabbit. If your hearts are willing but your budget doesn't allow for the fixed price meal, a less expensive bar menu is available in the firelit tavern.

◆ **Romantic Note:** Reservations made well in advance and a jacket and tie are a must for dinner.

Boston Area

Boston is alive with history, culture, beautiful architecture, and picturesque parks. At this premier destination for natives and world travelers alike, romance waits to embrace you around every corner. One of the best places for outdoor kissing is in the famous **PUBLIC GARDEN SWAN BOATS.** For kisses with a view, soar to the top of the gleaming 62-story **JOHN HANCOCK TOWER** or the 52nd-floor observatory of the stately **PRUDENTIAL CENTER.** Surprisingly, even one of the city's unique museums inspires romance: the **ISABELLA STEWART GARDNER MUSEUM** encompasses a glorious courtyard, reminiscent of a European palazzo, that makes a stunning setting for masterpieces collected from around the globe.

Although Boston's luxury hotels can be more businesslike than bohemian, they'll pamper you with the sort of extras that you can enjoy only at world-class accommodations. Be sure to ask about discount packages and weekend rates; you're almost guaranteed to find a significantly lower room rate than those officially listed.

Hotel/Bed and Breakfast Kissing

BOSTON HARBOR HOTEL, Boston
70 Rowes Wharf (on Atlantic Avenue)
(617) 439-7000, (800) 752-7077
Very Expensive to Unbelievably Expensive

Rowes Wharf is on the inner harbor, south of the Callahan Tunnel, near Congress and Broad streets.

Many guests arrive by boat at the Boston Harbor Hotel, but you can come by car or foot and still feel like your ship has come in. The location is enviable, as close to the water as the deck of the airport water shuttle that stops regularly at the dock just outside the hotel's entrance. After you're whisked up to your room, slip into something more comfortable—they provide terry robes and slippers—and gaze out your window at the shimmering water and city wharves below. The harbor views are definitely preferable to the city views, which, although they look over Boston's splendid skyline, are also above the raised highway that will soon be under major construction in the Big Dig. All rooms offer plush, executive hotel amenities, with Oriental vase lamps, quilted bedspreads, and Italian marble bathrooms. The Governor's Suite is the hotel's most extravagant accommodation. You can watch airplanes glide in and out of Logan from your private deck. From the sitting room, French doors open to the bedchamber, with its masculine half-tester done up in grays and ivories. If all that water below makes you long for a cool dip, make a splash in the hotel's 60-foot lap pool.

THE COPLEY PLAZA HOTEL, Boston   ◆◆
138 St. James Avenue, (617) 267-5300, (800) 8-COPLEY
Very Expensive to Unbelievably Expensive

At the corner of St. James Avenue and Dartmouth Street, across from the Boston Public Library.

You may wonder whether you've entered the inner sanctum of the shah's palace as you step into this 370-room hotel's majestically opulent lobby. Marble and gold dominate the palatial room, as immense, dripping crystal chandeliers, soaring columns crowned with gilt fleur-de-lis, and furnishings reminiscent of Versailles create an almost theatrical setting. After all this splendor, guest rooms can be somewhat disappointing. Standard rooms are, well, standard, and tend to be dark as adjacent buildings obstruct sunlight from penetrating the windows, especially on the lower floors. Suites have nonworking fireplaces but are spacious, and some face pleasant Copley Square. Deluxe rooms are preferable, as they face the outside and are brighter and more welcoming. Still, you will enjoy comfortable furnishings, a convenient location, and the pampering that any city hotel can provide.

◆ **Romantic Note:** Even if you don't stay overnight, the opulent lobby's **TEA COURT** is one of Boston's most splendid settings for afternoon tea. High-backed chairs with gilt woodwork, soaring arched mirrors, and marble columns provide a regal backdrop for miniature sandwiches, light lunches, desserts, specialty coffees, and, of course, a selection of fine teas.

FOUR SEASONS HOTEL, Boston
200 Boylston Street, (617) 338-4400, (800) 332-3442
Expensive to Unbelievably Expensive

From the Massachusetts Turnpike, take Exit 22 and follow signs to Copley Square. Take the first left onto Dartmouth Street and drive for two blocks. Turn right onto Boylston.

The velvet green of spring, swan boats sparkling in the summer sun, trees aflame in autumnal finery, snow muffling the city in white—every season is glorious when observed from your window at this world-class hotel facing Boston's most resplendent Public Garden. From the higher floors, you can see above leafy treetops for an even better view, including the golden dome of the state house. Even those rooms facing away from the garden overlook enchanting city views. Each newly refurbished bedchamber is elegantly adorned in deep blues, soft greens (our favorite), or peaches; estimable wood furnishings; and such distinguished touches as Oriental vase lamps and marble vanities. Executive Suites are especially spacious, with vistas from both the sitting room and bedroom. On the eighth floor, you can exert yourselves with a swim, then luxuriate in the bubbling whirlpool that also overlooks the garden.

◆ **Romantic Note:** A pianist, often one from the Boston Pops, fills the hotel's **BRISTOL LOUNGE** with soft rhapsodies in the evening. Enjoy a cocktail, casual dining, or the decadent Viennese dessert buffet as you relax by the marble fireplace.

LE MERIDIEN, Boston
250 Franklin Street, (617) 451-1900, (800) 543-4300
Moderate to Unbelievably Expensive

Take the Massachusetts Turnpike to Highway 93 North. Take the Atlantic Avenue exit and turn left onto High Street. Drive two blocks and turn right onto Oliver, then left onto Franklin.

This old-guard hotel with a French accent brings a whisper of Paris to its cosmopolitan sister across the sea. The structure, built in 1922 as a bank, was refurbished in 1981 by discriminating French hoteliers; their knack for drama is especially inspiring in the ninth-floor Contemporary Suites. Touch a button in the sitting room where floral love seats echo the colorful greenery of Post Office Square far below, and electric drapes pull slowly aside to reveal a stunning cityscape. The drama continues in the bedroom. Touch another button and the drapes slide away again, this time exposing the panorama on two sides of your corner room. Flop onto the king bed and you'll feel on top of the world. A dozen little toiletry bottles and extras pamper you in the bathroom, along with bathrobe, slippers, a hairdryer, and a scale.

Two of the city's top restaurants wait downstairs. The **CAFÉ FLEURI**, with its soaring six-story garden atrium, is an elegantly cheerful setting for the contemporary French and American cuisine. At the five-star **JULIEN**, with its stunning crystal chandeliers and castle-like walls, you will be treated like royalty.

THE LENOX HOTEL, Boston   ◆◆◆
710 Boylston Street, (617) 536-5300, (800) 225-7676
Expensive to Unbelievably Expensive

Near Exeter Street, Copley Place, and the library.

While some big-city hotels forsake historic ambience for modern amenities and plush but sometimes impersonal decor, the Lenox cherishes its rich heritage. Old-world charm, not sleek opulence, rules the 222 guest rooms and suites of this turn-of-the-century hotel. One of the few hotels in Boston with working fireplaces in the guest rooms, the Lenox seems more like a casual country inn. Rooms on the 11th floor offer the best views of the city rooftops around you, especially Room 1125, where you can see the Charles River and Cambridge beyond the city. In the John Hancock Suite, you can relax by the fire in the spacious parlor or sink into the carved wood bed. In Room 1111, our favorite, a corner hearth and a crystal chandelier add a romantic glow to the soft blues of the spacious bedchamber. You may feel as though you've taken a time machine back to the Boston of yesteryear, although you're only a short walk from one of today's most vibrant neighborhoods.

◆ **Romantic Note:** Ask about the Romantic Rendezvous package, which includes a fireplace room, champagne, and a continental breakfast in bed for less than $200 per night.

THE RITZ-CARLTON, Boston   ◆◆◆
15 Arlington Street, (617) 536-5700, (800) 241-3333
Very Expensive to Unbelievably Expensive

Call for directions.

Hurry through the cramped lobby of this top-notch hotel. A white-gloved elevator operator waits to whisk you up to an evening of "puttin' on the Ritz," Boston-style. If your budget allows, spring for a Club Room on the 14th through 16th floors. The splendid view overlooks the Public Garden, Boston Common, and the skyline beyond, and you'll be so pampered that you may never want to leave. In the Club's plush but cozy common room, a seemingly endless selection of complimentary snacks and beverages is presented to Club-floor guests, including a continental breakfast, light lunch, afternoon tea, hors d'oeuvres, wines, cordials, premium liqueurs, and late-night sweets (including luscious chocolate-covered strawberries). A wood-burning fireplace and crystal chandelier glow in the sitting room of a 15th-floor suite overlooking the garden, although, sadly, the bedchamber has no view. In the Superior Rooms, French country flair is reflected in the cream-colored, gold-trimmed furnishings. Downstairs, in the firelit gentleman's club of a bar, whisper over what locals rate as the best martinis in Boston.

THE WESTIN, Boston ◆◆◆
10 Huntington Avenue, (617) 262-9600, (800) 228-3000
Expensive to Unbelievably Expensive

At Copley Place, on the corner of Dartmouth Street.

A room with a view is all but guaranteed at this 36-floor jewel of a hotel rising above ritzy Copley Place. The nearby John Hancock Tower is its only competition for a piece of the sky. Stay in a corner room on one of the higher floors and you will feel as if you're looking over the rim of heaven onto a spectacular vista of the city skyline and the Charles River. The Westin's spacious rooms are furnished in plush, upscale-hotel style, with teal and mauve accents, cream-colored walls, and Early American-inspired furnishings. Share a warm embrace as you gaze out the window to watch the sunset wash the city in a rosy glow as lights from the buildings downtown blink on, creating fluorescent constellations.

Restaurant Kissing

ANOTHER SEASON, Boston
97 Mount Vernon Street, (617) 367-0880
Moderate to Expensive

Call for directions.

Gaslights cast a soft amber glow over the old brick sidewalks of historic Beacon Hill as you stroll to this charming restaurant. Inside, the mood of a French café is enhanced by *fin de siecle* murals depicting chic Parisians promenading along sunny boulevards.

Banquettes hug the wall for cozy dining, and lighting is low. The room may get somewhat too noisy for sweet talk, but that's all the more reason for a romantic couple to move closer.

The menu finds inspiration in the changing seasons, hence the restaurant's name. French-born chef Odette Bery, internationally acclaimed for her culinary talent, uses only the freshest ingredients to create a menu with flair and flavor. Order such regional favorites as codfish cakes and Boston baked beans or opt for such inventive fare as salad with Hubbard squash and greens laced with apple-lemon dressing.

AUJOURD'HUI, Boston   ◆◆◆◆
200 Boylston Street, at the Four Seasons Hotel
(617) 338-4400
Very Expensive

From the Massachusetts Turnpike, take Exit 22 and follow signs to Copley Square. Take the first left onto Dartmouth Street and drive for two blocks. Turn right onto Boylston.

A grand staircase leads to this premier Boston restaurant, but it's more than luxurious decor that impresses the culinary mavens who flock to Aujourd'hui. Fine food, flair, and scrupulous service crown what many regard as Boston's most outstanding dining room. The corn chowder is legendary, the sliced roast duck with red raspberries wins praises from the regulars, and a well-known food critic confesses that he "absolutely swooned over the vermouth and white chocolate sorbet with bittersweet confection." Everything here is the ultimate in elegant, intimate dining. Considered by many to be the most romantic restaurant in the area, it is worth a taste and a kiss or two. Also, outside lies one of the most romantic walking areas in Boston, around the Public Gardens, swan boats, and the ice skating ring in winter.

◆ **Romantic Alternative:** The hotel's café with piano bar is another romantic setting. Hot chocolate poured from a silver service, paired with a plate of sophisticated pastries, makes a sweet nightcap after the theater, while cushiony love seats abet hand-holding and kissing.

THE CAFÉ, Boston   ◆◆◆
15 Arlington Street, at the Ritz-Carlton Hotel
(617) 536-5700
Moderate to Expensive

Follow the Massachusetts Turnpike (Route 90) eastbound to Exit 22. Follow signs to Copley Square. At a traffic light, turn left onto Dartmouth Street. Follow it for four blocks and turn right onto Commonwealth Avenue. In three blocks, at its end, turn right onto Arlington. The hotel is on the right.

The Ritz-Carlton embraces many of the classic, regal amenities of a fine European hotel, but the Café leaves no doubt that you're in the heart of Boston. The dining room's large windows front on Newbury Street, the city's premier shopping avenue, and murals by artist Ruth Lyke depict local scenes: the State House, the Custom House, Beacon Hill, and the Public Garden.

Candlelight, fresh flowers, heavy silver, and meticulous service are evidence that you're in the company of proper Bostonians who eschew excess, yet appreciate quality. It's easy to pick out the locals—men in classic double-breasted suits and women wearing their best pearls—among the chic international guests staying at the hotel. Harp music wafts through the room between

6:30 p.m. and 9:30 p.m., and even staid New Englanders have been known to hold hands and sneak a kiss in public. Their devotion extends to such delectables as veal medallions sautéed with cognac and apples, and New England-style chicken pot pie.

◆ **Romantic Note:** The Café serves dinner until midnight every night, a reliable late-night romantic plus.

CAFÉ BUDAPEST, Boston ❖❖❖
90 Exeter Street, (617) 266-1979, (800) 531-1979
Expensive to Very Expensive

From the Massachusetts Turnpike, take Exit 22 and follow signs to Copley Square. Go around the block to the café.

Have you ever walked into a valentine? Well, that's how you'll feel upon entering Café Budapest, a rococo warren of old-fashioned rooms wrapped in infinite shades of pink. As constant as true love, this Hungarian restaurant has been a favorite romantic rendezvous for more than 30 years. After you taste the chicken paprikash with nokkedli (homemade noodles), you'll know why. Even the iced cherry soup, served in glass bowls, is delivered like a love note by a tuxedoed waiter.

By the way, if you experience a feeling of deja vu the first time you visit Café Budapest, it may be because you saw the film *Housesitter*, in which Goldie Hawn plays a waitress at the restaurant.

CHOCOLATE BAR, Boston
250 Franklin Street, at Le Meridien
(617) 451-1900, (800) 543-4300
Moderate
(Open Saturdays from 2:00 p.m. to 4:30 p.m; reservations required)

Take the Massachusetts Turnpike to Highway 93 North. Take the Atlantic Avenue exit and turn left onto High Street. Drive two blocks and turn right onto Oliver, then left onto Franklin.

Scientists confirm what chocoholics have always known: chocolate is a real aphrodisiac. In fact, it's such potent stuff that just a whiff can set the brain's endorphins astir and ignite feelings of ardor. Romantics who wish to indulge their consuming passion are accommodated at Le Meridien's chocolate bar. Be forewarned, however; this is a serious affair, for couples well beyond candy kisses.

Here, chocolate reigns supreme in columned and marbled splendor. Gorgeously presented on richly swagged cloths with lace doilies and sparkling silver servers, the bountiful all-you-can-eat buffet offers a cornucopia of white, milk, and bittersweet chocolate concoctions, often in creative combinations.

Choices vary from week to week, and may include such confections as chocolate ganache, chocolate trifle, chocolate cheesecake, chocolate fondue, chocolate eclairs, chocolate ice cream, chocolate cream puffs, chocolate pasta, and chocolate bread pudding. Did I mention chocolate mousse? Well, you get the idea.

The prix fixe orgy includes coffee, tea, or milk served at your private table by an attentive wait staff.

THE COLONNADE'S "NIGHTS AT THE OPERA," Boston ◗◗◗
120 Huntington Avenue, (617) 424-7000, (800) 962-3030
Moderate (Saturdays at 8:00 p.m.; reservations required)

Take the Massachusetts Turnpike eastbound to Exit 22. Follow signs to the Prudential Center, 300 yards past the tunnel. The hotel is on the left.

Grand opera celebrates grand passions, paying homage to enduring love with memorable music. Still, when a friend told me that eating at the opera can be great fun, I was more than a bit skeptical. That was before I attended the Colonnade's "Nights at the Opera," where the atmosphere suggests a festive house party and people dress for the occasion.

Six actor/singers, collectively called the Opera Un Met, wander about the pink dining room like troubadours of old, performing a musical love story they have cobbled together using well-known arias. In addition to a menu, guests receive a program that makes it easy to follow the action.

The performers seem to have a good time choosing couples to serenade. Who can resist a kiss or two when listening to the love calls of *"La ci darem la mano"* (*"Give me your hand; answer your lover's plea ..."*) from Mozart's *Don Giovanni?*

The four-course meal is as imaginative as the music, and the presentation is visually exciting. Among the artful choices are roast salmon with grilled corn, red pepper, and Red Bliss potato compote, and a salad of bitter greens and pears with cider vinaigrette.

◆ **Romantic Note:** "Nights at the Opera" generally sell out early in the week. If you're too late for a reservation, leave your name on the waiting list. You may be lucky and get a call-back when there's a cancellation. Also, complimentary parking in the hotel garage is included in the dinner package.

FINE ARTS DINING ROOM, Boston ◗◗
465 Huntington Avenue, at the Museum of Fine Arts
(617) 266-3663
Moderate

From the Massachusetts Turnpike, take Exit 22 to the Prudential Center. Keep to the left and get onto Huntington Avenue. Stay on Huntington for three-quarters of a mile; the museum is on the right.

The art of love and the love of art go hand-in-hand at the Fine Arts Dining Room. The menu takes a pleasant turn with each featured exhibition in the Gund Gallery of the West Wing, designed by architect I.M. Pei. French impressionists are paired with French cuisine, while a recent exhibition on "The Lure of Italy—American Artists and the Italian Experience" inspired such culinary masterpieces as Sicilian monzu (swordfish stuffed with Parmesan cheese, basil, and grilled shrimp on roasted peppers) and delicate lemon and herb ravioli. The salad bar is outstanding; the European dessert table is irresistible.

Even though the gray and green dining room seems too large and too modern for traditional romantics, it manages to feel intimate. Tables are well spaced, and sitting by the window wall overlooking the sculpture garden removes you to a hushed world of your own. The wait staff draws heavily on foreign students, who lend the restaurant a charming continental cachet.

◆ **Romantic Note:** Museum admission is not charged to restaurant goers who do not visit an exhibition. Admission to the museum is free on Wednesdays between 4:00 p.m. and 9:45 p.m. At 6:15 p.m. on Wednesdays, there's a free introductory walk through all the collections, and on the first Wednesday of each month at 6:30 p.m., there's also an introductory walk in Spanish.

L'ESPALIER, Boston   ◆◆◆◆
30 Gloucester Street, (617) 262-3023
Very Expensive

Call for directions.

Elegant and serene, L'Espalier indulges all of the senses. Indeed, dinner here is such a sybaritic event that even the most hardened heart couldn't fail to respond amorously to the seductive fare.

Nonetheless, it tickles my funnybone to ascend the circular staircase from the foyer to the second-floor dining rooms and behold an army of waiters, busboys, and the maitre d' lined up with military precision. Perfectly attired in black and white, they seem to have just stepped out of a *New Yorker* cartoon.

The fashionable brownstone townhouse, with ornate marble fireplaces and soft gray walls accented with intricate snow white fretwork, is a soothing and understated setting for such offerings as fresh Wellfleet oysters and caviar with champagne-watercress cream and cucumber. The sautéed veal rib eye encased in pistachios and accompanied by forest mushrooms, truffled potatoes, and fried shallots in a black truffle port sauce, is worth celebrating. Dainty love potions, complimentary treats from the chef, begin and end each meal.

◆ **Romantic Alternative:** Nearby, in the same building that houses Cheers, the model for the TV show *Cheers*, **THE HAMPSHIRE HOUSE,**

84 Beacon Street, Boston, (617) 227-9600, (Moderate), offers gracious townhouse dining with a less dramatic price tag. A window table in the library is the perfect perch for viewing the Public Garden swan boats and making like lovebirds.

MR. LEUNG, Boston
545 Boyston Street, on Copley Square, (617) 236-4040
Moderate to Expensive

From the Massachusetts Turnpike (Route 90), head eastbound and take Exit 22. Stay to the right and follow signs for Copley Square.

Stylish, sleek, and sophisticated aren't words ordinarily used to describe Chinese restaurants, but then Mr. Leung isn't your ordinary Chinese restaurant. From the moment you descend into the striking black and white dining room, you experience the mysterious Orient. The ambience promises a most exotic evening.

Dramatic lighting suffuses this underworld so that, like the difference between infatuation and true love, it's sometimes difficult to know what is real and what isn't. (The sculptural floral arrangements appear to be artificial but, in fact, are real.) Service veers on the pretentious. The chef, however, more than meets the challenge of satisfying discriminating diners, and vegetarians will welcome the menu's variety. Ordering a dish with meat, fish, or poultry catapults a meal into the Expensive category.

◆ **Romantic Alternative:** For more moderately priced urbane dining, cross the Charles River and visit **CHANGSO RESTAURANT,** 1712 Massachusetts Avenue, Cambridge, (617) 547-6565. The gourmet Chinese food is enhanced by an array of distinctive sauces. Don't miss the best littleneck clams in black bean sauce this side of Hong Kong.

THE WINE CAFÉ AT ICARUS RESTAURANT, Boston
3 Appleton Street, (617) 426-1790
Inexpensive

Call for directions.

When your taste exceeds your pocketbook, it takes ingenuity to enjoy the finer things in life. But it can be done. Head for Icarus, one of Boston's classier restaurants and a romantic hideaway for city sophisticates. The dining room may be off-limits to the strictly budget-conscious, but on Sundays, from 5:30 p.m. to 10:00 p.m., you can revel in pleasures that are usually reserved for the well-heeled.

The secret is not to wander from the bar area, a handsome balcony filled with rich dark woods, polished brass, and lavish floral arrangements. Cozy up in the comfortable lounge, where soft lighting and soft jazz set the mood for an intimate tête-à-tête. Order a glass of wine and share bites of such tasty tidbits as a trio of pork medallions or warm wedges of focaccia garnished with a large bud of roasted garlic. All 10 items on the special menu carry paltry price tags.

Cambridge

Restaurant Kissing

CHEZ NOUS, Cambridge
147 Huron Avenue, (617) 864-6670
Moderate

Call for directions.

Step across the threshold of Chez Nous and enter a cozy world where you'll bask in the sincerity of a warm welcome. With seating for barely 30 guests, unadorned teal blue walls, dropped ceiling, low lighting, and classical music, Chez Nous offers an understated romantic atmosphere much appreciated by Cambridge intellectuals. There are no distractions for lovers who wish to gaze into each other's eyes.

The eclectic menu, which changes so frequently that it is handwritten, offers such cosmopolitan choices as stuffed pheasant, wolf fish with lobster sauce, pasta dishes, and roast chicken. To savor each delicious moment, ask your waiter to serve slowly.

Outdoor Kissing

CHARLES RIVER, Cambridge

Near MIT (Massachuttes Institute of Technology) on Vasser Street, near Harvard University on Oxford Street.

For a pastoral pleasure in the city, consider a picnic on the Memorial Drive side of the river. The lunch wagons that congregate around Boston University, Massachusetts Institute of Technology, and Harvard College dish up Chinese, Indian, Near Eastern, and Italian goodies that the most impecunious student can afford. Take your purchases to the grassy banks of the Charles River, spread a blanket under one of the venerable maples, and enjoy the water view framed by Boston's distinctive skyline of historic and contemporary buildings. There's no more romantic setting for outdoor kissing.

Watertown

LE BOCAGE, Watertown
72 Bigelow Avenue, (617) 923-1210
Moderate to Expensive

At the intersection where Bigelow crosses Mount Auburn Street (the main thoroughfare between Cambridge and Watertown).

Never mind the dreary facade or the commercial street. There's a delightful surprise waiting inside this little restaurant. The subtle aura cast by the dining room's flickering candlelight illuminates a magical setting for dinner *a deux*, and behold the view: a miniature garden all atwinkle with little lights.

At Le Bocage, tables are spaced so far apart you'll quickly forget there's anyone else around. And that rare commodity, quiet, is in ample supply. Waiters, too dignified to crash silver or clatter plates, silently anticipâté your every wish.

The menu, classic French cuisine with contemporary attention to healthy eating—less fat and sodium—is an indication of the care that the husband-and-wife team of Ed and Susanna Tolini lavish on their restaurant. Such tasty dishes as smoked chicken and apple sausages, and poached salmon with sorrel and watercress sauce pose difficult choices. Bibb lettuce and radicchio salad is served after the main course in the continental manner. The crowning achievement is dessert, an ambrosial assortment that includes crêpes Suzette, crème brûlée, and a sensuous bittersweet chocolate mousse torte.

Rockport

For generations, artists and tourists alike have painted Rockport as the quintessential New England seaside town. Here you will find "Motif #1," a weatherbeaten shack perched at the tip of a rocky pier, colorful lobster-trap markers slung along its rooster red shingles. The scene, made famous in paintings and photographs, is still magically preserved, as though it had been tucked inside a picture frame. Nearby, you can join the crowds on the narrow lanes of Bearskin Neck, a pier clustered with gift shops and chowder houses that sways between fun and funky. Persevere to the end of the pier and you'll be rewarded with a splendid view of the harbor, busy with fishing boats, and the ocean beyond. If summer's heat bears down, nearby beaches offer a refreshingly cool Atlantic dip.

Hotel/Bed and Breakfast Kissing

ADDISON CHOATE INN, Rockport
49 Broadway, (508) 546-7543
Inexpensive to Moderate

Call for directions.

This old-fashioned country inn greets you with a warm smile and breezy style. If a winter chill nips the air, a crackling fire warms the living room, with its plaid wing chairs and contemporary sofa. Just beyond, black leather lounge chairs set before the television are the first hint of this inn's mix of nostalgic antiques and modern furnishings. The seven guest rooms are cozy and comfortable. Old-fashioned beds, glowing pine floors, a marble-topped bureau, Shaker rocker, or even a white brick chimney rising up through your room are some of the telling details that fill this 130-year-old home. In the morning, a continental breakfast is served in the firelit breakfast room. On a sultry summer day, you're invited to splash in the pool, a refreshing start to a day of touring the Atlantic coast.

PLEASANT STREET INN, Rockport
17 Pleasant Street, (508) 546-3915, (800) 541-3915
Inexpensive to Moderate

Call for directions.

Step onto the front porch of this splendid Queen Anne Victorian crowning a quiet knoll and look up. Above you is a mural of a dreamy sky brushed with billowing clouds. A blend of beautifully restored architectural detailing, modern enhancements, and homespun hospitality awaits inside. From the foyer, with its pressed tin ceiling, to the homey living room to the collection of china and porcelain in the family dining room, where a continental breakfast is served each morning, you will be impressed with your surroundings. A turreted sitting area in Room 1 overlooks the village, its two steepled churches, and a wink of ocean beyond. In Room 7, a bed is tucked into the first level, and a spiral staircase leads to a snug sleeping loft in the turret's faceted crown. Cozy rooms, swagged draperies, hardwood floors, antique bureaus, and paintings inspired by local scenes all add to the inn's inviting, nostalgic ambience.

SEACREST MANOR, Rockport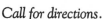
131 Marmion Way, (508) 546-2211
Inexpensive to Moderate (Open April through November)

Call for directions.

Two lighthouses stand on the island viewed from this seaside inn's sunken living room. Contemporary furnishings fill the room, and afternoon tea adds a breath of sedate refinement. The ambience is breezy and casual, the decor simple and homespun in the eight guest rooms, six with private bath. Two rooms open to a sun deck overlooking the blue ocean horizon beyond Rockport's wooded, residential shore. Prints of sailing ships remind guests of the home's heritage; turn-down and shoeshine service pamper with panache. In the morning, a country breakfast is served in the firelit dining room.

YANKEE CLIPPER INN, Rockport   ❤❤
96 Granite Street, (508) 546-3407, (800) 545-3699
Moderate to Very Expensive (B&B), Expensive to Very Expensive (MAP)
(Closed January through mid-February)

Call for directions.

The serene blue water of Rockport's harbor shimmers in the summer sun, softly caressing the rocky shore, smoothing its stony face so that all is soft and sleek as the coast curves gracefully to this quintessential New England seaside village. This is where Jackie and John F. Kennedy held hands in 1959. Though the Clipper's sails are a little weathered, this venerable inn still boasts one of Rockport's best views.

Of the three buildings that comprise the inn, the more secluded Quarter-deck building takes best advantage of this enviable location. Vintage Queen Anne antiques and reproductions add a nostalgic touch to this seaside home with picture windows overlooking the harbor. In the main inn, housed in an old mansion, highlights include private sun porches, sleigh and fishnet canopy beds, and cheerful fabrics. The ambience is comfortable and homespun, if occasionally dated. The vintage Bullfinch House is across the street, so it has no view, but all guests are invited to wander back for a quick kiss in the inn's oceanfront gazebo or a refreshing dip in the saltwater pool. Breakfasts and dinners are served in **THE GLASS VERANDAH** (see "Restaurant Kissing"), an intimate restaurant located on the mansion's enclosed porch.

Restaurant Kissing

THE GLASS VERANDAH,
127 Granite Street, at the Yankee Clipper Inn
(508) 546-7795, (508) 546-3407
Moderate to Expensive (Open April through November)

Call for directions.

Your hearts will set sail as you gaze over Rockport's harbor from your table in this enclosed-porch dining room off the Yankee Clipper Inn's parlor. Waves lap at the rocky shore as it curves around the azure cove to the tiny village center, creating a spellbinding scene. Inside, Spode china, crystal stemware, and candlelight add a touch of elegance, while white iron chairs provide a summery café feel. Shrimp sautéed with apple chutney, Dijon mustard, wine, and garlic; seafood au gratin; and poached salmon with sweet red pepper sauce are some of the specialties. Other noteworthy dishes include veal marsala, stir-fried beef tenderloin, Rockport lobster, and broiled steak, sole, and swordfish. Toast the sea view with a nonalcoholic wine or beer or bring a bottle of your favorite to sip while the sun sets (Rockport is a dry town, so wine and alcohol are not available here).

Gloucester

Hotel/Bed and Breakfast Kissing

THE GLOUCESTER ADVENTURE, Gloucester   ❖❖
State Fish Pier, off Parker Street (winter)
Downtown Gloucester (summer), (508) 281-8079
Inexpensive to Moderate (inn, dining)

Call for directions.

The only American tall ship that is also a bed and breakfast, or, as Cape Ann's old salts are fond of saying, "bunk-'n-board," the *Adventure* offers the thrill of romance on the high seas in the comfort of a historic home port. Although the 66-year-old schooner is listed on the National Register of Historic Places, there's nothing stuffy about this dreamboat. Overnight guests snuggle up in a private cabin on a double bunk bed, lulled to sleep by the lapping of ocean waves.

Gulls and cormorants announce breakfast, which is cooked on the original galley wood stove and served windjammer style in the quaint red-and-white-checked foc's'le, or al fresco on the deck overlooking Gloucester's working harbor.

Even if you don't stay overnight, you can enjoy Sunday breakfast aboard ship. Each week's menu is different, reflecting the inclinations of the day's guest chef. A meal may include Mexican or Portuguese dishes, pancakes with New England maple syrup, or something completely original. The only guarantees are juice, lots of freshly brewed aromatic coffee, and an appetite sharpened by sea air.

◆ **Romantic Warning:** Overnight guests share bathroom facilities.

Restaurant Kissing

WHITE RAINBOW, Gloucester   💋💋
65 Main Street, (508) 281-0017
Moderate to Expensive

Call for directions.

A brick building squeezed into Main Street houses this stellar restaurant in the heart of Gloucester. Formal and informal menus here suit a variety of tastes. Casual meals are served in the refreshingly contemporary café, with its chrome and black leather chairs, framed art posters on deep mauve walls, and black-stemmed glassware on white linen. Maui onion soup, pâté, lobster stew, crab cakes, and soft-shell crab are some of the specialties. In the more formal main dining room, the menu offers a creative twist on old favorites, with such specials as Jamaican jerk pork, grilled sea scallops Thai style, and sautéed lobster. The delectable cuisine is your pot of gold at the White Rainbow.

Lowell

Restaurant Kissing

SOUTH EAST ASIAN RESTAURANT, Lowell   💋💋
343 Market Street, (508) 452-3182
Inexpensive

Call for directions.

To cap off an excursion to **LOWELL NATIONAL PARK** (see "Outdoor Kissing"), stroll over to the gaily painted South East Asian Restaurant and sample the authentic open-air market cuisines of Thailand, Laos, Cambodia, and Vietnam. Inside everything glows pastel pink, from the walls to the floor and tablecloths. Potted palms separate the tables.

The coded menu identifies dishes by ingredients, country of origin, and degree of spiciness. The most popular appetizer is goi cuon, five little logs of shredded garden vegetables, herbs, and ground pork wrapped in delicate rice paper crêpes. Like many dishes here, it is also available in a vegetarian version. Be adventurous. One of the thrills of discovering a new cuisine, like a new love, is exploring the possibilities.

◆ **Romantic Note:** Lovers who wish to satisfy their passion for lots of fine food won't want to miss the all-you-can-eat luncheon buffet, served Monday through Friday, from 11:30 a.m. to 2:30 p.m., or the all-you-can-eat dinner buffet on Monday, Tuesday, and Wednesday from 6:30 p.m. to 9:30 p.m.

Outdoor Kissing

LOWELL NATIONAL PARK
(508) 459-1000
$3 for adults

Call for directions.

One of my favorite day trips is to **LOWELL NATIONAL PARK** (the nation's first urban park), where free (yes, free) canal boat rides take you through an area that will remind you of Venice. True, the canal boats here are shared, which inhibits romantic inclinations. Nevertheless, especially in fall, when leaves are aflame with color, cruising is an appealing way to see America's first planned industrial city, the birthplace of painter James McNeil Whistler and beat poet Jack Kerouac. Many of the buildings have been restored and refurbished. This historic mill town comes to life for tours and education, with tour guides in period costumes who act out their roles authentically.

Tyngsboro

Hotel/Bed and Breakfast Kissing

STONEHEDGE INN, Tyngsboro
160 Pawtucket Boulevard, (508) 649-4342
Moderate to Expensive (inn, dining)

Call for directions.

With horses grazing in fenced paddocks that line the sinuous driveway, and a putting green on the side lawn, Stonehedge seems more like an estate in Texas than a country retreat in New England. The relaxed rural atmosphere lends a casualness to **SILKS,** the inn's comfortable dining room, that belies its ambitious French menu. ("Silks" refers to the colorful caps and blouses worn by jockeys, and drawings of racehorses punctuate the walls of the spacious restaurant.) The well-spaced tables, an attentive, almost pampering wait staff, high banquettes, and cozy atmosphere meet anyone's definition of romance.

I became a fan of chef Jim Overbaugh on tasting his fabulous fresh breads. The waiter had to refill our bread basket more than once. The dinner menu features classic French dishes plus innovative specialties such as haddock served with a light white wine and grapefruit sauce. Any serious French restaurant presents an assortment of dessert cheeses as well as pastries, and Silks is no exception. It also boasts a well-stocked wine cellar. The continental service is conscientious without being cloying.

After dinner, it's tempting to head upstairs to a comfortable suite. Unfortunately, the ersatz Early American decor of the bedrooms is disappointing, but the pleasant common rooms, deep Jacuzzi tubs, king-size beds, and working fireplaces offer romantic consolation.

◆   Romantic Note: An especially good value, if you plan to stay the night, is the special package that includes dinner for two on arrival, a suite, and breakfast the next morning.

Lexington

Restaurant Kissing

VERSAILLES, Lexington   ◆◆◆
1777 Massachusetts Avenue, (617) 861-1711
Moderate

From the Massachusetts Turnpike, take Route 95 North. Turn off at Exit 31A and go one and a half miles. Versailles is on the left.

Only a few steps from Lexington's famed Minuteman statue and the Battle Green that commemorates the first shots of the American Revolution, chef Isaac Dray is sparking a gastronomic revolution. Versailles' lush beige interior glitters with mirrors, gilt-framed paintings, and rich dark woods. Old-world charm is reflected in the personal, relaxed service; a continental menu stars such favorites as moulles au vin blanc (mussels steamed in white wine and herbs) and individual beef Wellington.

What makes Versailles different, however, is that each day the chef includes a few specials from his native Morocco. Such dishes as poulet à la Marrakesh (chicken breast with onions and green olives), poulet bastilla (chicken with walnuts, raisins, herbs, and Moroccan spices wrapped in filo dough), and lamb with caramelized onions and prunes are sure to make your hearts beat a little faster.

In summer, Versailles sets out sidewalk tables shaded by large market umbrellas, ideal for an open-air lunch or a cool drink.

Concord

This fair village sparked the American Revolution with the "shot heard round the world" in 1775, and was home to the revolution in American literature forged by Ralph Waldo Emerson, Henry David Thoreau, Louisa May Alcott, Nathaniel Hawthorne, and other Concord writers. Today, you can visit the splendidly preserved historic sites and literary homes in this classic Colonial town. Bring a picnic to the **OLD NORTH BRIDGE**, the birthplace of the American Revolution, now a pastoral scene of a rude wooden bridge spanning an idyllic river. Climb the hill to the terraced gardens of the **BUTTRICK ESTATE** and embrace for a moment overlooking this sylvan setting. The town center is ideal for strolling, window shopping in the shops, and relaxing on the lawn of Monument Square, punctuated with a steepled church on one end and the Colonial Inn on the other.

For one of the best country drives or bike rides in the area, explore the neighboring town of **CARLISLE**. You'll be rewarded with splendid old Colonials, tranquil farmlands, and the best chocolate chip ice cream in the world, made by the **BATES DAIRY FARM** and served at an old-fashioned roadside stand in a bucolic setting highlighted by the resident cows, bunnies, and geese. Although it's only 20 miles from Boston, Concord feels worlds away.

Hotel/Bed and Breakfast Kissing

THE COLONIAL INN, Concord
48 Monument Square, (508) 369-9200, (800) 370-9200
Moderate to Expensive (inn), Expensive (dining)

In the center of town, facing the green in Concord Center.

History is more than water under the bridge in Concord. It's as alive and vibrant as ever, especially at this centuries-old inn. Built as a home for one of the town's first settlers in 1716 and expanded as a hotel in 1889, this landmark offers dining and lodging in a casual country atmosphere with a Colonial emphasis. In the main dining room, unusual sconces evoking the gas lights of yesteryear flicker on the rich wood posts that rise between the tables. Multipaned windows, leather chairs, white linens, and fresh flowers set the stage for such traditional specialties as chicken or lobster pie; roast duckling; prime rib; chicken sautéed with tomatoes, olives, mushrooms, and scallions in white wine; and fettuccine Alfredo with scallops, shrimp, lobster, and mussels. A rustic tavern and a Colonial café overlooking the village offer lighter fare, including sandwiches, salads, and burgers.

More than 100 rooms now accommodate Concord's scores of tourists and business travelers. The main inn is the more charming of the two buildings.

Although the fireplaces can no longer be used, your room is likely to feature a four-poster bed, patchwork quilt, wing chair, and crewel-look draperies. The Prescott Wing rooms are smaller and simply decorated with country furnishings, plaid wing chairs, and writing desks for visiting executives. Ask for a room overlooking the town, and take a quick peek outside at midnight.

HAWTHORNE INN, Concord   ◆◆◗
462 Lexington Avenue, (508) 369-5610
Moderate to Expensive

Call for directions.

The location is ideal, in the same neighborhood as the Louisa May Alcott and Ralph Waldo Emerson homes, now open to the public, and it's just a short walk to the town center. This bed and breakfast feels more like a private country home than an inn, with its eclectic blend of American antiques, South American artifacts, and modern sculptures created by the innkeeper. On cold evenings, guests gather around the hearth in the Victorian parlor for conversations. The seven guest rooms are country cozy, with an assortment of vintage writing desks, nostalgic beds, hand-crafted quilts, Japanese Ukiyo-e prints, and soothing hues.

After a breakfast of home-baked breads, yogurt, cereal, and fresh fruit, take time to explore the yard. Here, the Alcotts planted fruit trees and tended a garden, and Hawthorne planted pines, two of which still grow today, a living reminder of Concord's heritage.

Restaurant Kissing

AIGO BISTRO, Concord
84 Thoreau Street, (508) 371-1333
Expensive

On the second floor of the Concord train depot, just off Route 126, adjacent to the center of town.

This cheerful bistro is your ticket to refreshingly contemporary cuisine in Colonial Concord. One intimate room overlooks the railroad tracks. There, in the warmer months, the sun washes diners in golden warmth; in winter, the sight of a train emerging from a snowstorm is almost magical. The back room is accented with a mural of a delightful Mediterranean scene and the motto "Garlic soup saves lives," penned in an old Provencal language. Golden walls, terra-cotta oil lamps, and rosewood tables add a European panache. Aigo, or garlic, features prominently on the menu. The roasted garlic soup, with caramelized squash, parsleyed walnut oil, and grilled bread, is a favorite appetizer. Seasonal main courses might include veal stuffed with leeks, sage, juniper, and roasted wild mushrooms; chicken with Berber spices, eggplant relish, and pomegranate couscous; and steak with garlic confit. Garlic may not save your life, but in the hands of the talented cooks here, can enhance it considerably.

Outdoor Kissing

CANOEING IN CONCORD, Concord ❖❖❖
South Bridge Boat House, 496 Main Street, (508) 369-9438
About $8 per hour or $26 to $36 per day
(Open April through November)

From Route 2 westbound, turn right onto Main Street, at the third traffic light after Route 2 turns sharply left. The boat house is on the left, just before the bridge over the river.

The ballet of a sunbeam on rippling water, the flash of a songbird as it flits from tree to tree, the soft lapping of the river on the hull of the canoe, the green velvet of the trees caressing the shore—all embrace you with serenity as you glide along the Concord and Sudbury rivers. Immortalized in Thoreau's writings, these waterways have been navigated by generations of Concordians and visitors alike. A favorite excursion begins at the South Bridge, where you can rent canoes, and journeys through town to the historic North Bridge, about one and a half hours round-trip. Here, you can picnic where the "shot heard round the world" was fired, or walk up the hill to the Buttrick estate to wander the splendid terraced gardens overlooking the placid river that curves into the distance.

Sudbury

Hotel/Bed and Breakfast Kissing

LONGFELLOW'S WAYSIDE INN, Sudbury
Wayside Inn Road, (508) 443-1776
Inexpensive (inn), Moderate (dining)

From the Massachusetts Turnpike (Route 90) westbound, take Route 128 northbound. Take Exit 26 onto Route 20 west for 11 miles. Bear right onto the Wayside Inn's access road; the inn is on the right.

"As ancient is this Hostelry as any in the land may be," are the words Longfellow used in his *Tales of a Wayside Inn* back in 1863. Today, America's oldest inn still provides "Food, Drink, Lodging for Man, Woman and Beast" as it has since 1716, half a century before the American Revolution. Perhaps it is the long heritage of hospitality or the splendid manner in which the Colonial ambience is preserved in the architecture, decor, and cuisine, but visitors will be hard-pressed to find a more hospitable inn.

When you arrive for dinner, you'll most likely be greeted at the door by a gentleman in tricornered hat and Colonial garb. To the right, a blazing fire helps you shake off winter's cold in the Old Bar Room, where pewter steins hang from the low beamed ceiling and guests stop in for a Coow Woow, supposedly the nation's first mixed drink. To the left, a period-style room recreates the Wayside's beginnings, the mission of the nonprofit organization that operates the inn. Beyond, a casual, festive air prevails in the expansive main dining room, with its Colonial-style chandeliers, tin sconces, tabletop tapers, hand-painted valances, and muted green woodwork. The low-slung Tap Room is more intimate, with brown-checked cloths and subtle lighting. Wait staff in period dress present hearty four-course dinners of prime rib, roast goose, broiled scrod, chicken with cranberry-walnut stuffing, and lobster or crabmeat casserole. The price also includes a relish dish, appetizer, salad, rolls made from grain from the ancient grist mill down the lane, and dessert.

Ten upstairs guest rooms are filled with such details as antique furnishings, hardwood floors, plaid wing chairs, six-over-six windows, crewel-look draperies, and deep green woodwork. In keeping with tradition, you can lodge your horse in the stables across the street, just as travelers did when the new world was truly new.

◆ **Romantic Note:** Advance reservations for the inn or restaurant are highly recommended.

Sherborn

Hotel/Bed and Breakfast Kissing

SHERBORN INN, Sherborn
33 North Main Street, (508) 655-9521
Moderate

Take the Massachusetts Turnpike (Interstate 90) to Exit 13 (Natick). The inn is located at the intersection of Routes 16 and 27, on the right side.

You will fall in love with the Sherborn Inn the first time you see it, and successive visits will confirm your initial impression. It's the perfect place to escape the hassles of the 20th century. Built in 1716, the white colonial sits amid old-fashioned gardens, sprawling lawns, and fieldstone fences.

Once the home of decorated Civil War hero Colonel Samuel Bullard (1733-1807), the inn is a lovely blend of Early American atmosphere and charm seasoned with modern appointments. Its four overnight rooms, all in the original house, are romantically decorated with four-poster canopied beds, yet include such modern amenities as hairdryer, clothes steamer, refrigerator, and television.

The quiet dining room (open to the public) pampers guests with local delicacies, including Maine crab cakes with Pommery mustard sauce and red pepper puree, American field greens salad, and roasted pheasant with cornbread and chestnut stuffing.

◆ **Romantic Note:** Sunday brunch—a lavish smorgasbord of made-to-order waffles and omelets, meats, fishes, fruits, and desserts—gives you a front-row seat when croquet tournaments are held on the front lawn. In a thoroughly enchanting tableau, couples dressed in white—women in flowing skirts and straw bonnets, men in white shirts and trousers—pursue their genteel but ruthless sport.

Pioneer Valley

Deerfield

Hotel/Bed and Breakfast Kissing

DEERFIELD INN, Deerfield　　　　　　　　　　◆◆◆
The Street, (413) 774-5587, (800) 926-3865
Moderate

Call for directions.

Old Deerfield has attracted generations of visitors to its beautifully preserved village, and this inn is its centerpiece. From the Colonial parlor, with its cheery fire, comfy furniture, and exquisite secretary desk, to the 23 welcoming guest rooms, this is the epitome of an old-fashioned inn, forgoing spectacular modern luxuries for sedate charm. Although all rooms cost the same, those with a view of the village are decidedly more romantic. Your bedchamber may hold a four-poster with faux tester, antique marquetry bedside tables, swagged valances, books and reading chairs, and artwork depicting village scenes. The fresh Colonial look is enhanced by reproductions and antiques, some acquired from museums, and rich fabrics custom-made to evoke the inn's heritage.

Candles and brass chandeliers lend a nostalgic radiance to the inn's dining room (open to the public), where high-backed and shield-back wooden chairs surround oak tables topped with fresh flowers. Some of the world's most discriminating travelers, as well as celebrities and royalty whose children attend Deerfield's eminent prep schools, have enjoyed meals here. Menus change monthly, but may feature appetizers such as smoked salmon ravioli with Alfredo sauce or local hickory-smoked trout, and select entrées including luscious veal sautéed with wild mushrooms, deglazed with white zinfandel, and finished with fresh tarragon, or beef with jumbo shrimp, fresh rosemary, and whole-grain mustard. In the morning, you're invited to choose anything on the inn's extensive menu, from delicious eggs Benedict to specialty waffles.

Outdoor Kissing

HISTORIC DEERFIELD, Deerfield
(413) 774-5581
Access to the village is free; entry to all of the period houses is $10 per person.

From Interstate 91 northbound, take Exit 24 and drive six miles north on Routes 5 and 10, which run along together. Turn left onto the village street (called The Street—you'll see a sign). Drive one-half mile to the Hall Tavern, across from the Deerfield Inn, for tickets, parking, and a picnic area.

Walk hand-in-hand through this centuries-old New England village and explore not only its history but the simple beauty of its 12 splendidly preserved buildings from the 18th and 19th centuries. This is truly one of the most beautiful towns in Massachusetts. Just a stroll around the village delights the eye, whether its tree-lined pathways gleam with the green leaves and lawns of summer or sparkle with winter snow. Inside the crisp Colonials, you can view period rooms and collections of hand-wrought pewter, textiles, ceramics, and other examples of decorative arts.

Sturbridge

Hotel/Bed and Breakfast Kissing

PUBLICK HOUSE HISTORIC RESORT, Sturbridge
On the Common, Route 131, (508) 347-3313, (800) PUBLICK
Inexpensive to Expensive (inn), Moderate (dining)

Call for directions.

Well known since revolutionary times for its good cheer and fine lodging, this resort approaches landmark status in Massachusetts. Popular and busy at any time of year, it caters to visitors to nearby Old Sturbridge Village, families, and business travelers. The inn seems a little weary of all this hospitality, but all guest rooms have been recently revamped in rich fabrics that enhance the traditional furnishings. Four-poster and canopy beds, hand-hooked rugs, porcelain table lamps, pedestal sinks, ticking wall clocks, prints of sailing ships, and botanical etchings contribute to the updated country look.

Of the sprawl of dining rooms, the low-slung Tap Room is most romantic, especially in winter, when a fire blazes in the immense, walk-in brick hearth. An atmosphere of easygoing finesse is imparted by the beamed ceiling, brass wall sconces, and wooden tables topped with candles, paper place mats, and linen napkins. In another dining room, The Barn, tables are set in the original stables and a grand brass weathervane of Gabriel soars below the high peaked ceiling. Traditional Yankee repasts of lobster pie, prime rib, broiled scrod, chicken with cranberry and walnut sauce, and pork chops with spiced apples highlight the menu. A turkey dinner comes complete with all the fixin's and a price that will please even cost-conscious Yankees.

◆ **Romantic Note:** In the Colonial tavern downstairs, you can make a toast to the past by the hearth or make a pledge to the future in the high-backed wing chairs.

◆ **Romantic Alternative:** The **COLONEL EBENEZER CRAFTS INN,** Fiske Hill Road, Sturbridge, (508) 347-3313, (Inexpensive to Moderate), also owned by the Publick House, is one mile but worlds away. This 1786 home is more a traditional bed and breakfast than bustling Colonial hotel. A low-key, homespun feel prevails in its eight guest rooms.

STURBRIDGE COUNTRY INN, Sturbridge
530 Main Street (Route 20), (508) 347-5503
Moderate to Expensive

Take the Massachusetts Turnpike to Exit 9 (Sturbridge). Go through toll booths onto Interstate 84, then take Exit 3B (Route 20 west), which is Main Street. Go two miles; the inn is on the right.

This 1840s homestead in the heart of now-bustling downtown Sturbridge has nine rooms, each with its own fireplace and whirlpool. As upscale as that may sound, the ambience is intimate rather than opulent. In the commodious corner rooms, you can nuzzle in an alcove sitting area. In the premier Loft Suite, with its Early American king-size bed and gracefully arched windows, the immense whirlpool is set beneath a skylight, near the corner hearth. Even standard rooms are nicely trimmed with Colonial-style furnishings and wall treatments, some four-poster beds, wing chairs, and gas hearths. In the morning, a continental breakfast is brought to your room or served in the airy post-and-beam parlor, where a player piano provides nostalgic entertainment.

Restaurant Kissing

THE WHISTLING SWAN, Sturbridge
502 Main Street (Route 20), (508) 347-2321
Expensive

Take the Massachusetts Turnpike to Exit 9 or Interstate 84 to Route 20 westbound (Main Street). Go about one mile; the restaurant is on the right.

This is Sturbridge's most intimate restaurant. White linens and high-backed chairs blend perfectly with the architectural details of this splendidly restored 1855 Greek Revival home, aglow with elegant etched glass wall sconces and flickering tabletop oil lamps. The kitchen prepares traditional favorites with a creative flair; we recommend beginning your meal with the crab- and scallop-stuffed mushrooms, escargots bourguignonne, or carpaccio con salsa, then moving on to coq au vin, scampi with clams, veal Oscar, or filet mignon béarnaise.

◆ **Romantic Alternative:** Upstairs, the **UGLY DUCKLING LOFT,** (508) 347-2321, (Moderate), has matured into a favorite eatery for locals and visitors alike. On most evenings, a pianist or guitarist sends cheerful melodies through the high-peaked former hay loft. The ambience and cuisine are casual, with internationally inspired dishes such as chili, quesadillas, calamari, Swedish meatballs, Jamaican jerk chicken, and lasagne.

Outdoor Kissing

OLD STURBRIDGE VILLAGE
1 Old Sturbridge Village Road, (508) 347-3362
$14 adults

From the Massachusetts Turnpike, take Exit 9 (Sturbridge) onto Interstate 84. Go through the toll booths, then take the first exit (3B) onto Route 20 westbound. Continue on Route 20 for one mile; the entrance is on the left.

The thump of an axe chopping wood still echoes through this beautifully preserved 1830s village comprising more than 30 vintage homes, mills, farmhouses, shops, and more. The aroma of apple pies baking still wafts on the breeze as costumed interpreters relive the era. And lovers can still steal a kiss beneath the covered bridge near the steepled church.

The Berkshires

South Egremont

Restaurant Kissing

JOHN ANDREWS RESTAURANT, South Egremont   ◆◆
Route 23, (413) 528-3469
Moderate to Expensive

Five and a half miles west of Great Barrington on Route 23.

Like the modern art highlighting the porch room's wall, this dinner house is a study in unfettered imagination—in both cuisine and decor. In warmer months, sliding glass doors surrounding the porch invite the outdoors in. Colder weather calls for a fire in the inner room's hearth, placed high enough in the wall so that all diners in this tiny room can enjoy it. Stenciled peach-colored walls, plus matching linens and candles, are all there is to distract you from the blaze. Appetizers and entrées are equally straightforward and fresh: start with lobster ravioli or venison sausage, then feast on grilled swordfish with lemon, oregano, anchovy, and olive oil; lamb with rosemary and straw potato pancakes; or a veal chop with braised fennel and onions.

◆   **Romantic Alternative:** Locals flock to **THE OLD MILL**, Main Street, South Egremont, (413) 528-1421, (Expensive), a rustic building atop a sprightly stream. The main dining room, though enhanced by a roaring fire, is a bit too large to be intimate, but the back room, open in the warmer, busier months, is a delightful spot for an early dinner, with its picture window overlooking the old mill stream. The food is some of the best in town. Choices include antipasto, pâté, black bean soup, grilled Cornish game hen, veal chop with rosemary sauce, and steak with grilled onions and sautéed red and yellow peppers.

Great Barrington

Hotel/Bed and Breakfast Kissing

THORNEWOOD INN, Great Barrington   ◆◆◆
453 Stockbridge Road, (413) 528-3828
Moderate to Expensive

At the junction of Routes 7 and 183.

Maintaining an inn is a little like maintaining a special relationship: you do your best to make a good situation even better. Such is the case at the Thornewood, where innkeepers devote a steady flow of tender loving care to the charming digs. Gas fireplaces now cast a soft glow in two guest rooms, enhancing the already romantic lacy canopy beds and soft springtime hues. Bedchambers in the newer wing are farther from traffic noise, and all are feminine without being too frilly. Before retiring, you may want to dance all night in the cozy dinner-dance restaurant. After sharing an onion tart, baked Brie, brandied pork, or raspberry duck, you may be lured by old-fashioned love songs to repeat—or practice—your wedding waltz. Your evening here, like a song you'll most likely hear, will be "Unforgettable."

WINDFLOWER, Great Barrington
684 South Egremont Road (Route 23)
(413) 528-2720, (800) 992-1993
Expensive to Very Expensive (MAP, dining)

Across from the Egremont Country Club, about three miles from Great Barrington center, on Route 23 West.

After walking in the winter wonderland of the Berkshires, you can cuddle by the fire at the Windflower. One blazes in the parlor, where home-baked pastries and tea welcome you in the afternoon, served on a marble-topped coffee table ringed by sofas and wing chairs. Six of the 13 guest rooms also are warmed by fireplaces. All the rooms have antique carved wood, brass, or canopy beds. For an unusual treat, you can take a whole-body shower in Room 7's antique bath. A stunning hand-hooked rug and lavender satin canopy highlight Room 4. In Room 12, you can watch the wood fire crackle in an immense fieldstone hearth, or, in summer, slip out the back door to a wide veranda overlooking the lawn, meandering stream, swimming pool fringed with perennials, and organic herb and vegetable gardens.

These gardens play an important role in the inn's dining room, which is well known for its exquisitely prepared cuisine and relaxed atmosphere. A choice of three entrées includes meat, seafood, and poultry; specialties include marinated lamb, salmon with sorrel sauce, and duck with purple plum sauce. Despite all these luxuries, the 1800s Federal-style inn is a casual, down-home kind of place where you'll feel comfortable wearing faded jeans while working on a jigsaw puzzle in the library.

◆ **Romantic Note:** If you're not staying at the inn but want to dine here, advance reservations are a must. When the inn's restaurant is not open, on certain nights in the off-season, bed-and-breakfast rates are $60 less per couple. Ask about winter ski packages, too.

Restaurant Kissing

THE PAINTED LADY, Great Barrington
785 South Main Street, (413) 528-1662
Moderate

Follow Route 7 south for three-quarters of a mile after Route 23 bears off for New York.

When you see this odd-shaped, colorfully painted Victorian home, you'll know you're in for a special treat, one that's courtly but not pretentious, sweet but not too precious. Former parlors and bedchambers have been converted to ladylike dining rooms, with gilt-framed impressionistic renderings of Victorian women, flower-and-bow wall coverings, swagged drapes, and smoky pink tulip glass lampshades over glowing candles on each table. The dishes here have an Italian accent, including the eggplant Parmesan, chicken primavera, and veal marsala. Daily specials change per "the mood of the chef," including the Painted Lady's luscious cheesecakes.

◆ **Romantic Alternative:** LA TOMATE, 293 Main Street, Great Barrington, (413) 528-3003, (Moderate), is an upbeat eatery with understated cosmopolitan flair. Red fan-motif wall coverings and candlelit tables add a festive touch to the two narrow, long dining rooms. Unpretentious French specialties include onion tart, garlic sausage with warm potato salad, bouillabaisse, chicken with morel sauce and cognac, steak with red wine vinegar and cream, and crème caramel and chocolate mousse for dessert.

Stockbridge

Hotel/Bed and Breakfast Kissing

THE INN AT STOCKBRIDGE, Stockbridge
Route 7, (413) 298-3337
Moderate to Very Expensive

From Main Street in Stockbridge, take Route 7 north for one and a quarter miles to the inn's driveway.

Coming to this classic country manor is akin to sinking into a cloud. Fluffy down cushions on the parlor's sofas are a sure remedy after a long day of touring the Berkshires by foot, auto, or skis. A roaring fire and complimentary wine and cheese make it all the more welcoming. In summer, splash in the pool. Stay in the delightful Terrace Room and you can sip champagne on your private back porch overlooking a wooded alcove and a fountain, then sink into your private whirlpool tub beneath a skylight framing the stars. More down-filled furnishings highlight the spacious Blagden Suite and the Rose Room. Other bedchambers feature Laura Ashley prints, Williamsburg highboys, rich chintzes, and king-size beds in six out of eight. In each, a cut glass decanter holds brandy to warm even the chilliest evenings. In the morning, a three-course breakfast is served around the long mahogany table in the formal dining room, a hearty farewell for when you leave this bit of heaven and journey through the garden of Eden known as the Berkshires.

RED LION INN, Stockbridge
Main Street, (413) 298-5545
Very Inexpensive to Unbelievably Expensive (EP), Expensive (dining)

Call for directions.

Imagine rising to your guest room in an elevator crafted of gold-toned filigree, more intricate than any Victorian birdcage. This original 1896 lift is just one of the many antiques at home in the Red Lion's aristocratic old lobby, made even more grand by the fireplace, red velvet settees, collection of china, and voluptuous bouquets of flowers. "Venerable" is the word that best describes this landmark hotel, where five presidents have been guests through the years. Begun as a coach stop in 1773, it's grown into a six-building estate housing more than 100 rooms. Guest rooms embrace their share of antiques, including some step-up or canopy beds, but the bricked-in hearths and televisions on stands are somewhat cold and the personal touch is a bit lacking. It's best to avoid the "bed-and-breakfast" rooms, where four to five rooms share one hall shower.

In the palatial dining rooms, crystal chandeliers, bouquets of fresh flowers, pewter plates, cane-seat chairs, and a deep red carpet keep alive an era of elegance. In keeping with the inn's New England heritage, traditional favorites on the menu include broiled scrod, grilled swordfish, and a turkey dinner complete with dressing, mashed potatoes, and homemade cranberry sauce. An amazing two dozen desserts include Indian pudding, pecan ball with butterscotch sauce, and good old apple pie with ice cream or cheddar cheese.

South Lee

Restaurant Kissing

FEDERAL HOUSE, South Lee
Main Street (Route 102), (413) 243-1824
Expensive

Approximately one and a half miles east of Stockbridge on Route 102.

Four classical columns rise two stories high to shoulder the weighty pediment of this Federal-style home. Built in 1824 by an industrialist who developed a paper mill and, for the most part, the town around it, the distinguished home is still the center of tiny South Lee. A first-class restaurant now delights patrons in the country-home dining room, appointed with a black marble hearth, ladder-back chairs, tall tapers, and bouquets of flowers blooming in silver bowls and pitchers on each table. Dining in the former front parlor and billiard room is equally inviting. As befits this stately setting, seasonal courses such as smoked salmon pâté, country terrine of rabbit with lingonberry sauce, rack of lamb with minted herb sauce, and boneless roast duckling with maple, pecan, and bourbon sauce will satisfy the most sophisticated palate.

◆ **Romantic Note:** Upstairs, the antique-filled guest rooms are enhanced by soft colors, feminine prints, and pumpkin pine floors and range from commodious to cozy in size. Be aware that the popular restaurant constitutes the first floor, leaving little space outside of the bedchambers for overnight guests to linger in.

Lee

Hotel/Bed and Breakfast Kissing

APPLEGATE BED AND BREAKFAST, Lee
279 West Park Street, (413) 243-4451
Moderate to Very Expensive

From Route 7 North, bear right onto Lee Road, which becomes West Park Street. The inn is two and a quarter miles farther up on the right, across from the golf course.

With its cast-iron gate, venerable apple trees, and pillared edifice, this noble Georgian hints of the old South, but inside you'll encounter pure Yankee hospitality. A large brick hearth warms the spacious parlor, furnished with ball-and-clawfoot settees, built-in bookshelves, and a baby grand. In the afternoon you'll be welcomed like a respected friend, with wine, cheese, and cheerful cordiality. In the summer, relax Southern-style on the screened-in porch or splash in the pool. Float up the curved staircase and you'll find six tastefully appointed guest rooms. The most indulgent one easily accommodates a sofa and Queen Anne chairs, a second sitting area with tufted wing chairs, a step-up four-poster canopy bed, a wood-burning hearth, and, in the bath, a steam shower that rivals any club's sauna in size. All rooms offer something special, whether it be lace billows over canopies, stylish Early American furnishings, or a sleigh bed. In each, a decanter of brandy and a petite box of chocolates ensure sweet beginnings.

◆ **Romantic Note:** The inn loans bicycles so guests can enjoy one of the Berkshires' favorite good-weather pastimes.

BLACK SWAN INN, Lee
Route 20, (413) 243-2700
Very Inexpensive to Very Expensive (inn, EP), Expensive (dining)

Take Exit 2 off the Massachusetts Turnpike (Route 20), turn right, and continue for a mile and a half down the road.

Nested snugly along the shore of tranquil Laurel Lake, this is a comfortable, modern hotel with bed-and-breakfast flair. The best rooms are in the new wing, where children are not allowed; many feature lakeshore decks. Special touches include four-poster and canopy beds. Gas fireplaces, ample televisions, and hydra-tubs are standard.

Like its namesake, the restaurant is graceful and looks right at home on the water's edge. Its glass walls and ceiling invite in sunlight, and moonbeams, to play across the rose-colored linens and dried flowers arranged on each table. The cuisine is European, the wine list a real globe-trotter, with selections from every major wine-producing region in the world.

CHAMBÉRY INN, Lee
Main Street (Route 20) and Elm Street
(413) 243-2221, (800) 537-4321
Inexpensive to Very Expensive

Take Exit 2 off the Massachusetts Turnpike. Stay to the right, which will bring you to Main Street. Look for a white picket fence on the left.

Listen up, students of love. This was the Berkshires' first parochial school, constructed in 1885. Today it's the area's most unusual inn, owned by a woman who graduated from here in 1953. Suites are stunningly spacious, dwarfing the canopy or four-poster queen-size beds beneath 13-foot-high, pressed tin ceilings. Climb the separate girls' and boys' stairs to upstairs rooms that are equally spacious and serene. Each suite has a sitting area by a gas hearth, single whirlpool tub, television, phone, and, best of all, blackboards lining one wall where guests can draw hearts and scribble inspirational thoughts. If you mind your p's and q's, a basket of pastries and tea will be brought to your door in the morning.

◆ **Romantic Note:** Less expensive guest rooms are located, along with a modern art gallery, in the basement level, but these are as tiny as the suites are spacious and not nearly as special.

Lenox

Nestled like a priceless jewel in the green velvet hills of the Berkshires, Lenox is the epitome of culture in the countryside. **TANGLEWOOD,** the summer home of the Boston Symphony Orchestra, is the most sublime attraction; call (413) 637-1940 in summer or (617) 266-1492 year-round for program information. Here you can spread your blanket on the lawn and feast on a picnic while classical melodies fill the fresh mountain air and float down the ridge to the sparkling blue Stockbridge Bowl far below. Even if a concert isn't being held the day you visit, a picnic here is still a wonderful way to spend an afternoon.

Yesterday's and today's millionaires have built their castles in the hills surrounding the village. Galleries, inns, and restaurants cater to them with surprisingly sophisticated offerings. Prices can be high, reflecting the influence of New Yorkers who frequent the area, but one of Lenox's best attributes is the stunning scenery. In **KENNEDY PARK,** a short walk out of the village, you can stroll hand-in-hand through woodland to panoramic views, especially delightful during foliage season. In winter, the park offers superb, though sometimes demanding, cross-country skiing.

A short drive from town, the **PLEASANT VALLEY WILDLIFE SANC-TUARY,** where birds and deer—and lovers—find refuge, is ideal for longer hikes.

Hotel/Bed and Breakfast Kissing

APPLE TREE INN, Lenox
224 West Street, (413) 637-1477
Moderate to Unbelievably Expensive (inn), Expensive (dining)
(Open May through January 1)

At the monument in the center of Lenox, take Route 183 South for one and half miles. When the road forks, take the right fork; the inn is the first driveway on the right.

When you see this imposing white mansion cresting the hill above Tanglewood, you might expect a more upper-crust crowd inside, the kind that intimidates others for a living. Happily, this splendid inn is much more easygoing than elitist. True, performers find a home away from home here, as evidenced by autographed photographs of Isaac Stern, Midori, Yo-Yo Ma, and the like. But the parlor's grand arched colonnade, brick hearth, and velvet wing chairs stand in syncopâtéd contrast to wacky artworks such as a lady falling into the innards of a grand piano or a shadowbox depicting a scene from *Charlotte's Web.* Raggedy Ann dolls line the curved staircase leading to the guest rooms, which range from well-worn cozy to stunning suites. Rooms in the front of the house have mesmerizing views of the blue Stockbridge Bowl and rolling green Berkshires. Several have wood-burning fireplaces. All have antique furnishings and intriguing mementos, such as the decorated egg collection on the wall of marvelous Suite 8 and the petite eau de cologne bottles hemming the hearth in Room 3.

For concertgoers, dining here before the show is a Tanglewood tradition. The main restaurant is akin to a music tent, with lights trailing up to the pink domed ceiling and windows overlooking one of the best restaurant views in the Berkshires. Char-grilled steak, wiener schnitzel, and blackened fresh fish are some of the entrées that may be offered. In winter, the cozy, casual Tavern opens for dining, warmed by a huge brick hearth. In summer, you can splash in the outdoor pool that shares the inn's premier panorama, stop and smell the more than 450 varieties of roses, or simply sit under the namesake apple tree, with nobody else but you know who.

◆   **Romantic Note:** For pre-Tanglewood dinners, reserve well in advance. After the show, a stroll up the inn's steep drive for dessert and coffee will save you from post-concert traffic.

BLANTYRE, Lenox   ◆◆◆◆
Route 20 and East Street
(413) 637-3556 May through November
(413) 298-3806 December through April
Very Expensive to Unbelievably Expensive

On Route 20, at the corner of East Street, just south of the Route 7 junction.

Envision a magnificent Scottish Tudor-style mansion, crowning 85 rolling acres of prime Berkshire property. Now imagine swirling up the grand staircase to a room fit for royalty, flawlessly decorated in regally restored antiques, with elaborate window and wall treatments, ceramic tile hearths, gilt-framed oils, Oriental carpets, and fresh flowers. A tray of fruit, cheese, and crackers and a bottle of Evian welcome you, as you peer out over terraced lawns where hot-air balloons and helicopters have been known to land. Special occasions are Blantyre's raison d'être. A Sunday-morning carriage ride, lunch for two aboard a private boat on Laurel Lake, croquet on two tournament courts (appropriate white outfits only, please), or an enviable picnic basket for Tanglewood can all be arranged—for a price, of course. But even the smaller, less extravagant bedchambers are pleasantly decorated in Laura Ashley prints, with the occasional canopy bed and crystal chandeliers.

As you may have envisioned, your castle harbors a show-stopper parlor, with a fire glowing in the hearth. As befits its proximity to Tanglewood, the music room is so spacious and regal that Beethoven would feel at home performing for kings and queens on the ornately carved grand piano. The marble hearths at both ends, crystal and gilt chandeliers, tapestried sofa and chairs, museum-quality antique desks, doors opening to the covered patio, and gilt harp before the window are just a part of its splendor. In the baronial dining room, with its dark wood paneling, green tile hearth, and tapestry along one wall, prix fixe dinners are served on antique china, accompanied by vintage crystal, tapers in sterling holders, and fresh floral bouquets. Smoked salmon and trout soufflé or potato, fontina, and white truffle ravioli with caramelized onions and balsamic vinegar are just starters. Seasonal entrées may include grilled squab with native blueberries, chicken on barley risotto with sage and prosciutto vinaigrette, or rack of lamb with herbes-de-Provence. The bill might imply that you've flown to Scotland yourselves, and the castle verifies it.

BROOK FARM INN, Lenox
15 Hawthorne Street, (413) 637-3013
Moderate to Expensive

From the statue at Lenox town center (south end of Main Street), turn onto Stockbridge Road. Take the first right onto Hawthorne Street. The inn is on the left.

Like the poetry readings held here on most Saturday afternoons, this inn's parlor is at once grand and homespun. A hearth and high ceilings hint at high-toned beginnings, but shelves chock-a-block full of books and the jigsaw puzzle in progress on the table speak of simpler pursuits. More fireplaces warm the downstairs and some second-floor guest rooms. In one room, an antique mirror above the hearth reflects a canopy bed with eyelet ruffle, stenciled hope chest, and comfy floral wing chair. Another has a carved wooden bed and white wicker sitting area. Third-floor rooms can be tiny, with even tinier baths. If you like earthy Victorian decor, with little frou-frou, this is for you.

CRANWELL RESORT AND GOLF CLUB, Lenox
55 Lee Road, (800) 272-6935
Expensive to Unbelievably Expensive

On Route 20, near its junction with Route 7, south of Lenox center.

This century-old castle on the hill is one of Lenox's magnificent remnants of a well-heeled past. Recent renovations have given the structure additional elegance; most notable is the Venetian marble that transformed the lobby and bar into a sultry sea of deep green and guest-room baths into shimmering spectacles. Indeed, the setting, mesmerizing views, and spacious and serenely uncluttered bedchambers rank high for romance, but unfortunately are also ideal for decidedly unromantic conferences, what with state-of-the-art meeting rooms, a golf course, and tennis courts.

The delightful restaurant is done up in quiet colors and enhanced by windows on three sides that overlook the Berkshires. Seated below an intricately carved ceiling, diners can savor wild mushroom terrine, lobster and truffle ravioli, grilled swordfish, veal chops and salmon, summer bouillabaisse, and sautéed tuna. Come before sunset, request a table by the window, and sigh.

GARDEN GABLES, Lenox
141 Main Street, (413) 637-0193
Inexpensive to Expensive

Call for directions.

Recent refurbishments have spruced up this long-established inn a short walk from Lenox center. In the parlor, family-style furnishings are grouped around the copper-sheathed hearth and a 1924 Steinway. A fireplace also welcomes guests into the second parlor, with velvet love seats that are ideal for a long evening of snuggling by the fire. Floral and paisley wall coverings lend a decorative touch to the guest rooms. Upstairs, two large rooms each house a pair of queen-size canopy beds, corner brick hearth, private balcony, and whirlpool tub. Downstairs rooms can be extremely cozy, but are pleasantly decorated in true country-inn style. In summer, a 72-foot 1909 swimming pool rejuvenates wilted spirits.

GATEWAYS INN, Lenox
71 Walker Street, (413) 637-2532
Moderate to Unbelievably Expensive (inn, EP), Very Expensive (dining)

From the monument at Lenox town center, bear left and go approximately 1,000 yards. The inn is on the left.

Arthur Fiedler, venerable conductor of the Boston Pops Orchestra, slept here during his last four seasons at Tanglewood. Today, the inn is a symphony of refined elegance. Fiedler's Suite, the most expensive in this small hotel, is befitting any dignitary. Sofas gather about the hearth in the sitting room. A second fireplace warms the bedroom, with its Oriental rug and fishnet canopy bed. The dressing room is perfect for preparing for the concert, even if you're in the audience rather than on the podium. Fireplaces and ornate beds warm several other guest rooms. Standard rooms are also welcoming, but not as special. Overall, the notes of sophisticated decor are played precisely, though one might like to hear an impassioned trill once in a while.

The restaurant is as seductive as a sonata. Award-winning cuisine is presented in surroundings that echo perfectly the softened sophistication of Tanglewood. Gas fireplaces, gold wall coverings, brass chandeliers, art prints, tabletop candle lamps, classical music, starched and fanned napkins, and gold-trimmed china harmonize beautifully. Dishes may include rack of lamb, filet mignon, salmon topped with shrimp and lobster, or chicken with crawfish and truffles in a light honey-liqueur sauce. On certain nights, a limited prix fixe menu served before 7:00 p.m. is one of Lenox's best bargains; call for dates and times.

ROOKWOOD, Lenox
19 Stockbridge Road, (413) 637-9750, (800) 223-9750
Inexpensive to Very Expensive

From the statue at Lenox town center (the south end of Main Street), turn left onto Stockbridge Road. The inn is the first building on the left.

Built in 1885, this Victorian wooden castle has a turret that soars upward from one corner. Here, in an octagonal alcove in the sky, you can cuddle on the day bed and peek through the whimsical triplets of oval and multipaned windows. Steps lead down to the cozy bedchamber, with a four-poster tucked under the sloped ceiling. Each room at Rookwood has something special to offer: a private balcony in the treetops, a brass bed, an old-fashioned clawfoot tub. Seven out of 19 are warmed by fireplaces—two are tiny ones original to the home. Muted tones and dainty florals provide serenity throughout. Afternoon tea and a buffet continental breakfast are served downstairs. A day at Tanglewood may inspire you to tickle the ivories on the grand in the parlor, and relive the sort of popular evening entertainment enjoyed during this vintage Victorian's early years.

UNDERLEDGE, Lenox
76 Cliffwood Street, (413) 637-0236
Moderate to Expensive

From Lenox center, heading north on Main Street (Route 7A), bear left onto Cliffwood Street, opposite the Mobil station. The inn is the 14th house on the right.

On this street, once known as Millionaires' Row, majestic mansions stand as reminders of an era of unparalleled wealth. Then you reach Underledge, where you, too, can sleep like a millionaire. It may not be the most magnificent home on the block, but it is the most inviting: a white manor crowning a grassy knoll.

Despite baronial guest rooms, fireplaces galore, and stylish country-manor furnishings, the ambience speaks more of welcome than wealth. One spacious guest room is entered through heavy double doors off the entryway. Cheerful florals, a king-size brass bed, brick hearth, and private back entrance highlight Room 2. Second-floor rooms are equally regal; one has a private deck carved out of the tower overlooking the lawn and leafy trees. Our favorite was the Lavender Room, with its soft florals and antique china displayed above the hearth. Even the smaller third-floor rooms hold something special, such as stenciled walls, pressed flower designs in the lampshades, or candles for that romantic glow.

In the parlor, classical music sets the tone for antique furnishings, fringed lampshades, art prints, and a baby grand. In the warmer months, muffins and fruit are served in the glass-rimmed solarium, where you can survey the grounds of your estate before starting your day amongst the Berkshires' natural riches.

WHEATLEIGH, Lenox   ◆◆◆◀
Hawthorne Road, (413) 637-0610
Moderate to Unbelievably Expensive (inn)
Expensive to Very Expensive (dining)

Call for directions.

Built in 1893 in the style of a 16th-century Florentine palazzo, this magnificent, secluded mansion is destined for major redecoration, the details of which are being kept coquettishly hush-hush, no matter the extent of my frustrated queries. I will tell you that the foundation from which they are working is befitting royalty. Of course, so are the prices. Most bedchambers are enormous, but some are absolutely tiny, and one is squeezed into the upper half of an old elevator shaft.

In the dining room, the food is impeccable, a grand indulgence for even the most sophisticated clientele. Seasonal entrées focus on fresh, top-notch ingredients, including produce grown locally, exclusively for Wheatleigh. Caviar with crème fraîche and warm buckwheat blinis, or grilled rabbit with autumn root vegetable salad, may whet your appetite for grilled bass with a pinot noir-truffle sauce and scallop mousse flan, or roasted Texas antelope with fresh huckleberries. Brunch is also in the expensive range.

Restaurant Kissing

CANDLELIGHT INN, Lenox
53 Walker Street, (413) 637-1555
Very Inexpensive to Expensive (dining, inn)

One block from the monument on Walker Street (Route 83), across from Talbot's.

With candles flickering in pewter candlesticks, fires blazing in the hearths, and lacy curtains tied back with rosettes, this inn might make you feel like a casual Colonial out to celebrate the harvest. Four dining rooms have been carved out of this vintage home. Although fine china and linens grace the tables, the overall ambience is down-home friendly. Hearty seasonal fare may include crab cakes with black beans in curried scallion sauce, sautéed pork with apple-mint chutney, or fisherman's stew.

◆ **Romantic Note:** Upstairs, guest rooms also speak of earlier times, with a quaint, but unfortunately somewhat timeworn, feel of a small Colonial hotel. Although there are few knickknacks to impose a distinctive personality, the antique beds, white woven spreads, and an occasional wing chair add a charm of their own.

CHURCH STREET CAFÉ, Lenox
69 Church Street, (413) 637-2745
Inexpensive (lunch only)

Church Street parallels Main Street, one block to the east. The café is between Housatonic and Franklin.

With cuisine as creative and tasteful as the modern art displayed on its walls, this American bistro is a cozy spot for a refreshing lunch. Sandy mocha walls are the perfect backdrop for the intriguing watercolor, mixed-media, and sculpted works by local artists displayed gallery-style in the three petite rooms. Light wood chairs and tables and cheerful service lend an easy, contemporary atmosphere. Lunches feature seasonal specials such as a blackened chicken sandwich, white bean chili, Louisiana gumbo, or our favorite, a crêpe filled with corn, chiles, and jack cheese topped with spicy salsa. Everything is fresh and delicious.

◆ **Romantic Note:** This place might be too casual for a romantic dinner.

LENOX 218 RESTAURANT, Lenox
218 Main Street, (413) 637-4218
Moderate

On the north side of town, on Main Street (Route 7A), beyond the main business district.

As fresh as mountain air to a city slicker, this fashionable new restaurant is a daring, enticing departure from tried-and-true Colonial modes. The contemporary decor is a surprise, from the soaring cathedral ceiling to the soft gray and pink art deco-inspired wall coverings to the modern china placed on gray linens with black napkins. The cuisine, too, sets this restaurant apart from others in town. A flawless wait staff in white shirts and black bow ties serves appetizers such as Sicilian eggplant caponata, country pâté with cognac, and fresh homemade mozzarella cheese with red roasted peppers. Generous pasta dishes include rigatoni with Italian sweet sausage and a light tomato and basil sauce. Entrées include chicken with sun-dried tomatoes, prosciutto, and cheese; scrod with pesto on spinach greens and cheese; and veal piccata.

After dinner, you may just want to linger awhile in the bar, with its blazing fire in the winter and complimentary pub cheese and corn chips. Maybe it's because the owners are trying something new, or because the restaurant is removed from the busy village center, but they just seem to try harder here, and it shows.

Outdoor Kissing

MAIN STREET SPORTS & LEISURE, Lenox
102 Main Street, (413) 637-4407, (800) 952-9197
From the monument in Lenox town center, head north on Main Street for one and a half blocks; the shop is on the east side of the street, adjacent to the Mobil station.

This sporting goods shop is your ticket to romance in the great outdoors of the Berkshires. Whether summer casts a shimmering haze on the verdant hills or winter sifts snow over the forest, the staff can direct you to the best outdoor kissing spots, give you a trail map if needed, rent you the proper equipment, and even shuttle you to the starting point of your foray. Imagine canoeing down the pristine Housatonic River for two hours of no roads, no cars, no houses, and plenty of wildlife. In fall, admire the golden leaves on trail and tree. In winter, strap on a pair of cross-country skis to discover a snowy paradise. In the Berkshires, you're reminded that joy comes from simple things: the caress of a summer breeze, the crunch of leaves beneath your feet, the smell of snow in the air, the wonder of sharing it all together.

THE MOUNT, Lenox
Plunkett Street, (413) 637-3353 (box office)
Open late May through October

At the junction of Routes 7 and 7A.

As characters are forever intertwined in the enduring novels of Edith Wharton, so are ethereal literature and nature joined at the Mount, her summer residence. Now under restoration, the estate beckons lovers of beauty and culture to tour the mansion and gardens or attend a matinee performance of a play based on this Pulitzer Prize-winner's life, her works, or those of her friend Henry James. Along with a top designer, an architect, and her niece, who designed the idyllic Dumbarton Oaks in Washington, D.C., Wharton created gardens at once formal and welcoming, a celebration of color in spring, like a pastoral impressionistic painting on a hazy summer afternoon. The mansion, reminiscent of an Italian villa, can transport daydreamers to old Europe, and to an era when love, too, was a thing of refined beauty.

Hancock

Hotel/Bed and Breakfast Kissing

JIMINY PEAK, Hancock
Corey Road, (413) 738-5500, (800) 882-8859
Expensive to Very Expensive

From Route 7 North, turn left at the sign for Jiminy Peak onto Brodie Mountain Road. Drive three miles to Jiminy. (The ski resort is between Routes 7 and 43, north of Pittsfield.)

If you've come to the Berkshires for the Berkshires themselves, this compact mountain village is a great place to kick up your heels. (Don't try it on the slopes, though!) Nestled in the palm of a ski resort, you can hike through wildflowers in spring, splash in the pool in summer, admire the changing foliage in autumn, or ski from your door in winter. Thaw by the fires blazing in the mountainous stone hearths on the first floor or in the more private second-floor ski lodge parlors where cocoa and cookies are served. A third option is to duck into Drummonds copper-topped bar, and sip a potent hot drink by the hearth there. This casual but classy restaurant has Colonial-style chandeliers hanging from a peaked ceiling, and is designed so that many tables are placed by windows.

Guest rooms in the main lodge are the easiest to access when snow drifts outside. Each has a sitting room with television, a small modern kitchen, and bedroom. Plaid sofas, brass beds, knotty pine coffee tables, and country-inspired prints add unpretentious flair to these more modern hotel-style rooms. Condominiums are more secluded. The newer, "deluxe" models with two bedrooms and two baths are the most appealing, with contemporary design, cathedral ceilings, and a fireplace in the living room, but don't be seduced into staying inside all day. The Berkshires await.

◆ **Romantic Note:** Be sure to ask about the stay-and-ski packages, which offer savings off the regular rate. Children will be well entertained with supervised all-day ski programs and weekend-night videos while you entertain each other. Die-hard skiers will find the superb snow-making, long season, and extensive night skiing noteworthy kissing features.

> *"A kiss is something you cannot give without taking and cannot take without giving."*
>
> Anonymous

VERMONT

Southern Vermont

Bennington

Hotel/Bed and Breakfast Kissing

SOUTH SHIRE INN, Bennington
124 Elm Street, (802) 447-3839
Moderate to Expensive

From Route 7 North, which runs through the center of Bennington, turn left onto Elm Street. The inn is on the left, one block up, at the corner of Elm and Jefferson.

This grand Victorian entices you with hearths in seven of its nine rooms. In the main house, spacious rooms, intricately carved wooden beds, and serene colors reign. In the Gold Room, a cloud of white fabric floats above a carved four-poster. A ceramic tile hearth, marble-topped bureau, and plush window treatments add elegance to the Wentworth Room. If firelight doesn't warm your love in the Carriage House rooms, perhaps the whirlpools will, or the Victorian-style four-posters. What the common rooms lack in intimacy, they make up for in spaciousness. In the library, books beckon behind leaded glass doors, while the rich paneling makes one expect a pipe and slippers to be awaiting nearby. The breakfast room looks like a fine restaurant, with its crystal chandelier, intricate plasterwork, and peach-colored swags. A full country breakfast will revive you after last night's rendezvous.

Restaurant Kissing

BENNINGTON STATION, Bennington
150 Depot Street, (802) 447-1080
Moderate

From Route 9 West, turn right at the first light onto Depot Street. The depot is on the left-hand side, at the corner of River and Depot streets.

When this depot was constructed in 1897, trains promised romance and adventure for the traveler, rather than newspapers and naps for the commuter. Today, as you walk up the ramp crossing the tracks past a now-still boxcar, you'll discover a happy revival of that era. The lovingly restored exterior is crafted of locally quarried blue marble. The interior's rubbed wood paneling showcases historic photos of the depot's heyday. Old-fashioned cast-iron street lamps and art deco-inspired table lamps cast a sentimental glow for this journey. Casual service and such Yankee fare as prime rib, pot pie, and roast turkey seem right on track in this friendly establishment. All aboard!

THE FOUR CHIMNEYS
RESTAURANT AND INN, Old Bennington
21 West Road (Route 9), (802) 447-3500
Expensive (dining), Moderate (inn)

On Vermont Route 9 (same as New York Route 7) in the center of town, near the Bennington monument.

The sign seems superfluous at this stately mansion set back from the road. You can't miss the distinctive four chimneys that rise from its imposing white facade. Prestige and refinement top the menu in the well-respected restaurant, with its crystal chandelier, pink linens over floral cloths, oil lamps, cane-back chairs, and plush swags trimming bay windows. You may want to begin your evening with a cocktail on the sofa by the lounge's fireplace. With four chimneys, it's no surprise that hearths warm the dining rooms, too. The European-inspired cuisine includes an unusual mustard soup, stuffed quail or salmon, and scallop terrine as appetizers. Entrées such as beef Wellington for two, Cornish hen, and sweetbreads and ox tongue are creatively prepared.

◆ **Romantic Note:** In the guest rooms, soft colors and spaciousness soothe the spirit, but the look is somewhat sparse.

Arlington

Hotel/Bed and Breakfast Kissing

ARLINGTON INN, Arlington
Historic Route 7A, (802) 375-6532, (800) 443-9442
Inexpensive to Expensive (inn), Expensive (dining)

At the junction of Route 7A and Route 313.

Whether 'tis better to dine by the wood stove in the solarium or by the hearth in the formal dining room—that is the first difficult choice at this landmark 1848 Greek Revival mansion. In the lingering twilight of the warmer months, let your love bloom in the greenhouse room, with its bright floral cloths and glass enclosure overlooking beds of bright impatiens. In winter, ask for one of the five tables in the formal fireplace room, with its antique Oriental blue-and-white china, hand-blown glasses, candlelight, and fresh or dried flowers. Starters such as the house-cured gravlax, lemon linguine, and marinated artichokes, tomatoes, and pine nuts with a roasted garlic-basil-goat cheese dressing are all excellent. Entrées may include salmon with papaya-lime sauce, veal with peach-apple chutney, or game hen with dried cherry salsa. Difficult choices abound.

While the mansion is imposing and the cuisine is gourmet, guest rooms display a country ambience, decorated in antiques, with color schemes that range from cheerful blues and yellows in Pamela's Suite to dark browns in Martin Chester's Room. Some rooms in the main house are quite cozy in size. Suites in the Carriage House are secluded and spacious, with an Early American flair. In each, Lake Champlain chocolates ensure sweet dreams.

INN AT COVERED BRIDGE GREEN, West Arlington   ✪✪✪
River Road at Covered Bridge Road, (802) 375-9489, (800) 726-9480
Moderate to Expensive

From Historic Route 7A North, turn left onto Route 313, opposite the Arlington Inn. After four and a half miles, turn left and cross the covered bridge to the inn.

Norman Rockwell was inspired by a land of salt-of-the-earth Americans and scenery that would convince any interloper that this is indeed the best nation in the world. Where better to experience Rockwell's Vermont than in the home where the artist himself chose to live and work? The scene is picture-perfect. You drive through a red covered bridge spanning an icy brook, past a white steepled church, up to a 200-year-old Colonial that seems to smile with the glow of candles sparkling in each window. In the daylight, you'll see that the inn is hemmed by an apple orchard on one side and a horse farm on the other. The setting is so quintessentially Vermont that people pull off the rural route just to drink it in (even if they've never heard of Norman Rockwell).

Inside, you'll find charming, antique-filled guest rooms brushed with just the right touch of down-home country charm. Rest your heads upon the floral toss pillows on a four-poster bed. Admire the hand-hooked accent rug in front of the raised corner hearth. Sip water from crystal glasses set on marble-topped bureaus. Two studios are also available to overnight guests. The Colonial-era Corn Crib is cozy and cute, with tree-trunk beams and a wood stove. Rockwell's bright, airy studio now houses a fireplace living room, two bedrooms, and a small kitchen.

Breakfast, served near the hearth in the dining room, is a country extrava-
gance, with home-pressed cider, fresh fruit, and, perhaps, baked apples,
followed by walnut French toast. It's enough to coax sighs of joy and comfort
out of a Rockwell painting.

WEST MOUNTAIN INN, Arlington
River Road (Route 313)
(802) 375-6516
Expensive (inn, MAP), Expensive (dining)

One-half mile west of Arlington on Route 313.

This inn hosts a dinner party unlike any other we've attended, orchestrated
with finesse and discretion. A fire blazed in the parlor; trays of scallops wrapped
in bacon, cheese, and crackers, and crudités were cleverly placed to encourage
mingling. Some guests gathered at the bar for wine and cocktails, but no money
exchanged hands. After all, this was a private gathering. We settled on the sofa
in the parlor and struck up a conversation with another couple of romantics,
so engaging we decided to enjoy our meal together. Of course, tables for two
were offered as well. Firelight made the wood paneling glow and locally crafted
stoneware "face plates" added an ambience both elegant and country. The
pumpkin puree was superb, and the filet mignon with mushrooms, roasted
garlic, and rosemary deserved a standing ovation. The chocolate oblivion torte
was worth a second bow. Afterwards, guests didn't slink off to their rooms, but
lingered in the delightful common areas, playing backgammon in the game
room or admiring the collection of African violets.

A frilly African violet also adorns each guest room. Each bedchamber is
uniquely shaped and amply sized, serenely decorated in soft tones, and filled
with antiques or finely crafted wood furnishings that will be future generations'
honored antiques. A lacy canopy billows over the headboard in the Robert
Todd Lincoln Room. You can snuggle beneath the Wedding Ring quilt by the
gas fireplace in Sarah's Room, then sneak out the back door to follow the
hiking trails radiating from the inn. Some rooms have screened-in porches
overlooking the inn's family of llamas grazing in the hillside meadow. At the
end of your stay here, you're invited to take the African violet from your room
home with you, a sweet reminder of your stay.

Manchester Village

Hotel/Bed and Breakfast Kissing

1811 HOUSE, Manchester Village
Historic Route 7A, (802) 362-1811, (800) 432-1811
Moderate to Expensive

In the center of Manchester Village, immediately north of the church and across from the Equinox Hotel.

Authentic down to vintage 1770s windowpanes, wall coverings reproduced from Federal-period designs, painted woodwork, and period art, 1811 House has operated as an inn since 1811. You can easily imagine yourselves as guests of that time, smoothing out your skirt on the camelback settee by the hearth in the sitting room or pouring your love a sherry in the firelit parlor. Of the 14 cozy guest rooms, six are warmed with wood-burning fireplaces. In many, you'll find fishnet canopy beds, velvet tufted reading chairs, old-fashioned baths, and Oriental rugs on hardwood floors. For more contemporary pursuits, the basement recreation room houses pool and Ping-Pong tables, television, and VCR.

In the early evening, the petite Colonial pub is a local gathering place, where townsfolk come to imbibe some 26 varieties of single malt scotch or other potent potables. It's a warm place to toast the history you'll make together.

THE EQUINOX, Manchester Village
Historic Route 7A, (802) 362-4700, (800) 362-4747
Expensive to Unbelievably Expensive

Call for directions.

When you first see the Equinox, you may wonder how the ground beneath it can support such a mammoth structure. To say it is gargantuan would be an understatement. A three-page map is required just for the interior layout. Perhaps they should give you a compass, too. Some 136 guest rooms have been completely renovated as of June 1992, to the tune of $9 million. Much of this went into the lavish suites, which were inspired by the sort of stately decor preferred by presidents. With a stellar history dating back to 1769, the Equinox has hosted many of our heads of state. You can easily envision Abraham Lincoln penning a letter or speech on the leather-topped, gilt-edged desk in his namesake suite. Standard and Premium rooms are less special, decorated in neutral tones and light wood furnishings.

In keeping with the grand old hotel, the Colonnade restaurant is a monumental chamber. Six ample columns shoulder a gracefully bowed, hand-painted ceiling. An immense crystal chandelier shimmers above white linen tables and fringed floral swags crown soaring windows. This would be a fitting spot for a more personal inaugural dinner of your own.

INN AT MANCHESTER, Manchester Village
Historic Route 7A, (802) 362-1793
Very Inexpensive to Expensive

Call for directions.

In this village of marble sidewalks and grand 19th-century mansions, this is one inn that has stayed true to its heritage. Originally built in 1880 as a summer home, the inn is more casual and homespun than elegant and posh. A fire warms the parlor, where afternoon tea is served. Breakfast is enjoyed around family-size tables in the simply decorated dining room. In the colder months, you can snuggle by the fire in one of the suites. When the snow falls outside, spring blooms inside in Laura Ashley-inspired floral fabrics. When reserving, ask for one of the renovated guest rooms, and keep in mind that six of the 20 rooms have shared baths.

THE RELUCTANT PANTHER, Manchester Village
West Road, (802) 362-2568, (800) 822-2331
Expensive to Unbelievably Expensive (inn, MAP), Moderate to Expensive (dining)

Just past the Equinox Hotel as you enter the village on Route 7A, bear left onto West Road (at the library). The inn is immediately on the left, a purple building with yellow shutters.

Reluctant? Not for long at this plush inn and restaurant. Firelight glows in 10 of the 16 guest rooms, all decorated in plush fabrics and top-quality furnishings. The exclusive Mark Skinner Suite is the pièce de résistance. You can snuggle beneath the covers before the marble hearth in the bedroom or splash in the immense whirlpool tub by a second fireplace in the spectacular bathroom. Rooms in the main house are equally sleek, with tufted reading chairs, goosedown comforters, soft floral spreads, and a corner hearth or brass chandelier. An ample marble hearth, high-backed chairs, and botanical prints await you in the main dining room, but I preferred the patio room, with its fireplace, green stone floor, windows all around highlighted with potted flowering plants, and photos of spring gardens. Breakfast is served here, too.

Seasonal dinner menus in the restaurant may include terrine of pheasant with wild rice salad; smoked scallop chowder; pepper-crusted Atlantic salmon with black beans, tomatoes, and basil; or pumpkin-filled sage ravioli with smoked chicken and Vermont cheddar. It's an evening that will make you purr with delight.

THE VILLAGE COUNTRY INN, Manchester Village
Historic Route 7A, (802) 362-1792, (800) 370-0300
Expensive to Very Expensive (MAP)

Call for directions.

From a chilling October afternoon, we tumbled into this wonderland, past the French Rabbit gift shop, to the urn of hot cider set before the fire crackling in the fieldstone hearth. Ruffled pillows, Victorian fringed lamps, and flickering candles provided a genteel ambience. Our bedchamber was sheer perfection, with its canopy bed blooming in irresistibly rich florals, antiques and treasured mementos, a spacious bath with a clawfoot tub on a raised platform, and a fainting couch just to let you catch your breath. On slower evenings, doors to unoccupied guest rooms are left open and guests are welcome to choose one that suits their fancy—not an easy decision. Each is an Eden of chintzes and unusual bed treatments. Dream in an antique carved wooden or brass bed beneath a billowing swath of lace or a crown of ruffles or a canopy tied back with ribbons and silk flowers. Some rooms overlook the inn's fabulous spring gardens. The plush decor more than makes up for the lack of in-room hearths and the petite bathrooms. But the evening is just beginning.

A candlelit dinner is served in the firelit rose room, where tables are tucked into cozy niches formed by white garden trellises intertwined with ivy. This is a leisurely, multicourse affair, beginning, perhaps, with grilled duck breast with maple honey mustard or salmon cakes with Back Bay sauce. Entrées may include sensuous pecan-crusted duck breast with cranberries and maple syrup, New York strip sirloin with cabernet sauvignon sauce, or roast pork with Benedictine and oranges. A decadent dessert will provide the proper ending or, should I say, beginning, to your enchanted evening. An innkeeper surprise awaits you in your room. Although I'm sworn to secrecy, I will say that fun and fantasy are sometimes just what you need to set your love abloom.

◆ **Romantic Note:** Not a whisper about this inn's unique "Affairs of the Heart" packages. When you make a reservation, you're given just enough hints to whet your imagination, but details remain secret so you can be surprised together.

WILBURTON INN, Manchester Village
River Road, (802) 362-2500, (800) 648-4944
Moderate to Expensive

From Route 7A North, just around the bend from the winter entrance to Hildene, take a sharp right onto River Road. Follow the curving road about three-quarters of a mile until you see the entrance for Wilburton Inn on the left.

A long, curving drive bordered by an old New England stone wall brings you to this Tudor mansion and its commanding view of the voluptuous Green Mountains. The architecture is stately, the ambience and decor somewhat sparse but for the innkeeper's collection of contemporary sculpture placed around the grounds and in the common room. The formal dining room, open nightly during busy times and weekends in winter, is akin to a gentleman's club, with its huge hearth of green and brown tile, rugged Frederic Remington bronze horse on the mantel, and dark cherry paneling. Continental specialties include venison pâté, sautéed seafood cakes, and Vermont pheasant. Much sunnier, with a splendid view, is the breakfast room, a former terrace now enclosed.

Guest rooms are spacious, decorated in serene ivories, light yellows, or soft greens. In some, picture windows frame a view of the mountains that makes any other knickknacks or details unnecessary.

Outdoor Kissing

HILDENE, Manchester Village
Historic Route 7A, (802) 362-1788
$6 per adult
On Route 7A, two miles south of its junction with Route 11/30.

Your hearts will soar as you peer over the precipice upon which this grand estate resides. Descendents of Abraham Lincoln built this Georgian Revival mansion at the turn of the century. Recent restorations have revived its original beauty and grandeur. Tours of the home offer insights into this fascinating family, but the real beauty is outside. Bring a picnic lunch in the warmer months and spend the afternoon admiring the formal gardens or searching for a four-leaf clover in the meadow. In autumn, come just for the view of the valley below and the golden hills on the horizon. When snow blankets the countryside, ski cross-country along Hildene's trails, thawing out with a cup of cocoa in the warming hut. Occasionally, craft shows, concerts, and weddings are scheduled at this sought-after site, so call ahead for a schedule of special events.

SOUTHERN VERMONT ART CENTER, Manchester Village
West Road, (802) 362-1405
(Open May through October and for special exhibits or events)
From Historic Route 7A northbound, turn left onto Ways Lane, just past the Jelly Mill. Turn right at the T intersection onto West Road. Turn left into the Art Center drive and head uphill to the museum.

Far from staid, this secluded estate is a study in beauty created by nature as well as by man. The setting is serene, a 1917 Georgian Colonial mansion set deep in the woods, near Manchester Village, although it feels far away. On the grounds, modern sculptures are juxtaposed with slender birches. Ferns and wildflowers hem the **BOSWELL BOTANY TRAIL** and other scenic hikes that wind through the woodland. Inside, former parlors and bedchambers have been transformed into graceful galleries that showcase works by local and internationally renowned artists. Performing arts have a home in the adjacent pavilion.

During the summer, the **GARDEN CAFÉ** is an inspirational spot for lunch. The café tables, set on the outdoor terrace or inside the porch room with its soft green floors and stenciling between the multipaned windows, are a fine place to ponder the better side of human nature.

Dorset

Hotel/Bed and Breakfast Kissing

CORNUCOPIA OF DORSET, Dorset
Route 30, (802) 867-5751
Moderate to Expensive

From Route 7, exit at Route 30 north to Dorset. The inn is on the right, south of the village center.

A champagne greeting is just one of the delightful surprises at this amiable, homey inn. Bask in the happy sun room, where an overstuffed sofa invites you to sink down and survey the country yard and gardens framed by the wall of windows. Enjoy a backgammon game on the inlaid table in the front room with its corner hearth. On a wintry day, relax by the fire in the sitting room, with its dried floral arrangements and photos of regular guests. Pampering amenities include turn-down service and a beautifully presented wake-up tray of coffee and teas and more. Only four guest rooms are in the main house, each in the style of a refined but welcoming country home. A crocheted canopy arches over the bed by the corner fireplace in the Scallop Room. Needlepoint toss pillows highlight the pencil-post bed in Green Peak, while Dorset Hill offers a pleasant view of the backyard and garden. For complete seclusion, the Owl's Head Cottage, in back of the house, offers a fireplaced living room, open kitchen, and cozy sleeping loft with skylights to the stars. When you return from dinner, an oil lamp is lit in your room and gourmet candies are arranged on your pillow. But this cornucopia's bounty is truly complete at breakfast, a luscious affair of fruits (perhaps fresh raspberries in November) and heartwarming gourmet dishes that is a celebration all by itself.

Restaurant Kissing

BARROWS HOUSE, Dorset
Route 30, (802) 867-4455
Moderate to Expensive

From Route 7, exit at Route 30 north to Dorset. The inn is on the right, south of the village center.

Like its hometown, this restaurant offers a touch of polish without any pretense Tables topped with white linen overlays, tasteful china, baskets of dried flowers, and candle lamps fill the spacious main dining room. Even more enticing is the sunken greenhouse room, with its glass wall and ceiling overlooking the back lawn that comes alive with little white lights after sunset. For a casual night out, the tavern is a cozy choice, with its trompe l'oeil wall covering that looks like bookshelves. The formal and tavern menus will satisfy a variety of tastes, with entrées from Maine crab cakes to pork with pineapple, garlic, and sage.

◆ **Romantic Note:** Less impressive but nice are the guest rooms found in the main inn and several surrounding buildings. For the most part these are plain, eclectic, and homespun, although the fabrics and colors lend a cheerful ambience.

Rupert

Outdoor Kissing

MERCK FOREST AND FARMLAND CENTER, Rupert
Route 315 (Rupert Mountain Road), (802) 394-7836
$18 for a cabin

From Route 7, exit at Route 30 north. About two and a half miles north of Dorset center, turn left onto Route 315. Drive uphill to the forest entrance, on the left.

Sometimes you have to peel away layers of today's busy world to uncover the heart of romance. This expansive woodland and turn-of-the-century farm embrace the simpler pursuits of yesteryear. Trails wind through a forest where wildflowers bloom and songbirds flutter, leading to inspiring views and placid ponds. Best of all, you don't have to leave when the sun trundles below the hilltops. You can hike out to the five extremely rustic cabins (more like wooden tents than housekeeping units), that are available for a night completely unencumbered with the distractions of the 20th century (including running water and electricity). In spite of this the cabins are very popular. They provide shelter, and some of them have a wood stove. You carry in everything else, but leave your modern troubles far behind. Imagine awakening in your own remote mountain wilderness, where all you need to make the day complete is each other. Reserve early.

◆ **Romantic Warning:** It's best not to ramble through this forest during hunting season in late fall (usually November), and cabins are not rented at this time. Overanxious hunters occasionally mistake hikers for deer.

Wilmington

Hotel/Bed and Breakfast Kissing

THE RED SHUTTER INN, Wilmington   ◆◆
Route 9, (802) 464-3768, (800) 845-7548
Inexpensive to Expensive (inn), Moderate (dinner)

In the center of town, about a quarter mile west of Wilmington's only traffic light.

A recent face-lift has done wonders for this 1894 Colonial, saving the handsome exterior and freshening the bedchambers. A fireplace warms one suite, which also boasts a skylit high-peaked ceiling, exposed beams, and a bay window. The Carriage House has an even newer feel; its Molly Stark Suite features a corner hearth in the sitting room and a two-person whirlpool tucked beneath a skylight. The less expensive rooms are petite, but clean and pleasant. Antique furnishings and modern baths are found throughout. A fieldstone fireplace welcomes guests to the dining room, with its warm wood paneling, candle lamps, and Windsor chairs gathered around antique wooden tables.

The generous selection of mouthwatering dishes will satiate discerning appetites with appetizers such as lemon-dill shrimp and sea scallops with leek and thyme sauce, and extraordinary entrées including coquilles St. Jacques, prime rib, Vermont trout, charbroiled tuna steak, and more. Choose from a dozen desserts, ranging from liqueur parfaits and bananas Amaretto to maple-pecan pie. Guest and nonguests can both partake in this dinner.

TRAIL'S END, Wilmington   ◆◆◆
Smith Road, (802) 464-2727, (800) 859-2585
Moderate to Expensive

From Route 100 north of Wilmington center, turn right onto East Dover Road, then bear right onto Smith Road. Look for the inn's sign on the right, about a half mile from Route 100.

If only all our trails could end at an inn like this. The location is quiet and secluded; the ambience is unpretentious and relaxing; the look is artsy contemporary with a hint of ski lodge, an intriguing contrast to New England's many Colonial and Victorian inns. After a day in the snow, you can settle by the sunken fieldstone hearth in the sunken living room. An angled mezzanine above offers a second common area. Scaled-down, sunken fieldstone hearths can also be found in six of the 15 guest rooms. Fireplace suites squeeze a lot into a fairly small room, including canopy beds, whirlpool tubs (rubber duckies included), refrigerators, wet bars, televisions, and a sitting area. The updated country decor in the other rooms includes pottery-based lamps, printed throws, and a few well-placed antiques. Full breakfasts are served at mosaic-tiled tables for eight, a hearty start for your day in the outdoors.

THE WHITE HOUSE, Wilmington
Route 9, (802) 464-2135, (800) 541-2135
Very Expensive (MAP)

Set high on a hill, just east of town.

Cross-country skiers who opt to stay at the White House can virtually step from the front door onto 43 kilometers of groomed trails that traverse high meadows and forested valleys. When you return, relax with a mug of hot coffee at the sunken bar, warm up by the wood stove, and enjoy the nonstop view of Vermont's rolling countryside. You can cuddle by firelight in five of the 12 guest rooms, as well as in the spacious parlor with its leather chairs and Oriental rug.

Nostalgia and contemporary touches abound. Unfortunately, this turn-of-the-century summer home is feeling its age, and the somewhat dated interior is not helped by the occasional missing bathroom tile or threadbare chair. In the main dining room, candlelight and mahogany paneling create a warm setting for such continental specialties as veal saltimbocca, chicken cordon bleu, and filet mignon. Breakfast is served by firelight as well, and both impart enough warmth to carry you through the day.

West Dover

Hotel/Bed and Breakfast Kissing

THE INN AT SAWMILL FARM, West Dover
Route 100 (Crosstown Road), (802) 464-8131
Very Expensive to Unbelievably Expensive (inn, MAP)
Expensive to Very Expensive (dining)

From Interstate 91, take Exit 2 (Brattleboro). Turn right on Route 9, heading west to Wilmington. Turn right on Route 100 north, and drive six miles to West Dover. Past the village church, take the first left turn to the inn on the left.

Sometimes you have to ignore the rough edges to find a gem. Such is the case at this converted farmhouse and its bevy of cottages. Climb the stairs from the dated, somewhat ragged foyer to a commodious common room somewhat reminiscent of an alpine ski lodge, made cozier by blazing fireplaces and candles glowing on shiny copper-topped tables. Above, the mezzanine library, with a big-screen television in one room, offers a more secluded gathering area, away from the restaurant traffic. The dining rooms, located just off the common room, attract people from far and near. Colonial-style chandeliers, fresh flowers in sterling baskets, and plenty of silverware add an elegant touch. The sophisticated seasonal menu lists appetizers such as salmon mousse with caviar and fresh crabmeat; entrées might include grilled salmon in saffron sauce, chicken with white wine and chanterelles, or chateaubriand for two.

The cottage rooms, the inn's most intimate accommodations, feature a ruffled half-tester above a king-size bed, wood-burning hearth in the sitting room, and lots of florals. Some cottage rooms consist of one large firelit room. Main-inn rooms are spacious, with special touches such as Early American furnishings or a copper vanity, but may also have dated green carpet and somewhat standard hotel architecture. No matter what the season, the outdoors is still there, with nearby ski resorts, two trout ponds, a pool, and tennis courts.

West Townshend

Hotel/Bed and Breakfast Kissing

WINDHAM HILL INN, West Townshend
Windham Road, (802) 874-4080
Expensive (inn, MAP), Moderate (dining)

Call for directions.

Trundle down the back roads of Vermont, onto an even quieter dirt lane, and you will stumble upon this idyllic 19th-century farmhouse with a picture-perfect view of rural fields and mountains. Now is the time to forget about the outside world. Hiking paths, groomed cross-country ski trails, and beautiful sunsets abound. In the evening, guests gather in the candlelit dining room. Some choose to sit around the family-style table; those who seek a more intimate meal are seated in the Frog Pond Room, overlooking its namesake, which, in winter, is illuminated at night for ice skating. Six-course, prix fixe dinners may include an appetizer cheesecake, carrot-orange soup, game hens with Cumberland sauce, and frozen "grasshopper" parfaits. Only one entrée is served each night, so call ahead if you have special dietary requirements.

After dinner, cuddle by the fireplace in the refined, country-home living room or relax with a cup of tea by the Franklin stove in the sitting room. In the public Wicker Room, you can gaze out the windows at a mesmerizing view of the mountains. Many of the 20 guest rooms—15 in the farmhouse and five in the converted barn—share this view. The room's country-style decor has a fresh, updated feel, with pencil-post, sleigh, or canopy beds; hand-hooked rugs on hardwood floors; and perhaps a cozy window seat. In the Tree House, you can embrace on a private deck, then retire to the ruffled canopy bed. Jessica's Room, with its pencil-post king, overlooks the sylvan frog pond. The barn's entry is, literally, a barn, but rooms are warm and welcoming, with rustic wood highlights and the splendid view, as far-reaching and serene as the memory of your stay here.

Grafton

Hotel/Bed and Breakfast Kissing

OLD TAVERN, Grafton   ◆◆
Route 35 and Route 121, (802) 843-2231, (800) 843-1801
Moderate to Expensive

Located in the center of this tiny village, at the intersection of Routes 35 and 121.

In the beginning of the 19th century, stages stopped here on the route between Boston and Montreal. Recently restored by a local historical foundation, the Old Tavern invites you to join the likes of Hawthorne, Emerson, Kipling, and Thoreau for a respite in your travels through Vermont. The 35 rather petite guest rooms are nostalgically furnished with fishnet canopy beds with white woven spreads, braided rugs on wide plank floors, pressed-flower lampshades, and attractive wall coverings.

In the formal dining room, antique tables are adorned with candle lamps and a fascinating collection of 19th-century face plates. In the converted Phelps Barn, admire the patchwork quilts hanging on towering barn walls as you enjoy a cocktail by the fire downstairs, or sneak up to the mezzanine to cuddle on the love seat by the hearth there. The continental breakfast buffet is best enjoyed in the Garden Room. Skylights invite the sun in year-round to splash upon the verdant indoor garden. Pressed tin lamps and pewter plates on green cloths update the Colonial feel, while oils of New England scenes remind you to leave this old tavern to continue your exploration of Vermont.

Ludlow

Hotel/Bed and Breakfast Kissing

GOVERNOR'S INN, Ludlow
86 Main Street, (802) 228-8830, (800) GOVERNOR
Expensive to Very Expensive (MAP)

The town of Ludlow is situated where Route 100 and Route 103 intersect. The inn is two miles south of Route 103, on the village green, next to the public library.

Heartwarming details are what you can expect to find at this distinguished inn. Your stay begins with midafternoon high tea, a handsome study in sterling and porcelain. Graceful antiques, refined wall coverings, and well-chosen accessories adorn the guest rooms. They are not extravagant in size or decor, but all offer just the right amount of class and coziness. Room 5 has an understated Victorian flair, with its carved wood bed, stunning armoire, and marble-topped bureau; a stenciled screen hides an in-room sink. From Room 7, you can look over Ludlow's steepled Victorian church, then examine it more carefully through the telescope.

In the early evening, a fire is laid in the parlor's marbleized slate hearth, decorated with intricately painted inlays of sailing ships. Guests gather to enjoy a cocktail in anticipation of the fine dinner ahead. Nationally recognized gourmets, movie stars, even an ex-President, have raved about the innkeeper's culinary skill, which wins top awards year after year. Like the cuisine, the dining room is distinctive without being overdone or stuffy. Tables are set with antique china and Waterford crystal. Napkins are tucked into tiny baskets, and floral posies perch in antique pitchers. After a friendly, informative introduction by the chef, waitresses in pinafores and ruffled caps present each course. The tantalizing, delicately prepared courses might include mountain blueberry-Chablis potage, mushroom strudel, game hens Grand Marnier with orange-pecan stuffing, and chocolate-walnut pie with ice cream and crème de cacao—and that's just one dinner. (Breakfasts are equally special, with the added interest of the inn's wonderful collection of antique tea and coffee pots.) Foil-wrapped chocolates and a petite bottle of French cognac are presented on your turned-down bed, the sweetest stanza in this ode to romance.

Weathersfield

Hotel/Bed and Breakfast Kissing

INN AT WEATHERSFIELD, Weathersfield
Route 106, (802) 263-9217, (800) 477-4828
Expensive to Very Expensive (inn), Expensive (dining)
One-half mile south of the village of Perkinsville, on Route 106.

Welcome to a time before electricity, when candles and firelight invited weary travelers to shake the cold from their topcoats and be pampered for an evening. The hearth, wrought-iron candelabras, and table-top tapers in sterling bases are virtually the only light sources in the library turned dining room. You'll dine on antique china, surrounded by brimming bookshelves and oils reminiscent of the old masters as two grand pianists play in perfect harmony. A second dining room is akin to a sunken porch, with glass all around, hanging green plants, and fresh flowers on each table. Nightly dinner menus may include specialties such as three-onion soup, pan-smoked tuna, steak Diane, or grilled salmon. To whet your appetite for the multicourse dinner, afternoon high tea is served in the parlor between the main dining room and the porch. Complimentary wine, sherry, and local hard cider accompany dishes served piping hot in intricate sterling.

In keeping with your journey to the past, fireplaces glow in eight of the 12 guest rooms and suites. You may find a swath of lace tied with a posy of dried flowers above your black iron bed or a four-poster tucked beneath a beamed, sloped ceiling. A spiral staircase climbs to the Honeymoon Suite, with its cozy sitting area, jetted tub beneath the skylight, and private rooftop deck with a view of the lake over the inn's gabled roof. In the morning, a hearty buffet breakfast, elegantly served, invigorates you for another day of touring the lush Vermont countryside, just as other lovers did 100 years ago.

Windsor

Hotel/Bed and Breakfast Kissing

JUNIPER HILL INN, Windsor
Juniper Hill Road, (802) 674-5273, (800) 359-2541
Moderate (Closed April and first two weeks in November)
Call for directions.

You'll feel like millionaires as you wind up the long drive to this stately 28-room mansion crowning a wooded pinnacle. This is your castle for the evening, dating to the turn of the century, when the wealthy built homes on a grand scale and spared no expense in using the best materials available. The "great hall" is immense, a palatial room with rich wood paneling, leaded glass framing the front doors, and a large brick hearth. Oriental rugs blanket the hardwood floors; camelback sofas and velvet wing chairs define several sitting areas. More cozy is the firelit gentleman's library, with its leather wing chairs, cabinets full of books, and custom-made woodwork framing the windows. The dining room, too, has a hearth, this one surrounded by intricately carved fruits, laurels, and scenes inspired by ancient Greece. On busy nights when the inn is full, candlelit multicourse dinners are sometimes offered to inn guests. (Dinners are available only if there are enough requests to coax the innkeepers into the kitchen.)

All told, 13 fireplaces are scattered throughout the mansion, many in the elegantly decorated guest rooms. Old brass, four-poster, canopy, and other unusual beds are perfectly blended with antique furnishings and accessories. Elaborate stenciling decorates the hallway. Many rooms overlook the sublime view of Mount Ascutney and Evart's Pond that mesmerized the mansion's creator. Revel in the same panorama while sunning by the flower-bedecked pool, and count yourselves rich in love.

Cornish

Outdoor Kissing

THE SAINT-GAUDENS NATIONAL HISTORIC SITE,
Cornish, New Hampshire
Saint-Gaudens Road, off Route 12A, (603) 675-2175
$2 per person

Call for directions.

Although this is officially in New Hampshire, the site lies just two miles from Windsor, Vermont, across the Connecticut River through one of the world's longest covered bridges, which in itself is a fun detour. The site is more than the historic summer home and studio of famous American sculptor Augustus Saint-Gaudens. It is a slice of serenity, an embrace of peace for all who visit. Saint-Gaudens reveled in gardening, and his legacy is kept alive today in the splendidly designed lawns, hedges, and formal gardens. Take time to smell the flowers as you wander the grounds and admire the sculptor's works, many of them military memorials that somehow fit perfectly with the placid surroundings. On certain Sundays in the summer, the site is even more engaging, as music lovers gather for low-key concerts, a tribute to the site's artistic creator.

Quechee

Restaurant Kissing

SIMON PEARCE RESTAURANT, Quechee   ❤❤❤
The Mill, on Main Street, (802) 295-1470
Expensive

From Route 4 eastbound, turn right on Waterman Hill Road. Drive through the covered bridge and turn left onto Main Street. The Mill is the second building on the left.

Ask for a table with a view at this lively, popular restaurant. The setting is splendid. The Ottauquechee River crashes over the waterfalls just below the window, then races beneath a traditional New England covered bridge. Other windows overlook the river above the falls and the Victorian house perched on its opposite bank. The decor is as crisp and contemporary as the glass stemware sold in the shop next door, with a hardwood floor, cane chairs, exposed brick, and cheerful watercolors. Candles flicker in immense globes handblown at the Mill. Fresh, seasonal cuisine may include such house favorites as shrimp soufflé, beef and Guinness stew, or poached salmon with a vin blanc sauce. The wine list is award-winning, with plenty of selections for that special toast for two.

◆ **Romantic Note:** Before leaving the Mill, explore downstairs. You can watch artists magically transform blobs of molten glass into delicate stemware and clay into vases.

Woodstock

Hotel/Bed and Breakfast Kissing

THE JACKSON HOUSE, Woodstock
37 Route 4 West, (802) 457-2065
Moderate to Very Expensive

The inn is one and a half miles west of the village on Route 4 West.

On Saturdays, near twilight, a harpist fills the parlor with melodies that tug at your heartstrings. Guests emerge from their elegantly appointed rooms, drawn by the music and the complimentary champagne and hors d'oeuvres. This is a traditional country inn, where rooms are welcoming but not overwhelming and a generous gourmet breakfast is served at a round table for eight. In the bedchambers, you'll find elaborate antique beds, enhanced by plush window and wall treatments. Some rooms enjoy a view of the flower-bedecked backyard and the trail to the duck pond that encourages afternoon strolling. Third-floor rooms are the most commodious, with balconies over-looking this scene, peaceful and pretty whether spring flowers bloom or winter casts its snowy shawl over the land.

WOODSTOCK INN AND RESORT, Woodstock
14 The Village Green, (802) 457-1100, (800) 448-7900
Expensive to Unbelievably Expensive

In the center of the village, at the intersection of Route 4 and Route 106.

Looking for a piece of the big city in small-town Vermont? This grand, 146-room hotel offers all the modern amenities that today's cosmopolitan traveler has come to expect. Guests are welcomed by a roaring fire blazing in the lobby's immense stone hearth, but most do not tarry here. They're beckoned back to the Terrace Room, with its white wicker furniture and louvred shutters, where a grand pianist plays melodies and afternoon tea is served. Later, you can duck into the spacious den of a tavern for cheese and a cocktail. Like the property that embraces it, the dining room is sophisticated and palatial in size, with a gracefully curved wall of windows along one end and oil paintings, displayed museum-style, highlighting soft gray walls. Jackets are required during the busier season, requested at other times, to set the tone for traditional continental cuisine.

The guest rooms are abundant and anonymous. Patchwork quilts add a splash of color to standard rooms with light wood furnishings, desks for their many business travelers, and large, modern baths. The suites have fireplaces, but are really unbelievably expensive. Still, if city sophistication is what you seek, you can find it here.

Restaurant Kissing

BENTLEY'S FLORIST CAFÉ, Woodstock
7 Elm Street, (802) 457-3400
Inexpensive

In the center of town, on the corner of Central and Elm streets.

Springtime blooms year-round in this cheerful greenhouse café. Though tiny, it is alive with greenery, home to both a flower shop and an old-fashioned soda fountain crowned with a ceiling that replicates a frosted conservatory roof. Two spoons and Vermont's finest ice cream, Ben and Jerry's, are in order on a summer afternoon. The mosaic floor, bentwood chairs, and marble tabletops recall an era of innocent courting and simple pursuits. For heartier appetites and chillier days, sandwiches, baked goods, designer coffees, and hot spiced cider invigorate you for an afternoon of window shopping in Woodstock.

◆ **Romantic Note: BENTLEY'S RESTAURANT**, next door, proves that "casual Victorian" is not an oxymoron. Compact terraces create private spaces, softly lit with Victorian fringed lamps. Candles and linen napkins compete with tabletop ads and the occasional bottle of ketchup. The menu ranges from burgers to creative entrées such as maple-mustard chicken, almond-crusted trout, and pork filled with toasted walnuts, pecans, and almonds.

THE PRINCE AND THE PAUPER, Woodstock ◑◆◀
24 Elm Street, (802) 457-1818
Moderate to Expensive

Call for directions.

A pauper probably couldn't eat at this unpretentious but refined restaurant, one of Woodstock's best—but a prince and a few court attendants could. The more expensive fine dining menu includes such seasonal indulgences as oysters with champagne sauce gratinée, a bisque of butternut squash and pears, or wild mushroom ravioli with creamy garlic sauce. These savory starters serve to whet your appetite for boneless rack of lamb in puff pastry or Norwegian salmon with a vodka and green peppercorn sauce. For smaller appetites and budgets, bistro fare includes Cajun barbecued shrimp with spicy peanut sauce or eggplant crêpes. You can even sink your teeth into a creative, hearth-baked pizza. High-backed booths ensure privacy. In each, an original oil painting adds artistic flair. The pressed tin chandeliers hanging from the beamed ceiling, oil lamps, candles, and fresh flowers create a mood for love.

THE VILLAGE INN OF WOODSTOCK, Woodstock ◑◆◀
41 Pleasant Street (Route 4), (802) 457-1255
Moderate

The inn is located on Route 4, a quarter mile east of the Village Green.

Ask for a table in the intimate firelit back room and enjoy dinner in one of Woodstock's most romantic restaurants. The hearth glows with the graceful charm of the past in this delightfully restored 1899 Victorian. But even with the crystal lamp, pressed tin ceiling, deep mauve walls, dogwood china, and roses on each table, the ambience is casual and easy, not at all stuffy. Hearty

Yankee dishes include maple-glazed pork, Maine lobster, and baked scrod. The most popular dish is the very reasonably priced roast Vermont turkey dinner, complete with apple-sausage-bread stuffing, maple candied yams, mashed potatoes, and homemade cranberry sauce, perfect for giving thanks for each other year-round.

◆ **Romantic Note:** The inn also lets upstairs guest rooms, which are simple and old-fashioned, but not all that romantic.

Outdoor Kissing

BILLINGS FARM AND MUSEUM, Woodstock
Route 12 (River Road), (802) 457-2355
$6 per adult, $17 per family

One-half mile north of the Woodstock village green on Route 12. Signs will direct you to the museum.

As you tour the verdant hills of Vermont, you can imagine a time in the past when farmers worked land but recently cleared of trees and stones. You need not imagine at this living-history farm, where dairy cows graze in emerald pastures and farmers turn soil with horse-drawn plows. The setting defines pastoral in its truest sense, and visitors are welcome to picnic on the grounds overlooking the orchards and fields while they learn about a time when people lived with the earth, not high above it. When autumn brushes the land with bold strokes of gold and crimson, the scene is spellbinding.

South Woodstock

Hotel/Bed and Breakfast Kissing

KENDRON VALLEY INN, South Woodstock
Route 106, (802) 457-1473
Moderate to Very Expensive (inn), Expensive (dining)

Five miles south of Woodstock; call for directions.

More than 50 museum-caliber heirloom quilts are displayed throughout this inn, symbolic of the lovers brought together in the 27 rooms. Rooms in the main house are the most romantic, especially those with a Franklin wood stove or fireplaces raised so you can watch the flames as you snuggle on your step-up bed. Wide plank floors, antique beds, canopies with cutwork ruffles, hand-hooked rugs, and stenciled lampshades provide a finely crafted country look. The topmost suite is a favorite, with its canopy bed, sitting area by the fireplace, and sparkling white bath with an immense whirlpool tub.

No need to drive to Woodstock for dinner. When the dining room is open, it's one of the best in the area. A fireplace is tucked into one corner of the candlelit main room. A raised hearth glows in the terrace room, with its slate floor, hanging plants, windows on three sides, director's chairs, and brass oil lamps. Creative internationally inspired dishes flavored with Vermont's fresh bounty include chilled blueberry soup; terrine of rabbit, veal, and pheasant; and such entrées as pork with hickory-smoked fennel and honey-roasted garlic or lemon-almond sole. Breakfasts are the heartiest around, with your choice of entrées.

◆ **Romantic Note:** In summer, a spring-fed pond with a sandy beach invites a refreshing dip. In winter, sleigh rides and cross-country ski tours led by the innkeeper will brush your cheeks with that rosy glow of love.

Bridgewater Corners

OCTOBER COUNTRY INN, Bridgewater Corners
Upper Road, (802) 672-3412, (800) 648-8421
Moderate to Expensive (MAP)

Call for directions.

Welcome to a folksy, old-fashioned country inn that's both convenient to and worlds away from the Killington ski area and its sprawl of development. In the living room, a blazing fire chases away the winter chill, while puzzles from the inn's extensive collection, congenial conversation, and books provide entertainment. Televisions are happily banished from this rambling 10-room farmhouse. Dinners, served family style, focus on international themes, and always warrant raves from the guests. Italian and Greek repasts are favorites, but the North African and Mexican menus are equally delicious.

Bedchambers share the homespun feel. You might find a lobster-trap coffee table, old bureau, and a Jenny Lind bed beneath a skylit sloped ceiling or set off by a stenciled wall. Two rooms share a bath and some are set up to accommodate the bike groups that frequent the inn (the innkeeper will let you know when the bicyclists are coming). Several downstairs rooms were recently revamped and look over the back gardens, the inn's jetted hot tub, and a terraced lawn with swimming pool. This is not the best place for low-light smooching, but it's just right for put-your-feet-up relaxation after a day in Vermont's great outdoors.

Killington

Restaurant Kissing

HEMINGWAY'S RESTAURANT, Killington
Route 4, (802) 422-3886
Expensive to Very Expensive (Closed most Mondays and Tuesdays and for four weeks in April and May, dependent on the weather)

Call for directions.

Many connoisseurs consider Hemingway's to be one of the finest restaurants in the nation. The exceptional American cuisine and varied wine list consistently live up to its esteemed reputation. The ambience is a perfect marriage of intimacy and indulgence, while the decor and service remain refreshingly unpretentious. In anticipation of this special dinner together, enjoy a cocktail in the parlor, as if visiting an elegant home. Relax by the blazing hearth and take a moment to admire the modern, flowing sculptures created by local artists. Each of the three dining rooms is sensual and intimate. The largest, with just nine tables, is where you will find vintage crystal chandeliers, plush valances, salmon-colored walls, and candles flickering on each table. A second room basks in the glow of a fireplace and lovers sighing over each nibble. Downstairs, a petite room with just four tables is akin to the wine cellar of a gracious host. Candles glow on the cool stone walls while bottles of enviable vintage tempt you from behind an iron grill. Fixed price menus focus on fresh ingredients and creative cookery.

Begin your meal with a seasonal appetizer such as the applewood-smoked salmon and sturgeon with seaweed salad, wild mushroom tart with morel sauce, or their famous garlic soup. In addition to the gamebird specials in honor of the restaurant's literary namesake, main courses include halibut and lobster with vanilla and sweet corn, wood-roasted pork with polenta and wild mushrooms, and beef tenderloin with balsamic sauce and rosemary. Pumpkin charlotte, lemon crème brûlée, or Vermont maple ice cream with a caramel cage ensure a sweet ending to your remarkable evening here.

Chittenden

Hotel/Bed and Breakfast Kissing

MOUNTAIN TOP INN, Chittenden
Mountain Top Road, (802) 483-2311, (800) 445-2100
Very Expensive (EP), Unbelievably Expensive (MAP)

Call for directions.

You could spend a week at this rustic 1,300-acre resort hotel and still find more new activities to try together. The room rate covers all recreation, including boating, sailing, windsurfing, canoeing, fishing (they provide rods and bait), horseback riding, horsedrawn wagon rides, golf on the inn's five-hole par-three course, tennis, shuffleboard, croquet, badminton, fly-fishing instruction, trap shooting, and mountain biking. In winter, ice skating, cross-country skiing, and sleigh rides will coax you away from the fieldstone fireplace in the lobby. If rain dampens your spirits, the game room has billiards, Ping-Pong, foosball, and air hockey. And you can soothe your muscles in the sauna or the small whirlpool (no windows) located next to the game room.

With all that activity, dinner is in order, served in a large, lively room decorated with Colonial pressed-tin chandeliers, snowshoe-inspired chairs, and tabletop oil lamps. With the emphasis placed squarely on the outdoors, 35 guest rooms in the main buildiing are simple, highlighted with Shaker-style rocking chairs and comfortable, contemporary sofas to sink into after a long day of playing together.

◆   **Romantic Note:** There are a few cottages with multiple guest rooms that have the same decor as the main inn. There are also chalets scattered throughout the huge property. These are rather large and are more appropriate for families.

TULIP TREE INN, Chittenden
Chittenden Dam Road, (802) 483-6213
Expensive to Very Expensive (MAP)

From Route 4 in Mendon, turn north onto Meadow Lake Drive. Drive to its end and turn right onto Chittenden Road. Continue three miles to the inn, on the left.

After a long day of schussing down the slopes at nearby Killington or hiking in the autumn woods, nothing beats slipping into a hot, bubbling whirlpool bath. In five of the eight guest rooms of this country inn you can do just that, although there is only room for one in the tub at a time.

There's no need to leave this country hideaway after your soak. Gourmet candlelit dinners, complete with a sorbet course, are served to guests—but there is only one seating and one entrée. One recent night, the menu offered a savory curried carrot soup, salad, pork with orange-apricot sauce, orzo, and pumpkin cheesecake with maple syrup. After dinner, guests can relax in two parlors; one is decorated with sailing ship prints and decoys on the mantel of a hearth with a fireplace insert, the second has a fieldstone fireplace. Return at your leisure to your simple, country-style room, where the stenciled walls, antique bureau, tufted side chair, and carved wooden or four-poster bed create a soothing setting for a long winter's nap. But first, treat your two lips to a lingering kiss.

Fair Haven

Hotel/Bed and Breakfast Kissing

VERMONT MARBLE INN, Fair Haven
12 West Park Place, (802) 265-8383, (800) 535-2814
Expensive to Very Expensive (MAP)

From Route 4, take the Fair Haven exit and drive south into town. The inn is a three-story marble mansion facing the town's square.

Which is best: the exquisite cuisine, the impeccable decor, or the gracious but friendly hospitality you receive at this marvelous marble mansion? You can decide while you experience one of the finest and most surprising inns in Vermont. Open the splendid etched-glass front doors and enter the Victorian era, recreated and updated to provide the utmost in elegant comfort. To your left, a cozy firelit library invites relaxing with a magazine or chess game. To the right, a formal double parlor opens before you, with a resplendent crystal chandelier, two intricately sculpted marble hearths, even more elaborate plasterwork, and plush but inviting furnishings, perfected by such details as a gilded mirror, seasonal bouquet, and display of antique collectibles. In the guest rooms, you're welcomed with fresh flowers, sherry, and afternoon nibbles. Eight of the 12 rooms have fireplaces. Elizabeth Barrett Browning would have felt at home in her namesake room, with its canopy bed, lacy ruffled toss pillows, peacock wall coverings, fireplace, and marble-topped vanity with wash basin. No fewer than nine coordinated accent pillows top the step-up canopy bed in the Henry Fielding Room. In the T.S. Eliot, a tasteful art deco-inspired look with blacks, pinks, and arching lines prevails.

But the ultimate indulgence—the inn's exquisite cuisine—still awaits you. In the evening, a stunning Austrian crystal chandelier bathes the dining room in soft light. Tables cloaked in white linens with pink overlays are resplendent with lead crystal stemware, graceful silver, and flickering oil lamps. Trompe l'oeil wall coverings look like satiny drapes, soaring to intricately plastered ceilings. Each course promises unusual taste temptations, all of them beautifully presented and absolutely delicious. The menu changes monthly and, as strange it sounds, there is a different menu for those guests staying overnight than for those who are there only for dinner. Overnight guests receive a seven-course repast; dinner guests receive only a five-course repast. Both, however, are absolutely unsurpassed in quality and presentation. Our spectacular dinner featured spiced apple soup; grilled beef with pineapple, apricot, and artichoke hearts; Southwestern black bean salad; piña colada sorbet; smoked duck with corn relish; quail stuffed with wild rice; and a dessert plate with truffles, a decadent cake, and luscious tart. Five-course meals are $30 fixed price. In the morning, your pampering continues with a candlelit five-course breakfast.

◆ **Romantic Note:** For an extraordinarily special evening, ask about the inn's "Celebration of Romance" package, with champagne, roses, and a private dinner for two in the library. It's a night to remember forever.

Northern Vermont

Middlebury

Hotel/Bed and Breakfast Kissing

THE MIDDLEBURY INN, Middlebury
14 Court Square, (802) 388-4961, (800) 842-4666
Inexpensive to Expensive

On Middlebury Common.

A small, red satin heart-shaped box sits on my bureau. Inside, it holds two heart-shaped pewter napkin rings and some of my fondest memories of our visit to northern Vermont. The rings, along with a bottle of bubbly and a bouquet of blooms, are just the overture to the Romantic Innterlude package at this stately 45-room Colonial-style hotel, built in 1827, where they treat every guest like an honored friend. Step across the threshold and you'll enter the era of gracious hospitality. Furnishings are elegant, but comfortably so—the ambience is anything but stuffy. The multipaned window arching over the front door, the grand piano, leather-tufted chairs, a fireplace with silver candlesticks on the mantel, Oriental rugs, and fluted columns rising through the spacious lobby add a sense of majesty. In the afternoon, a complimentary tea, complete with pastries and finger sandwiches, is served. Commodious guest rooms are gracefully appointed with Early American reproductions, velvet wing chairs, and plush draperies. Televisions are tucked away in attractive cabinets.

Upper-crust colonists would feel at home in the Founders Room restaurant, with its exquisitely restored woodwork and wainscoting, muted blue-on-white floral wall coverings, bronzed chandeliers, and white classical columns rising up to the ceiling. Shrimp cocktail and baked Brie whet your appetite for sirloin steak, veal Madeira, roast duck, bourbon shrimp, and other continental dishes. A salad bar, freshly baked breads and the inn's famous popovers, and plain-folk service tone down the posh atmosphere. In the morning, a full buffet breakfast is served, with everything you could possibly want or imagine, from bacon and eggs to muffins and cereals to sausage and pancakes, with real maple syrup, of course. Just to make sure your appetite is satiated, Romantic Innterluders are handed a willow basket, large enough to carry an infant (not to give you any ideas), that is brimming with picnic goodies. The basket, and memories, are yours to keep.

SWIFT HOUSE INN, Middlebury   ◆◆◆
25 Stewart Lane, (802) 388-9925
Inexpensive to Expensive

Call for directions.

Charm runs in this family of three 19th-century homes, but each, like kissing cousins, has a unique personality. The 1814 Main House, the most sociable of the three, offers traditional luxury. You'll be seduced by arched canopy or brass beds, wood-burning fireplaces, jetted or clawfoot tubs, candle sconces, and fine antiques. You'll find the parlor here, done up in muted peachy tones with an upright piano, marble hearth, and a television tucked away in a cabinet. Gourmet dinners are served in the hunter green dining room highlighted with rosy lavender detailing, where fireplaces warm patrons as they enjoy entrées such as Green Mountain trout, veal with shiitake mushrooms, or rack of lamb with garlic and rosemary. The Carriage House is cosmopolitan, with spacious rooms, bleached wood furnishings, whirlpool tubs, fireplaces, and a steam room and sauna (and, unfortunately, a small conference room) down the hall. The Gate House, set on the busy road, is old-fashioned, with a turreted parlor, lincrusta wall coverings along the carved wood staircase, and bright, feminine florals in the guest rooms.

Sociable, sophisticated, nostalgic: all three form a first-class group that will bewitch you with their hospitality.

Restaurant Kissing

CAFÉ CHATILLON, Middlebury
Frog Hollow Mill, (802) 388-1040
Moderate

From Middlebury Common, cross the Main Street bridge and turn right onto Frog Hollow Alley. The café is on the right, past the bottom of the falls and a scenic footbridge.

On a sunny day, this is one of the best spots in town for a casual lunch or early dinner. Umbrella-topped tables are set on a small patio on the bank of Otter Creek. The falls thunder just upstream, but here the waters are placid, the scene serene. After dark, little white lights shine like the Milky Way around the patio, while oil lamps sparkle on the cozy tables inside. Along with creative sandwiches and soups, lunch specials may include local rabbit and black beans with cornbread or linguine with clam sauce. Seasonal dinner menus are equally creative, with such entrées as lamb with feta cheese and polenta or bourbon-and-mustard-marinated chicken breast. With this proper romantic setting, you're guaranteed to feel as mellow as the river passing by.

Waitsfield

Hotel/Bed and Breakfast Kissing

THE INN AT ROUND BARN FARM, Waitsfield
East Warren Road, (802) 496-2276
Moderate to Expensive

From Route 100 South, turn left onto Bridge Street in Waitsfield center. Drive through the covered bridge and bear right at the fork. After a winding country mile, you'll see the round barn and inn on the left.

O'er the covered bridge and though the fields, to the Inn at Round Barn Farm you'll go, delighting in every moment you share in this Currier and Ives print come to life. Set on 85 acres of rolling Vermont hillside, complete with cows and a calico cat, this 1810 farmhouse and its graceful round barn, one of only a few remaining in the state, rise golden from the green lawns, capturing the beauty of autumn year-round. Inside, farm life is left behind for a blend of charm and sophistication. Vivaldi and Mozart set the tone for elegant country decor as you bundle by the hearth. Guest rooms are equally heartwarming, at once elegant and comfortable, with such details as wide plank floors warmed with Oriental carpets, corner gas fireplaces, private Jacuzzis and steam showers, hand-hewn beamed cathedral ceilings, canopied beds, and rich floral fabrics. Most rooms share the lovely view of the inn's terraced flower beds and placid duck ponds backdropped by the Green Mountains. On a warm afternoon, you and your loved one should swing on the hammock or settle on the park bench to drink in the beauty of it all.

Flowers abound inside the inn as well, down to a colorful pansy on your breakfast fruit cocktail. The morning meal is served in a sunny room with windows overlooking this epitome of Vermont countryside, and may include treats like cottage cheese pancakes with raspberry-maple syrup, served with freshly baked muffins and breads.

◆ **Romantic Note:** The Round Barn is host to a variety of country get-togethers, including weddings. Inn guests often receive free tickets to the Mozart, piano, or bluegrass concerts. Art exhibits are hosted on the lower level. Below that, a 58-foot lap pool invites guests in for a refreshing dip. True romantics will brave the spiral staircase that climbs up the silo to the cupola crowning the barn for a lofty kiss.

Outdoor Kissing

SUNSET ROCK HIKING TRAIL
Green Mountain National Forest

From Waitsfield, follow Route 100 South past the Sugarbush ski area turnoff and West Hill Road. Turn right onto Lincoln Gap Road and drive three miles up the very steep, narrow road to the crest of the gap. The trail starts in the parking area on the left. The hike takes about one hour round-trip.

For a panorama that stretches without end, like your love for each other, follow this rugged, forested trail to the place the locals seek out for outdoor romance—Sunset Rock. You'll clamber over boulders, past birches, and, in the autumn, through a kaleidoscope of red and gold leaves to a view of verdant mountains and rolling valleys that is inspiring at any time of day. The smooth rock invites picnicking. If you're feeling adventurous, tarry for the sunset over the peaks, but be sure to bring a flashlight and take care on the hike down.

◆ **Romantic Alternative:** When in Vermont, court your love where locals have for nearly two centuries. Young-at-heart couples search out secret swimming holes to satisfy their thirst for light-hearted romance, and this is one of the best around. To reach it, head south on Route 100 from Waitsfield center for about eight miles. Look for the abandoned, dilapidated white house on the right, park in the dirt drive, and follow the trail to the stream. The stimulatingly cold brook trips and tumbles over smooth rocks, splashing into a cool pool. Sharing a mountain-stream kiss on the sandy, sunny bank is sure to warm your body and soul.

Warren

Hotel/Bed and Breakfast Kissing

BEAVER POND FARM INN, Warren   ●●
Golf Course Road, (802) 583-2861
Very Inexpensive to Inexpensive

From Route 100 South, turn right onto West Hill Road. Drive uphill, then bear right onto Golf Course Road. The inn is on the right.

What better way to enjoy a Vermont winter afternoon than to ski cross-country to your inn's door, kick off your boots, and feel the warm caress of your lover's hand as you cuddle by the wood-burning hearth? Just a snowball's throw from Sugarbush ski area, this restored 1860 farmhouse provides a charming interlude removed from the villages of alpine-style condominiums. In the warmer months, the snowmelt reveals a private one-hole golf course that serves as the inn's backyard, punctuated with the namesake beaver pond and backdropped by mountains. Guest rooms are welcoming any time of year with their homespun, country-inn furnishings, smattering of antiques, hardwood floors, brightly papered walls, and skylighted eaves upstairs. A full breakfast, served family style in the beamed dining room, is sure to lend a hearty start to any outdoor Vermont adventure.

Restaurant Kissing

CHEZ HENRI, Warren   ●◖
Sugarbush Village, (802) 583-2600
Moderate

Call for directions.

A taste of France will delight your senses in this cozy and casual bistro. Red tablecloths, café-style tables, a stone fireplace, and high-backed booths lend it a buoyant Parisian air. This is one of the longest-lived restaurants in the Sugarbush area, and its gourmand's menu is the highlight. If you lust for frog's legs and calamari, you'll fulfill your desire here, along with such specialties as asparagus ravioli with roasted garlic and goat cheese or rabbit in red wine sauce. In snow season, energetic skiers may trundle in to enjoy the dancing in back, but the disco is well separated from the dining room, and even though no one would call disco dancing romantic, it can be sexy. So why not take a break on the dance floor between courses?

SAM RUPERT'S RESTAURANT, Warren
Top of the Sugarbush Access Road, (802) 583-2421
Moderate

Call for directions.

Little white lights sparkle like constellations in this surprising sugar house turned dining establishment. Pottery oil lamps with hurricane globes capture flickers of light on each table, as though a star was brought down from the night sky just for the two of you. A profusion of green plants and the pot-bellied stove at one end make you feel as though you're dining in a spring garden even when snow drifts outside. The cuisine is heaven-blessed as well, with such seasonal specialties as herb-grilled tuna with tomatillo salsa, pan-roasted lamb chops with warm Middle Eastern caponata salad and curry butter, or pork au poivre with brandied Hungarian sauce. Decadent desserts, too, are out of this world.

Waterbury

Hotel/Bed and Breakfast Kissing

THATCHER BROOK INN, Waterbury
Route 100 North, (802) 244-5911, (800) 292-5911
Inexpensive to Expensive

From Interstate 89, take Exit 10 to access Route 100 North. The inn is approximately one mile up on the left.

Although it has abundant charm, the inn is on a busy street and traffic noise is a problem in all the guest rooms. Also, the public rooms are too public, with patrons of the restaurant and tavern leaving little privacy for overnight guests. What a shame, because every other aspect is so thoroughly engaging.

Downstairs, in the little tavern with the large fireplace, dollar bills are pinned to the wall above the bar. A Thatcher Brook tradition, they're signed by couples celebrating their anniversary, a memorial to romance. Perhaps they reavowed their love over a dinner of baked Brie and oysters Rockefeller, veal Marsala and grilled swordfish, served in the intimate, candlelit rooms of this Victorian mansion. Or perhaps they stayed the night in one of the Laura

Ashley-style rooms, embracing by the fire or soaking in the whirlpool. All guest rooms, whether spacious or small, are attractively decorated. Be sure to bring an extra dollar bill with you.

Restaurant Kissing

VILLA TRAGARA, Waterbury Center
Route 100, (802) 244-5288
Moderate to Expensive

Follow Route 100 North through Waterbury. The inn is six miles on the right side.

Legend holds that ghosts inhabit this 1820 farmhouse restaurant. Is it the aroma of spirited Italian cuisine that holds them to this mortal coil? Or perhaps they can't bear to miss the sunset as it casts a golden glow on the hills along the horizon. To share this immortal view (sadly, now, with Route 100 just outside), choose a table in the front room, with its billows of ruffled white curtains above the west-facing windows. In another larger room, exposed timbers from the original barn and a collection of plates on the wall create a cultured country look. In between, smaller rooms are partitioned by arched porticos and glow with the light of candles in pewter bases with hurricane globes. Fresh pastas and such delicacies as veal with prosciutto and asparagus or linguine with scallops, mussels, baby clams, and shrimp are sure to keep your spirits happy.

Stowe

Like the crimson and gold leaves taking flight in the autumn breeze, alighting where they please on mountain, stream, and meadow, the area called Stowe blankets nearly an entire mountainside with its vibrancy. Stowe Village is a compact cluster of historic buildings, shops, and a steepled church lining busy Main Street (Route 100). At the three-way stop in town, turn onto Mountain Road and you'll find hotels, inns, restaurants, and shops dotting both sides as you wind uphill. Stowe is one of New England's premier ski resorts, but outdoor enthusiasts also come here in the warmer months for mountain hiking, scenery, and a fresh breath of romance.

Hotel/Bed and Breakfast Kissing

EDSON HILL MANOR, Stowe
1500 Edson Hill Road, (802) 253-7371, (800) 621-0284
Very Expensive (MAP only December through March)
Moderate to Expensive (B&B in April through June, and October through December)

From Mountain Road (Route 108), turn right onto Edson Hill Road. Follow it uphill, past the Stowehof Inn. Look for the sign for Edson Hill Manor on the left, about one and a half miles up from Route 108.

If you've ever fantasized becoming earl of your own country estate, this is the place to make your dream come true. This European-style manor is set amidst 200 acres of rolling woodland, complete with riding stables, cross-country ski trails, and a pond that gleams like a jewel in the warmer months and invites skaters in winter. Nothing sparks romance more than a wood-burning fire warming a bedside hearth, and the Edson Hill Manor boasts fireplaces, some framed in Delft tiles, in 20 of its 25 rooms. Sleek four-poster beds, ceiling eaves, and braided rugs on hardwood floors lend charm to the guest rooms. Hand-painted murals transform ordinary, dated bathrooms into whimsical scenes featuring tropical fish or flitting songbirds. In the surrounding carriage houses, commodious rooms with more modern four-posters and large brick hearths prevail.

A chef from northern California's famous Lark Creek Inn rules the manor's fine dining room, with its garden trellis effect made complete by murals of intertwined ivy, vases of fresh flowers, pink linens, and tapers on each table. A slate floor and hearth blend nicely with the windows on three sides overlooking the verdant lawn and forest. Breakfast is a scrumptious affair of fresh fruit and muffins, granola, and your choice of such entrées as waffles with raspberries and homemade syrup or a zucchini and cheddar omelet with ham or home-fries. A brick patio in back offers umbrella-topped tables in warm weather that look down on the crescent-shaped pool below.

Rub noses on a special sleigh ride for two and even the coldest winter day will remain a warm memory in your heart. Skates, skis, and horses are also available.

GREEN MOUNTAIN INN, Stowe
Main Street, (802) 253-7301, (800) 445-6629
Moderate to Expensive

Take Interstate 89 North to Exit 10, where you will access Route 100 North. Drive approximately 10 miles into the village of Stowe. The inn is on the right.

When you've been schussing on the slopes of Stowe all day, or hiking through spring wildflowers or fall foliage, nothing is quite as soothing as thawing by a crackling fire or unwinding in a swirling whirlpool bath. Several suites in this 54-room, century-old inn feature these modern luxuries, while the decor remains purely Colonial with stenciled walls, folk art, and some canopy beds custom-made for the inn from 18th-century designs. Other modern additions, like the televisions, are a bit intrusive, along with a location on a busy street and the too-public common rooms, including a popular restaurant and smoky lounge.

◆   **Romantic Warning:** Who could have known in the 1800s that thousands would drive automobiles to Stowe? Street noise, unfortunately, permeates the inn's otherwise pleasing blend of nostalgic decor and modern amenities.

THE INN AT THE BRASS LANTERN, Stowe   ◆◆◀
717 Maple Street (Route 100 North), (802) 253-2229, (800) 729-2980
Inexpensive to Expensive

From Interstate 89, take Exit 10, then Route 100 North to Stowe Village (approximately 10 miles). Continue through the village on Route 100, Maple Street, for approximately a half mile. The inn is on the left.

Breakfast is pure Vermont at this restored 1800s farmhouse, whether you're starting your day off with blueberry pancakes, Cabot cheese, or locally grown fruits and vegetables. The decor, too, is as clean and crisp as Green Mountain air, with a touch of old-fashioned charm. A dainty teal sofa, love seat, and rose accent chair gather around the brick hearth that glows on the parlor's exposed beams, café curtains, and ongoing jigsaw puzzle. Each guest room holds something special—a fireplace, a canopied bed, a patchwork quilt—but the most indulgent is spacious Room 9, with its heart-shaped head- and footboards, brick wood-burning fireplace, and tiny hearts in the wallpaper that hint of the romantic encounters in this honeymooners' favorite.

◆   **Romantic Warning:** Most street noise is blocked out by considerate restoration, but some still sneaks through the cracks.

THE SIEBENESS, Stowe   ◆◀
3681 Mountain Road, (802) 253-8942, (800) 426-9001
Moderate to Expensive (MAP only in winter)
Very Inexpensive to Inexpensive (B&B in off-season)

From the village of Stowe, take a left on Mountain Road and drive approximately four miles. The inn is on the left.

Take a country stroll along Stowe's paved recreation path and you'll come across the backyard of this simple, old-fashioned country inn. A shaggy sheepdog fits right in with the homespun, well-used furnishings in the living room. The television room is downright frumpy, but who wants to spend time in front of the set? Upstairs, guest rooms have been recently redecorated, with a four-poster in one, two doubles and a plaid sofa bed (for the kids) in another. A favorite for romance is the room done in sky blue with a cloud white brass bed and wicker accent tables, a breath of fresh, down-home air in sometimes too trendy Stowe.

◆   **Romantic Note:** Breakfast is included in the room rate, but available à la carte to the general public.

STOWEFLAKE INN, Stowe
Mountain Road, (802) 253-7355, (800) 253-2232
Moderate (EP), Expensive (MAP)

Call for directions.

One of the most luxurious resort hotels in Stowe, this sprawling, modern complex makes up in amenities what it lacks in personality. Newly renovated rooms are spacious and modern, some with light pine furnishings, others with stately Colonial reproductions, all with plush window treatments and soothing color schemes. The lobby is grand and cosmopolitan. Fires warm the sunken living room. Several more elegant sitting areas look over the landscaped grounds and pool. A palatial indoor swimming pool and comprehensive exercise room will get you in shape for the hotel's popular golf school. Try your hand at the chip-and-putt course, the driving range, or the professional putting green before hitting the tennis and volleyball courts. A sauna, whirlpool, and massage will soothe you afterwards.

◆ **Romantic Warning:** As you might have guessed, this is a popular spot for conventions, but they are generally kept low-key.

STOWEHOF INN, Stowe
Edson Hill Road, (802) 253-9722, (800) 932-7136
Moderate to Expensive (EP), Expensive to Very Expensive (MAP)

From Mountain Road (Route 108), turn right onto Edson Hill Road. As it climbs uphill, the inn is on the right.

Two mighty maple trunks support the porte cochere of this Tyrolean-style inn. They seem firmly rooted in Stowe's recent past, guarding against any intrusion that is too 1990s. Today, the overall feel of the inn is dated, down to the firelit sunken living rooms in the lobby, but the public and guest rooms are fresh rather than worn. Some guest rooms are warmed by whitewashed, adobe-style corner hearths, with a valance and drapes above the headboard adding a designer touch. Many open onto private balconies, which take full advantage of this 46-room lodge's location high above Stowe's hustle and bustle. A large stone hearth warms the Seasons restaurant, where petite table lamps with lavender shades glow on pink-clothed tables as you enjoy creative appetizers and a classic continental menu.

TEN ACRES LODGE, Stowe ◆◆◆
14 Barrows Road, (802) 253-7638, (800) 327-7357
Very Inexpensive to Expensive

Call for directions.

When the cold autumn air blushes your cheeks as rosy as the maple leaves falling around you, cuddling by the fire will warm you the old-fashioned way (though which warms you more quickly, the cuddle or the fire, is entirely up to you). The eight contemporary Hill House rooms, all with fireplace, are as crisp as the mountain breeze. Neutral or pastel tones, cathedral ceilings, bleached wooden canopy beds, and private balconies add to the sense of airiness. Guest rooms in the 1840 farmhouse are touched with nostalgia by the use of antiques, reproductions, and patchwork quilts alongside contemporary pastel sofas and lamps. Two cottages on the property, however, are weatherworn and uninviting.

Invigorated by the great outdoors, jovial diners gather in the restaurant, where oil lamps flicker on white linens in a series of dining rooms carved out of the farmhouse. Deep grays, greens, and mauve surround you with country charm as you enjoy such seasonal specials as clams with smoked salmon or duck with spinach, followed by grilled partridge, squid-ink pasta with prosciutto, or steak with green peppercorns and onions. The inn's common rooms, with wood-burning fireplace, are adjacent and partially open to the restaurant. Better to snuggle in your Hill House room by your private flame for two.

TRAPP FAMILY LODGE, Stowe
42 Trapp Hill Road, (802) 253-8511, (800) 826-7000
Very Expensive to Unbelievably Expensive (MAP only)

From Mountain Road heading north, about two miles up from Route 100 in Stowe Village, bear left at a fork onto Luce Hill Road, which eventually becomes Trapp Hill Road. The lodge is at the crest of the hill.

What romantic could resist visiting this alpine lodge, whether to stay the night, enjoy dinner, or indulge in dessert at the Tea House? The Trapps lived one of the most compelling love stories of their time, retold in *The Sound of Music*. This is their slice of Austria, an expansive hilltop lodge with peaked gables and roofs built by the Trapp family. Popular and prosperous, it's grown to a sprawling complex with many buildings, from the gift shop to the time-share condos. Hundreds of tourists come by just to see the place, but only overnight guests are allowed free rein in the hotel and exquisite grounds. Spacious guest rooms are pleasantly decorated in the style of a modern hotel. Some have private balconies overlooking the voluptuous mountains that reminded Maria so much of her native Austria. Fireplaces are lit on demand in the generous common rooms on the upper floor. On the ground floor, a gentleman's library is lined with shelves full of books. The garden room, a lush greenhouse of hanging plants and immense vases filled with cut flowers, is a good place to soak up the high mountain sun.

The renowned multicourse dinners are sure to keep you satisfied on the snowiest winter evening. Appetizers include a trout fillet sautéed with grapes and hazelnuts, and crabmeat under cheese. Soups are homemade and hearty. Many entrées are enhanced by delicate sauces—white wine sauce on the game hen, béarnaise sauce on the poached sole, brandy sauce on the chicken with artichoke. The wiener schnitzel is sautéed with lingonberries. All are served in a simply decorated dining room with Colonial-style chairs and tables. Lighter (and sweeter) appetites will be satiated in the Tea House overlooking the verdant Vermont hills; the homemade European desserts are all irresistible.

◆ **Romantic Note:** You may feel as though you really can climb every mountain from the hiking trails that radiate from the lodge. After snowfall, enjoy gliding over the groomed trails of America's first cross-country ski center.

YE OLDE ENGLAND INNE, Stowe
433 Mountain Road, (802) 253-7558
Moderate to Very Expensive

From Interstate 89, take left onto Mountain Road. The inn is a third of a mile down on the left.

There are many ways to make merry at this Old English inn. Plunge into the sunken Jacuzzi in your guest room or lounge beneath a cloud of lace canopy surrounded by classic Ethan Allen furnishings and Laura Ashley prints. Toast each other's health and share a laugh in one of Stowe's best taverns, an authentic-looking pub pouring more than 120 ales, cognacs, and wines. If tea is your cup of tea, relax in the firelit parlor with afternoon finger sandwiches, scones, cookies, and tea breads, all baked at the inn and served with Britain's favorite hot beverage. Enjoy dinner in Copperfield's, a classic Tudor-style room with black half timbers on white walls highlighted with copper pots. Look for beef Wellington, venison, and pheasant alongside more common continental entrées. A proper breakfast is served here as well, from hot porridge to your choice of eggs any style to pancakes, omelets, Welsh rarebit, and, naturally, English muffins.

Restaurant Kissing

STUBB'S RESTAURANT, Stowe
Mountain Road and Edson Hill Road, (802) 253-7110
Moderate

Follow Mountain Road two and three-quarters miles. The inn is at the intersection of Mountain Road and Edson Hill Road.

Frank Sinatra playing in the background and glowing fireplaces; what more do you need for romance? Pink and burgundy linens, low lighting, ladder-back chairs, exposed beams, and a brick hearth in each of the two intimate dining rooms create an ambience both casual and polished. The menu is creative, with appetizers such as chilled lobster, spicy lamb sausage, smoked salmon, and baked clams. International entrées include crispy fish with Szechwan sauce, veal with sage and shiitake mushrooms, and lamb with sweet roasted pepper salad. Penne with puttanesca sauce is also on the menu, just in case Old Blue Eyes comes for dinner.

Lower Waterford

Hotel/Bed and Breakfast Kissing

RABBIT HILL INN, Lower Waterford
Route 18, (802) 748-5168, (800) 76-BUNNY
Expensive to Very Expensive (MAP)
(Closed April and first two weeks in November)

From Interstate 91 (north or south), take Exit 19 to Interstate 93 south. From Interstate 93 take Exit 1 to Route 18 south. Drive seven miles; the inn is on the right.

In love you long to share the best you have, to create a perfect world, to cherish your time together. Follow your hearts to Rabbit Hill Inn, serenely nestled in a tiny white village on the back roads of rural Vermont. You're welcomed with tea and cookies into the two firelit parlors, to peruse a picture book from the inn's vast and varied collection as you sink into a plush wing chair or love seat. Beyond, a quiet, congenial Irish-style pub promises more potent potables as you settle into a locally crafted Windsor chair or try your hand at darts. But resist lingering too long. Your beautiful bedchamber awaits, and each of the 12 rooms, harbored in two Federal-period buildings, greets you with one-of-a-kind decor. In the grand Music Room, you can play your own antique pump organ, which once sang in the church across the street, or crank up the Victrola and listen to an old love song as you embrace by the fireplace or on the fishnet canopy bed. The Nest Suite has a fireplace, a handsome wrought-iron canopy bed, and a large bathroom with a white wicker vanity and chaise and an immense Jacuzzi for two. A secret door opens to the firelit Loft, with its canopy bed, Shaker clock, and American Country decor. Below the window, the garden bursts with colorful flowers, including some 200 tiger lilies, hundreds of daffodils and narcissus, and chrysanthemums in the fall.

You'll cherish the garden view from the dining room, too, until the sun sets and candlelight directs your gaze inside. Sophisticated country describes the delightful setting, with Hitchcock chairs around wooden tables, Oriental carpets warming wide plank floors, swag draperies over multipaned windows, and, in one of the two intimate rooms, a fireplace to further warm your hearts. Mouthwatering multicourse dinners are artfully prepared and presented. Seasonal specials may include appetizers such as chicken galantine stuffed with pork, raisins, pecans, and oregano, or grilled ravioli of smoked veal sweetbreads, goat cheese, and wild mushrooms served with a Vermont maple-bourbon sauce and apple, pear, and currant compote. Entrées, say the pan-seared beef garnished with a three-onion confit or the sautéed duck with kumquats, prunes, and a Moroccan spiced sauce with pistachio-red pepper couscous, are remarkable. After dinner, walk hand-in-hand to your room to see just what kind of perfect world, at least for one evening, love can create. In the morning, a full, delicious breakfast highlights the beginning of another glorious day together.

Lyndonville

Hotel/Bed and Breakfast Kissing

THE WILDFLOWER INN, Lyndonville
Darling Hill Road, (802) 626-8310, (800) 627-8310
Inexpensive to Moderate

Call for directions.

What is a wildflower but a metaphor for love, blooming somewhere high on a hill or deep in the woods, perhaps never found unless you venture off the safe, well-worn road and stumble upon its unique beauty? This is also true of the Wildflower Inn, a magical farm cresting 500 acres of rolling fields and sugar pine forest in Vermont's little-traveled Northeast Kingdom. Black-eyed susans and daylilies bloom in abundance along the white picket fence by the farmhouse and rooster red barn, and hug the banks of a rocky waterfall that tumbles into the outdoor pool.

The theme continues in the uncluttered Carriage House rooms, each with a border depicting a particular flower. No need for weeding here. The few select antiques, handcrafts, and magazines don't distract from the serene view from the small balconies on the second floor looking over the duck pond (which turns into a skating rink in winter) and back hay fields. Housed in its own cottage, the Grand Suite is aptly named, being a spacious, modern apartment where you could easily live happily ever after. Its full kitchen, featuring rich, locally crafted cherrywood cabinets and table, opens onto a plush living room.

In the master bedroom, open the French doors and step up into your huge whirlpool, then recline upon the four-poster bed.

On certain nights (depending on the season, so call ahead), dinner is served on the enclosed patio of the farmhouse as the sun casts its farewell smile on the wildflowers, Morgan horses grazing in the rolling field, and forested hills on the horizon. A luscious, five-course repast in this unparalleled setting is yours for less than $20 per person. Appetizers may include seafood-stuffed mushrooms or an assortment of pâtés, followed by soup, then salad, then baked stuffed shrimp, stuffed rolled veal with Frangelica sauce, blackened tuna, or pesto linguine. Save room for Black Forest cake, raspberry-white chocolate cheesecake, or a wickedly indulgent hot fudge sundae. Everything is delicious.

◆ **Romantic Note:** Children are welcome here, a blessing for parents who need romance but lack a sitter. Yet the little ones will be totally unobtrusive, if getting away from them is what you seek. They are encouraged (and prefer) to participâté in daily jaunts to fishing holes, nature hikes, and hay or sleigh rides (adults are invited, too). The barn, with its family of rabbits, goats, and, perhaps, a newborn calf, is a treat for everyone. Children dine before 6 p.m. and can play games and watch videos afterward, as romance blooms in the restaurant.

Westmore

Restaurant Kissing

WILLOUGHVALE, Westmore
Route 5A, (802) 525-4123, (800) 541-0588
Inexpensive to Moderate

Follow Route 5A North until you come to the inn on the right, on the shore of Lake Willoughby.

Sometimes the best places to kiss are those far off the beaten path, down a country road that others were in too much of a hurry to explore. Such a place is Willoughvale. The view of the crystalline lake glistening across the road from the restaurant is intoxicating. The decor is simple, with Windsor chairs, hardwood floors, stenciled walls, and little else to clutter and distract from the splendid setting. Menus change daily, but lunch may include chilled blueberry bisque, marinated shrimp, prime rib sandwich, or baked cod. For dinner, which is not served every day, especially in winter, more entrées are added. The airy guest rooms in the main hotel feel as pure as the lake waters, with modern, Shaker-inspired furnishings. Across the street, on the shore, the lake nearly laps at the front door of separate, affectionate (read small but quaint) cottages, each with its own private dock. For all guests, a canoe is provided for pleasant paddles in paradise.

Outdoor Kissing

LAKE WILLOUGHBY BEACH, Westmore
On Route 16, near its intersection with Route 5A.

This quiet body of water doesn't shout with beauty, it whispers, echoing amongst the forested cliffs that climb from its shores to the sky. Lake Willoughby isn't one of Vermont's best-known lakes, but it is one of the most beautiful. On the north shore, a small beach beckons you to picnic. Pause for a spell, enjoying a repast of maple-smoked ham and Vermont sharp cheddar from a local general store, and share the simple serenity of the locale.

Shelburne

Hotel/Bed and Breakfast Kissing

THE INN AT SHELBURNE FARMS, Shelburne
Junction of Bay and Harbor Road
(802) 985-8498 (late May through mid-October)
(802) 985-8686 (mid-October through late May)
Moderate to Very Expensive (inn-EP), Expensive to Unbelievably Expensive (inn-MAP), Expensive (dining), (Open late May to mid-October)

Call for directions.

This is, quite simply, the most magnificent place I've ever seen in which the public can stay the night. Four kisses don't do it justice, but neither would 40. As we drove past the acres of farmland that belong to the estate, we spotted a Victorian palace across a field, with grand turrets and gables towering above a stone foundation. This was just the barn. The mansion, perched on the stunning shoreline of Lake Champlain, is a turn-of-the-century extravaganza, a brick and half-timbered castle of high-peaked gables and 11 chimneys, built in 1899 by William Seward and Lila Vanderbilt Webb.

Today, it looks as though William and Lila never left. Almost all the furnishings are original to the house, and everything has been masterfully restored by the nonprofit Shelburne Farms. Grand fireplaces blaze in all the common rooms, the only source of heat. You could almost get lost in the baronial library, with its 6,000 volumes. Gilded furnishings gleam in the tea room, where its namesake beverage is served in the afternoon along with cookies, breads, and indulgent cakes. You can easily imagine Mr. Seward smoking cigars in the game room, with its huge carved rock hearth, original billiards table, rich redwood paneling, and animal trophies mounted on the wall. The guest rooms are equally stunning, especially those with a lake view. The fireplaces no longer work, however, so you must rely on only your bedcoverings and each other to keep warm. Don't expect modern amenities here. The bathrooms, some shared, are original, too.

If you're not lucky enough to be an overnight guest, you can still come for dinner in the Marble Room, with its black-and-white floor, original silk wall coverings, and candles in sterling silver holders. Menus change daily but always feature local delicacies, many grown or made right on the farm. You may start your meal with potato and leek soup, their famous smoked cheddar, or risotto with pheasant, roasted peppers, and pistachios. Entrées could include Vermont lamb with pinot noir-rosemary sauce, sautéed snapper with thyme sauce and glazed pecans, or a beef fillet served with Maine lobster. It's all delicious, but frankly, peanut butter and jelly would taste like caviar in this setting. Reserve early; the room holds only 13 tables. I promise you will have an unforgettable evening.

Essex Junction

Restaurant Kissing

INN AT ESSEX, Essex Junction   ◆◆◆
70 Essex Way, (802) 878-1100, (800) 727-4295
Inexpensive to Expensive

Call for directions.

For cuisine on the cutting edge, come to this small luxury hotel that serves as a training ground for the New England Culinary Institute. Two dining rooms cater to contrary moods. Butler's Restaurant is posh, with sconces and brass chandeliers illuminating soft pink walls. Rich floral drapes are swagged above sheers, and candles flicker inside hurricane globes on each table. Sink into your high-backed upholstered chairs and indulge in lobster bisque or minted melon gazpacho, then share a spicy scallop appetizer. Grapefruit sorbet cleans your palates for such heavenly entrées as grilled tuna with roasted pepper sauce on black pasta or beef tenderloin with corn and onion timbale and smoked tomato jus. The menu changes daily. For a more casual and less costly affair, the bright, airy Birch Tree Café serves soups, salads, and sandwiches.

In the hotel, 30 of the 97 rooms have wood-burning fireplaces. Most are elegantly appointed with graceful Early American reproduction tables and armoires, plush window treatments, robust green and burgundy upholstery, and neutral walls. The modern baths boast brass fixtures and hairdryers. The less expensive Country Inn rooms aren't as special, with their rougher pine furnishings and obtrusive televisions, but those with a fireplace are invitingly quaint.

◆ **Romantic Warning:** The institute runs a popular catering business, and caters business meetings and weddings held in the conference center adjacent to the inn. In addition, you must pass through major construction on a new highway and retail shops at the entrance to the inn's drive, more of a city than country prelude, but be patient.

Burlington

Hotel/Bed and Breakfast Kissing

RADISSON HOTEL, Burlington
60 Battery Street, (802) 658-6500, (800) 658-4659
Very Inexpensive to Moderate

From Interstate 89, take Exit 14W. Follow Main Street to the lakefront and turn right on Battery Street. The hotel is one and a half blocks up on the right. Validated parking is offered in the garage.

Enter a room on the topmost floor of this city hotel and you will feel as though you've stepped onto the stairway to heaven. Below, Lake Champlain spreads a lavender-blue cloak across the land, its divine expanse held in check only by the cobalt mountains beyond. The setting sun enflames the sky as you sit, mesmerized, watching day turn to dusk then to dark, as the silvery moon rises and city lights wink on. This heavenly panorama raises the Radisson from typical city hotel to sublime kissing spot, but you must get a room with a view. The seventh floor is best; a corner room is spectacular. On this floor, you'll also be part of the Plaza Club. Though slightly more expensive, the price includes complimentary hot hors d'oeuvres, cheese, crudités, and wine in the evening; private cash bar privileges; milk and cookies when you return from dinner; and a generous continental breakfast. All guest rooms enjoy the amenities that only a first-class hotel can provide, including classy contemporary decor, an indoor pool, Jacuzzi and exercise room, a lounge with a weekend comedy club, and a posh restaurant overlooking the lake.

Restaurant Kissing

DEJA VU CAFÉ, Burlington
185 Pearl Street, (802) 864-7917
Moderate

Between Church Street and South Winooski Avenue.

As lively and open-minded as the university professors and students who dine here, Deja Vu isn't afraid to be different. A series of rooms offer a sense of intimacy in this expansive restaurant. In one room, an old brick and timber wall towers to a cathedral ceiling, while etched glass partitions in a coquettish fan motif attempt to restrain lively discourses from overflowing to adjacent tables. On the mezzanine, fringed lamps cast a Victorian glow. In the cozy courtyard, whitewashed walls, black ironwork over the windows, and a splashing fountain lend a Mediterranean air. The menu is equally eclectic, featuring flatbread pizzas, filled crêpes, and bistro specials such as seafood Hunan, pasta Tuscany, and Taos chicken. After indulging in Vermont maple custard or fresh fruit crisp with Ben & Jerry's ice cream, you may just want to see Deja Vu again—that is, if you haven't already.

LEUNIG'S OLD WORLD CAFÉ, Burlington
115 Church Street, (802) 863-3759
Moderate

At the corner of Church and College streets.

You will feel like an American in Paris stepping into this petite corner café. Squeezed along one wall, the marble-topped bar backed by a rococo facade of Roman statuary supports an immense, brass espresso machine. From the white pressed-tin ceiling, crystal chandeliers glint above an old-world street clock with a voluptuous round face and classic black numbers. Old Parisian songs play liltingly, while couples press around small café tables, sipping cappuccinos. The bistro-style fare has a domestic twist, featuring specials such as a baked artichoke and lobster terrine, Brie, quiche, and salad for less than $10. Sandwiches and salads will please the resolute Yankee. Tell your lover to meet you beneath the clock.

SWEETWATERS, Burlington
120 Church Street, (802) 864-9800
Moderate

At the corner of Church and College streets.

Phoenix rises in Vermont at this casual restaurant spiced with a slice of the Southwest. Bask in the glow of the sponged golden walls, highlighted with adobe mission-motif geometric details, an Indian blanket, and a Georgia O'Keeffe-style cow skull. In one dining room, behind cast-iron bars, a mural depicts an impressionistic party, with drunken nude dancers and other zany party goers, including a winged cherub on a pig. The enclosed streetside patio is more sedate, with pink linens and hanging plants; you can dine al fresco there no matter what the weather is like. Sweetwaters is trendy, young, and vibrant; the eclectic menu ranges from a smoked chicken and jalapeño flatbread pizza to bison burgers to hot Thai steak. In the evening it's popular and pulsing, with plenty of hot appetizers to be cooled off with a cocktail.

> *"A kiss is the shortest distance between two."*
> Henny Youngman

NEW HAMPSHIRE

Monadnock Region

Peterborough

Restaurant Kissing

BOILERHOUSE RESTAURANT, Peterborough
Route 202 South, (603) 924-9486
Moderate

In the Noone Falls Mill building, about three quarters of a mile south of the Route 101/Route 202 junction.

Dinner with a view is the specialty of this restaurant tucked inside the converted boilerhouse of an old mill. Ask for a table by the wall of picture windows, where you can dine overlooking the waterfall tumbling and coursing below. The open room counterpoints its historic past with a sleek, contemporary look. Begin your dinner with oysters, escargot, gravlax, scallop stew, or other aphrodisiacal appetizers. Now you're ready for veal sautéed with wild mushrooms, shallots, and thyme, deglazed with cognac, and finished with cream; New Zealand venison sautéed with sun-dried blueberries and cranberries; charbroiled sirloin with Madeira and ginger sauce; and other seasonal delights. Tempting desserts include almond and honey Bavarois with warm sugared apples, lemon and lime cheesecake, and "Death by Chocolate" ice cream. Our only complaint is that the restaurant is open to the downstairs lounge, and sounds of music and billiards tend to drift up to the diners. The lounge, however, is an inviting place for a fun drink, with copper-topped tables reflecting bud vases with bright blooms, flickering candles, and smiling faces.

LATACARTA, Peterborough
6 School Street, (603) 924-6878
Moderate

In the village center, just off Main Street.

Sometimes the best things in life are simple. Such is the case with this truly exceptional restaurant, a rare gem in small-town Peterborough. The decor is understated and serene, with bentwood chairs gathered around white-clothed tables topped with vases of dried flowers. Contemporary artwork and a stunning kimono highlight the rosy walls. The chef is of Japanese descent, esteemed for his Zen-inspired cooking techniques. His "Epicurean collage" combines fresh, natural ingredients and East-meets-West inspiration. Appetizers on the ever-changing menu range from Japanese dumplings to hummous to nachitos. Delectable entrées of beef with a subtle teriyaki sauce, ginger chicken, tempura, and vegetarian creations are excellent.

◆   **Romantic Note:** Classic flicks, e.g. *Casablanca* and *North by Northwest*, are shown in the recently restored, old-fashioned theater next door. Combined with dinner at Latacarta, this makes for one of the area's most romantic evenings. Here's looking at you, kid.

Jaffrey

Hotel/Bed and Breakfast Kissing

THE BENJAMIN PRESCOTT INN, Jaffrey
Route 124 East, (603) 532-6637
Very Inexpensive to Expensive

About two and a half miles east of the town center. Look for the pale yellow Greek Revival home with black shutters and candles in the windows.

All the particulars of a bona fide country inn are here: congenial atmosphere, pleasantly decorated historic home, pastoral location, all presided over by hosts who are friendly yet not clinging. This charming 10-room bed and breakfast is everything a country inn should be minus the posh extras of fireplaces and Jacuzzis. Housed in an 1853 Greek Revival home, it has a country ambience that is clean and uncluttered, but not too contrived nor too casual.

Stunning patchwork quilts highlight several bedrooms. A double wedding ring pattern and matching sham adorn the Early American-style four-poster bed in Phoebe's Room. A calico comforter and accent pillows lie on the brass bed in Susannah's Suite, with its small sitting room and gabled ceiling. The third-floor suite is the most indulgent, with a spacious sitting room that features conveniences such as a wet bar, television, microwave, and refrigerator, plus a private deck overlooking cow pastures, silos, and a cornfield. In the bedroom, a pencil-post bed trimmed with a floral canopy is tucked beneath a high peaked ceiling.

Special touches continue with the morning's repast. You may be pampered with three types of fruit breads or French toast cut in the shape of a maple leaf and served, of course, with pure maple syrup.

Rindge

Outdoor Kissing

CATHEDRAL OF THE PINES, Rindge
Cathedral Road, (603) 899-3300
About one-half mile south of Annett State Park. Follow Route 119 for one mile, to the cathedral on the left side.

Love is intangible, an aura, a feeling that is often more powerful than any material object. All who visit this extraordinary cathedral with the forest as walls and sky as ceiling sense this love, this ethereal magic that fills the soul. The setting, the way the light shafts through the towering pines crowning this hilltop, and the view of Mount Monadnock rising gracefully on the horizon are mesmerizing. Founded with loving devotion as a monument to a son killed in World War II, it's preserved as a memorial of loved ones lost in battle, with plaques and stones added through the years. Multifaith services are held at the outdoor altar among the trees.

The best time to visit may be on a quiet, off-season day. Embrace on this hilltop and feel one with love. When the carillon plays its melodious bells, it's almost like heaven.

◆ **Romantic Note:** Weddings here are unforgettable.

Mason

Restaurant Kissing

PICKITY PLACE, Mason
Nutting Hill Road, (603) 878-1151
Moderate

From Route 101, drive south on Route 31 to the blinking light near Greenville. Turn left onto Adams Hill Road, travel one mile to Nutting Hill Road, and turn right. The restaurant is one mile down, at the end of the road.

Once upon a time, a storybook cottage in a forest inspired an artist who was illustrating the tale of Little Red Riding Hood. This weathered 1786 shingle cottage with red trim and a rooster weathervane was immortalized in a 1948 storybook. You'll even find an exact, life-size rendition of the wolf in Grandma's bed illustration in one room of the petite gift shop. Better yet, two snug rooms have been transformed into intimate luncheon rooms, serving some of the most delicious and sought-after meals in the area. Blue ladder-back chairs are squeezed around white-clothed tables, oil lamps flicker, and drying herbs hang from the walls. The herbs are Pickity Place's strength. Grown in their delightful gardens, they fill a small shop with their scintillating scents and flavor the five-course luncheons. Whole wheat spice bread, pumpkin-curry soup, and sesame salad may start your meal. Chicken turnovers with sage and thyme, butter and herb baked fish, carrots with orange and fennel, and unusual quiches are some of the seasonal delights. Cardamom bars, New England bread pudding, and raspberry cheesecake would make any wolf's mouth water. Take a stroll through the "Please touch the herbs" gardens and visit the three little sheep in back of the cottage for a memory that will live happily ever after.

◆ **Romantic Note:** Reservations are a must at this popular spot way out in the woods. Seatings are at 11:30 a.m., 12:45 p.m., and 2:00 p.m. Call as far in advance as possible.

Outdoor Kissing

MOUNT MONADNOCK, Monadnock State Park   ◆◆◆◖
(603) 532-8862
The park entrance is clearly marked, four miles west of Jaffrey, off Route 124.

The view from the summit of this 3,165-foot mountain stretches forever. On a clear day, you can see all six New England states, particularly spectacular when the hills are aflame with autumn's crimsons and golds. This is the most climbed mountain in the nation, but 30 miles of hiking trails provide some secluded terrain. And the reward for your arduous ascent is unmatched; gaining the bald, rounded peak is akin to standing on a cloud, free from any trees and open to a 360-degree panorama. Not surprisingly, it can be windy and cool up top, so dress accordingly. The average hiker can complete the round trip in about three hours, but why rush? Find a sheltered spot and enjoy a picnic lunch together at this beloved mountain.

Fitzwilliam

Hotel/Bed and Breakfast Kissing

HANNAH DAVIS HOUSE, Fitzwilliam
186 Depot Road (Route 119), (603) 585-3344
Very Inexpensive to Inexpensive

Just beyond the town common, on Route 119.

Country quilts, braided rugs, and footed tubs lend warmth to this 1820 Federal home, a five-room bed and breakfast that revives old-fashioned charm without forsaking today's amenities. In the breakfast room, which opens to a commodious country kitchen, you can banish winter's chill before the Colonial brick hearth, with its mantel clock and dried flower wreath hinting of simpler times. A wood-burning hearth also warms the downstairs suite, with its pumpkin pine woodwork. Upstairs, firelight glows in boldly colored Chauncey's Room, shining on the white iron-and-brass bed. A pencil-post bed crowned with antique crocheted canopy invites nostalgic dreams in the Canopy Room, while a white iron bed fits snugly in cozy Hannah's Room. In the Loft, tucked into the adjacent carriage house, old barn doors highlight one wall, adding a country touch to the comfortable sitting room and mezzanine sleeping area above. An extravagant breakfast completes the country welcome, with granola, fruits, freshly baked breads, stuffed French toast or herbed cheese strata, eggs, bacon, and even green beans to see you through the day.

Marlborough

Hotel/Bed and Breakfast Kissing

THATCHER HILL INN, Marlborough
Thatcher Hill Road, (603) 876-3361
Very Inexpensive to Inexpensive

From Route 101 in Marlborough, turn south on Route 124. Drive about two miles to Thatcher Hill Road and turn right. The inn is the first farmhouse on the right.

This rambling farmhouse and its huge old barn rise from the surrounding fields like visions from the past. Here, you're welcomed with a pleasing blend of old-fashioned and contemporary details. The firelit entryway opens to a comfortable sitting room, where a patchwork quilt highlights the wall and you can play games or watch television. A second parlor provides a haven for quiet reading. A collection of free-standing vintage music boxes is scattered throughout the inn. You'll also find antiques in the seven guest rooms. In one cozy room, you can step onto the private porch overlooking the rustic barn. Another suite boasts a fireplace sitting room. Baths have footed tubs with hand-held showers, plus a touch of today—heated towel racks. Yet even with these modern luxuries, the inn retains its homespun friendliness.

Sunapee Region

New London

Hotel/Bed and Breakfast Kissing

HIDE-AWAY INN, New London   ◗◗◖
Twin Lake Villa Road, (603) 526-4861, (800) 457-0589
Inexpensive

Call for directions.

Built in the 1930s by a poet who wanted to ensconce herself in a tranquil setting to devote time to life's gentler pursuits, this home is a perfect place to spend time away together. In the afternoon, appetizers and wine are served in the parlor, with its wing chairs and swag drapes. Fires in the large fieldstone hearth are reflected on the resplendent Oregon spruce paneling. This supple wood stretches throughout the guest rooms, adding an easy continuity and earthy elegance. Simple furnishings, New England prints, and such considerate touches as bedside reading lamps welcome you with a hospitable embrace. If light amusement is your kind of relaxation, head down to the basement's Pipedream Pub, where darts and other games delight those who like to play at love.

PLEASANT LAKE INN, New London
125 Pleasant Street, (603) 526-6271, (800) 626-4907
Inexpensive

Call for directions.

Across the street from this country inn shimmers its namesake, Pleasant Lake, cloaked in a sylvan setting that seems frozen in time. There are nearby hiking trails, one proclaimed by *Yankee* magazine as a "walk to woo by." In winter, you can skate on the adjacent pond, then return to the brick hearth of the family room, with its spinning wheel and Americana crewelwork juxta-posed awkwardly with the television. The country look prevails in sunny guest rooms, in antique beds with white woven spreads and delicate wall coverings. Some have views of the lake or the rooster red barn on the other side of the inn. Eggs from the innkeepers' chickens are gathered for breakfast, as well as raspberries, blueberries, strawberries, and vegetables in season. The latter are also used for the three-course (about $20 fixed price) dinners served to guests on busier weekends.

Restaurant Kissing

BAYNHAM'S COUNTRY STORE AND CAFÉ, New London
180 Main Street, (603) 526-8070
Inexpensive

From Interstate 89 southbound, take Exit 12; from Interstate 89 northbound, take Exit 11. Follow signs toward New London. The café is near the center of town, on Main Street.

One milkshake and two straws are in order at the nostalgic soda fountain in this upscale country store. If you're in the mood for a light bite, the soups, sandwiches, and baked goods will tempt you to take a break from touring the town. But make no mistake: this is not a recreation of an earthy New England mercantile. Billed as a '90s version of an old-fashioned mom-and-pop shop, it's even more high-toned than that. Some Yankees would shudder at the prices of the unique merchandise imported from around the world, although you can find a few five-and-dime items tucked in amongst extravagances such as the $8,000 cookstove and a purse made from 200-year-old deer hide. Still, where else can you browse through local products while a fire blazes in the hearth? And the café is a fresh new alternative for a spot of tea or specialty coffees.

MILLSTONE RESTAURANT, New London
Newport Road, (603) 526-4201
Moderate

From Interstate 89 southbound, take Exit 12; from Interstate 89 northbound, take Exit 11. Follow signs toward New London; the restaurant is about three miles down, on the left.

Sandy peach walls and oil lamps on white linens add a touch of elegance to this subdued slice of serenity. In the warmer months, ask for a table by the multipaned windows overlooking the colorful back gardens. Throughout the year, watercolors and oils by local artists bring beauty inside the restaurant.

European-inspired seasonal dishes include sautéed chicken liver and smoked salmon appetizers, and such entrées as bluefish in pesto, sole almondine, lamb, and venison. Remember to toast the good time you are sharing as you leave the grind far behind.

PETER CHRISTIAN'S TAVERN, New London   ◆◀
Main Street, (603) 526-4042
Inexpensive

From Interstate 89 southbound, take Exit 12; from Interstate 89 northbound, take Exit 11. Follow signs toward New London. The restaurant is near the center of town, on Main Street.

One of well-heeled New London's favorite restaurants is this upbeat, low-key, old-world tavern. For privacy, ask for one of the high-backed booths, or compromise and settle at the burlwood tables for a draft beer and a hearty pub meal. Nachos, artichoke dip, or a cheese and bread board will take off the edge. Hearty onion soup, beef stew, and creative sandwiches are the tavern's forte, but the menu also features chicken cordon bleu, a hot Italian sausage burrito, seafood and asparagus puff, and quiche.

Sunapee

Hotel/Bed and Breakfast Kissing

SEVEN HEARTHS, Sunapee   ◆◆◆
Old Route 11, (603) 763-5657, (800) 237-2464
Moderate to Expensive

From Interstate 89 southbound, take Exit 12A. Follow Route 11 west for two and a half miles to Sunapee. A road sign will direct you to Seven Hearths.

Come in from a day of skiing, shake the snow from your coat, and settle in for a heartwarming night by the hearth in this 1801 country house. Fireplaces warm five of the 10 guest rooms, a sixth fireplace warms the dining room, and a seventh blazes in the parlor. The parlor also features a baby grand and tufted Victorian settees; hors d'oeuvres are served there in the evening and guests can relax with cocktails from the bar. Oil paintings and rich fabrics set a country cosmopolitan tone in the bedchambers. The Sultan Suite boasts a lovely Oriental carpet, and a forest green paisley spread on the four-poster bed. The firelit Freesia Room, with its brass and porcelain bed, is as full of color as a flower garden. Even the nonfirelit rooms are cheerful and welcoming, with brass, white iron, or carved oak beds and pastel decor.

In the evening, clear glass oil lamps flicker in the dining room, inviting overnight guests and visitors to enjoy upscale cuisine in a low-key setting. Baked escargot en croûte, sautéed chicken livers Dijonnaise, and Burgundy beef and orzo soup are some of the seasonal appetizers. Entrées, made with the freshest ingredients available, may include slow-roasted duck, veal medallions in a white wine sauce, or pork sautéed with apples and brandy. The blueberry bread pudding and winter fruit crumb tart are superb.

Bradford

Hotel/Bed and Breakfast Kissing

THE ROSEWOOD COUNTRY INN, Bradford
Pleasant View Road, (603) 938-5220, (603) 938-5253
Inexpensive to Moderate

Call for directions.

This inn blossoms with understated, delicate romance. In the entryway, stenciled roses trail up a soft gray wall, twirling around a brass candle sconce and up rose-carpeted stairs. To the right, a firelit parlor beckons you in from the cold. A spray of dried flowers hangs above the gas hearth; the carefully chosen furnishings echo the grace of the architecture. A table clothed in florals is tucked inside the Queen Anne turret. In a second common area, the Colonial-inspired tavern room, afternoon tea—strawberry kiwi is their specialty—is served near a cream-colored wood stove.

The softly stylish bedchambers welcome you with details such as ivy-motif stenciling, green paisley spreads, an Oriental carpet on a hardwood floor, or a stack of hat boxes tied with a black lace ribbon. In the Bridal Suite, grapevines intertwine to form a canopy over the pencil-post bed, and a white wicker love seat and table are tucked into the turret. Third-floor rooms are more Colonial in decor, with woven throws, a crocheted lace canopy, primitive portraits, electric candles in the windows, and an antique bedwarmer as a finishing touch. Luscious gourmet breakfasts, served in the firelit country dining room, or on the sunlit porch in warmer weather, will awaken you from your sweet dreams to welcome an even sweeter day together.

Henniker

Hotel/Bed and Breakfast Kissing

COLBY HILL INN, Henniker   ◆◆
The Oaks, (603) 428-3281, (800) 531-0330
Inexpensive to Expensive

Call for directions.

Strap on your skates and glide hand-in-hand over the frozen pond that the innkeepers create each winter. If you grow tired, duck inside the gazebo between the two ancient apple trees that look out over the 1790 farmhouse and its massive old barn. Inside the inn, a wood stove in the parlor thaws cold hands while you enjoy hot cocoa and goodies from the always-full cookie jar. The flintlock and powderhorn above the hearth, the beamed ceiling, and well-used furnishings add to the casual Colonial ambience; the working Victrola is a reminder of the more recent past.

Bedchambers are as easygoing as the inn's friendly pooch, with braided rugs on painted wide-plank floors, rocking chairs, and white iron and brass beds or canopied four-posters. Most rooms have either a double or two twins, to accommodate students and visitors of the nearby college. Some king and queen rooms are warmed by fireplaces. Carriage House rooms are petite but pleasantly decorated with simple, Colonial-inspired detailing.

You can watch the skaters twirl, and the birds flit to and from the feeders hanging from the birch tree, from the picture windows in the dining room. In the evening, candles in hurricane globes and pewter bases lend a nostalgic air to the Colonial restaurant and original tavern. Their uniquely rich chicken stuffed with lobster, leeks, and Boursin cheese is noteworthy; the veal Wellington, pork chop with pineapple-cilantro sauce, Cornish hen, baked stuffed scrod, and bouillabaisse are also excellent. In the morning, a full country breakfast fuels you for a day of skating, skiing, or, in the summer, a refreshing swim in the outdoor pool overlooking New Hampshire's verdant hills.

Restaurant Kissing

DANIEL'S RESTAURANT, Henniker
Main Street, (603) 428-7621
Inexpensive

In the center of town, across the street from the bookstore.

The afternoon sun pours into this bright, casual café, filling it with warm golden light. Cozy wooden tables and chairs are set by windows overlooking the river. You can watch the blue waters tumble by as you enjoy a low-key lunch. Sumptuous soups, salads, and sandwiches such as the Sante Fe BBQ melt, Monte Cristo, and veggie croissant top the menu. Light entrées include quiche, fish and chips, crab cakes, chicken teriyaki, tortellini, turkey burrito, and other internationally inspired dishes that please visitors and local students alike. Homemade cheesecakes and apple crisp can make a day feel sunny even when clouds color the sky gray.

Lakes Region

Wolfeboro

Hotel/Bed and Breakfast Kissing

THE WOLFEBORO INN, Wolfeboro   ❤❤
44 North Main Street, (603) 569-3016, (800) 451-2389
Moderate to Very Expensive

At the corner of Sewall Road and Main Street, in the center of town, on the water side.

Old and new intertwine in this 43-room hotel. Unfortunately, the new includes the busy nearby street and views over the parking lot. But the old is indeed lovely. Sprouted from an 1812 home, the Wolfeboro shares the charm of one of America's oldest summer resort towns, but is fully equipped for today's traveler. A fireplace warms the spacious lobby, where a jigsaw puzzle lends a hint of home to the well-bred sofas and wing chairs. The guest rooms, some dating back to the last century, now look more like those in an upscale hotel, with modern baths, contemporary furnishings, and Americana prints. The Copple Crown Suite, the hotel's prize gem, delights with its four-poster king crowned with a lacy sheer canopy, soaring faceted ceiling, Queen Anne reproductions, and two balconies with partial water views.

The restaurant, which attracts a business crowd at lunch, is in the older arm of the home and still displays some of the original woodwork, set off by tulip candle lamps glowing on each table. In one room, pillars rise to shoulder the crown ceiling. A demicircle of arched windows frames a view of the lake, fronted, unfortunately, by a parking lot. Traditional dishes include Yankee pot roast, chicken piccata, and roast turkey.

Wolfe's Tavern is less formal, more popular with locals, and, in some ways, more intimate, with three cozy, firelit rooms. Pewter steins hang in abundance from the ceiling beams while diners at wooden tables enjoy hearty, reasonably priced pub meals such as fish and chips, hamburgers, and deli sandwiches, served with a frothy mug to toast the best of the old and new together.

Gilford

Outdoor Kissing

ELLACOYA STATE BEACH, Gilford   ◆◀
Route 11, (603) 293-7821
From Interstate 93 north, take Route 3 north, heading toward Laconia. Past Laconia, turn east on Route 11; the beach is four miles down on the left.

Some come to New Hampshire for the foliage in the fall, skiing in winter, and mountain climbing in spring, but in summer one of the best pursuits in the state is a refreshing swim in a cool mountain lake. Ellacoya Beach is a classic, nestled on the southwestern shore of Lake Winnipesaukee, its blue waters ringed with forest and mountains. Bring a picnic to enjoy at a table beneath the birches, particularly during the fall and spring when you will probably be all alone. In summer you will most likely be joined by others escaping the summer heat, not romantic but possibly fun.

Ashland

Hotel/Bed and Breakfast Kissing

THE GLYNN HOUSE INN, Ashland   ◆◆◆
43 Highland Street, (603) 968-3775, (800) 637-9599
Very Inexpensive

Take Exit 24 (Ashland-Holderness) from Interstate 93, and bear right onto Route 3. Drive seven-tenths of a mile into the village of Ashland, and turn left onto Highland Street.

The elegant exterior of this Queen Anne stands in direct contrast to the workingman's town of Ashland. Tiny white lights sparkle like champagne bubbles about the graceful veranda and handsome turret, celebrating the home's splendid restoration. Inside, the atmosphere is both refined and relaxed. A glass of wine greets each guest, sipped, perhaps, in the parlor with its vintage settees and chairs, square piano, marble-crowned table topped with dolls clad in Victorian finery, and soft rose curtains over lace.

One bedchamber has a bed with an antique lace canopy, and a whirlpool tub. The third floor is a private retreat, with a sloped-ceiling sitting room, and a day bed tucked into the turret with windows all around. Special touches, such as flowers in an antique pitcher, carved beds, rich floral draperies, a period armoire, and bowls of potpourri, are found throughout the inn. Private baths are cleverly tucked into guest rooms. One fireplace room has a shower just off the bedroom with an etched glass door that makes it more of a luxury than an inconvenience.

In the morning, a firelit breakfast is served on antique Bavarian china with a silver tea service, mementos of the gracious living of yesteryear for which this house was built.

Restaurant Kissing

THE COMMON MAN RESTAURANT, Ashland
Main Street, (603) 968-7030
Moderate

Take Exit 24 (Ashland-Holderness) from Interstate 93 and bear right onto Route 3 to Ashland. The restaurant is one-half mile down, on the left side.

Every person, regardless of status, will enjoy this down-to-earth restaurant, one of the best-loved dining establishments in the lakes region, if not the state. Like all matters of the heart, it is full of fun, romance, respect, and tender loving care. In the entryway are a paint can weighting the door, boxes full of vintage ads that you can purchase for your collection, and other oddities. The door opens to a low-slung dining room with dried flowers hanging from the beamed ceiling, oil lamps flickering on blue cloths, Colonial tavern chairs, and tufted leather booths. Seafood is the kitchen's specialty, including fresh scrod, crab-stuffed shrimp, and Nantucket pie. Half a dozen steak dishes and traditional chicken entrées round out the menu. Reasonably priced desserts, from their famous white chocolate brownie sundae to Toll House cookie pie, are worth the calorie sacrifice. Afterwards, stop for a nightcap in the upstairs lounge, where you can snuggle around the wood stove or sit down at one of the Chinese checkers or backgammon tables.

Holderness

Hotel/Bed and Breakfast Kissing

THE INN ON GOLDEN POND, Holderness
Route 3, (603) 968-7269
Very Inexpensive to Expensive

Take Exit 24 (Ashland-Holderness) from Interstate 93, and bear right onto Route 3. The hotel is about four miles from the interstate.

A stay at this bed and breakfast is akin to visiting your country cousins: everything is simple and laid-back. Guest rooms are plainly furnished, clean, and uncluttered. In the Porcupine Hollows Suite, a plaid sofa and two reading chairs invite quiet pursuits in the sitting room, while a king-size bed fills the bedroom. Although the third-floor Owl's Nest has a partial dormer ceiling, it feels more spacious than the second-floor rooms and is pleasingly decorated with stenciled drapes and a wall border inspired by an English cottage. In the evening, guests gather by the fire to work on the jigsaw puzzle or relax with a good read. A second sitting room harbors a television. Country blue woodwork and pineapple-motif wall coverings invite you into the breakfast room, where you can enjoy home-baked muffins before heading out to hike through the inn's 50-acre backyard.

THE MANOR ON GOLDEN POND, Holderness
Route 3, (603) 968-3348, (800) 545-2141
Moderate to Expensive (B&B), Expensive to Very Expensive (MAP)

Take Exit 24 (Ashland-Holderness) from Interstate 93 and bear right onto Route 3. The hotel is about four and a half miles from the interstate, on the corner of Route 3 and Shepard Hill Road.

Built in 1903, this grand English-style mansion rests high on a knoll above timeless Squam Lake, the location for the film *On Golden Pond*. The decor is sophisticated but slightly tired, with dated carpeting and worn furniture. General refurbishment seems in order, although several guest rooms boast mesmerizing views of the scenic lake. The Windsor Room is one of the best; you barely need to raise your head from the pillow of your four-poster bed for a panorama of the lake and mountains through picture windows. Several rooms have four-posters, enhanced by old-fashioned baths, velvet wing chairs, or a private Juliet balcony. Rooms in the Lake Wing, on the lower level, are cozier but still nicely decorated with Early American-style furnishings and window seats in bay windows overlooking the lake.

The two dining rooms, sadly, have no view worthy of mention, but are elegantly decked out in draperies swagged over diamond-paned windows, wood-burning hearths, and fresh flowers. European-inspired specialties include escargot, honey-glazed scallops wrapped in bacon, baked Brie en croûte, roast duckling, filet mignon, and pork with a bourbon-mustard glaze. Before you leave, drink in the view of Squam Lake one last time for memories that are truly golden.

Centre Harbor

Hotel/Bed and Breakfast Kissing

RED HILL INN, Centre Harbor
Route 25B, (603) 279-7001
Very Inexpensive to Moderate

Call for directions.

It is the quintessential New Hampshire countryside view: farmhouse, rolling mountains, and sylvan Squam Lake. This scene is framed by the picture windows in the firelit parlor of this mansion crowning Overlook Hill. Built in 1904, the home is showing its age and needs updating, yet it still offers a comforting (albeit weary) welcome for travelers seeking a quiet getaway. Half of the 10 rooms in the main inn are warmed by hearths or Franklin fireplaces. The firelit Osceola Suite is spacious, with a carved wood bed, old-fashioned bath, enclosed porch, and balcony with a partial lake view. Third-floor bedchambers are cozy, with more of a farmhouse feel and exceptionally tiny baths tucked into former closets, but several enjoy splendid views. In some guest rooms, you'll find antique typewriters and desks for composing your own inspired love story of the lakes region. Crackling fires and flickering candles glow in the dining rooms, where tempting but inconsistent continental cuisine is served, an inviting alternative for those who don't wish to venture out on a stormy night.

◆ **Romantic Note:** When snow blankets the land in white, Red Hill Inn offers nine miles of trails and complete ski rental packages.

Moultonboro

Hotel/Bed and Breakfast Kissing

OLDE ORCHARD INN, Moultonboro
Lee Road, (603) 476-5004
Very Inexpensive

From Route 109, coming from Wolfeboro, turn left onto Lee Road (look for the sign for the Woodshed Restaurant). The inn is on the left, after the restaurant.

Surrounded by 12 acres of mostly fruit trees, plus a pond and a gurgling stream, this inn is in quiet country, where two favorite pursuits are gazing out the window at autumn's crimsons and golds, and gliding through the snow on cross-country skis. The inn is simple inside as well as outside, with a homey firelit living room and a second sitting room with television and VCR. The downstairs Gray Room is the most special bedroom, with a hearth, stenciled bedspread, and an Oriental rug on the hardwood floor. In the four upstairs guest rooms, touches such as a patchwork quilt, embroidered bedspread, or twig wreath add rural charm. Not surprisingly, apples figure prominently in the hearty breakfast, in their home-made applesauce and apple cake. Be sure to try a bite.

Restaurant Kissing

THE WOODSHED RESTAURANT, Moultonboro
Lee's Mill Road, (603) 476-2311
Moderate

From Route 109, coming from Wolfeboro, turn left onto Lee Road (look for the sign for the Woodshed Restaurant). The restaurant is one-half mile down on the corner of Lee and Lee's Mill roads.

An authentically restored 1860s farmhouse and barn are home for this expansive restaurant. The porch room, one of several, offers you a perfect perspective on the setting sun, as you enjoy American specialties in a quintessential New England setting. In the evening, the interior of the massive barn is transformed into one of the region's most romantic dinner houses. Candles flicker in brass-based glass globes, sparkling points of light amidst soaring post-and-beam architecture, enhanced by the rustic wooden walls, old wagon wheels, and vintage farm artifacts. A seat on the mezzanine provides an owl's-eye view of it all. In the smaller farmhouse rooms, baskets hang from rafters and pewter sconces highlight rough wooden walls. Traditional seafood and beef dishes highlight the menu, including their signature prime rib, lobster, and king crab. Denver chocolate pudding, pecan pie, and hot fudge sundaes are some of the decadent desserts.

◆   **Romantic Alternative:** If Mediterranean dining suits your fancy, **THE SWEETWATER INN,** Route 25, (603) 476-5079, (Moderate), is Moultonboro's other recommended restaurant. The ambience is not as special, but the oil lamps, Colonial-motif chandeliers, and hanging plants in the two large dining rooms set a pleasant stage for pasta, *pollo*, and paella.

Outdoor Kissing

ABENAKI TOWER, near Moultonboro
Route 109
About one mile south of the Route 109A junction, between Wolfeboro and Moultonboro.

An old-fashioned Sunday drive through the forests and along the shore of Lake Winnipesaukee can be a passionate pursuit in New Hampshire. If you're following this scenic route, keep a sharp eye out for the pull-off to Abenaki Tower. A short uphill hike brings you to an unexpected wooden tower rising from a bald patch in the woods. Climb the stairs and you'll be rewarded with a splendid overall view of the lakes region. Sunshine sparkles on mirrors of water set in verdant forest, and green mountains challenge the horizon. No wonder couples have been kissing here for years. It's up to you to carry on the tradition.

Center Sandwich

Hotel/Bed and Breakfast Kissing

THE CORNER HOUSE INN, Center Sandwich
Main Street, (603) 284-6219
Very Inexpensive (inn), Moderate (dining)

At the intersection of Routes 109 and 113.

Snowflakes swirled around the tiny white village, its steeple churches and century-old homes more perfect than any postcard. It was the first snowfall of winter, a giddy celebration of the birth of a new season, made even more delightful in this 1849 inn. Duck inside and you can warm rosy cheeks by the fire in the parlor, with its country plaid sofa, rocking chair, and well-worn, tavern-style coffee table. Local artwork—unusual sculptures and patchwork paintings—overflows into the series of intimate dining rooms. Oil lamps on white over burgundy linens, braided rugs on wide plank floors, bay windows with ruffled curtains, and a marble hearth in one room set the stage for loving nostalgia. The much-praised meals deserve their accolades, especially the beautifully prepared lobster and mushroom bisque, roast raspberry duckling, sirloin steaks, filet mignon, fresh salmon, pastas, and their popular chicken and veal Oscars with lobster, broccoli, and béarnaise sauce.

In operation as an inn for more than 100 years, the Corner House offers upstairs guest rooms that are cozy and old-fashioned. One has a private bath; three more share one bath. Each is decorated in country style, with such details as patchwork quilts, dainty floral wall coverings, even a spinning wheel. A hearty and mouthwatering breakfast will be sure to warm your hearts for a day of play in the snow.

◆ **Romantic Note:** On Thursday evenings in the cooler months, the inn presents old-fashioned New England storytellers. Dinner and stories cost about $10 per person. This is not a typo: it really does cost $10, it is a full dinner including wine and dessert, and the food is great. If you don't believe me, call them and check for yourself. Be sure to reserve ahead.

Tamworth

Hotel/Bed and Breakfast Kissing

THE TAMWORTH INN, Tamworth   ◆◆◀
Main Street, (603) 323-7721
Inexpensive to Expensive (B&B), Moderate to Expensive (MAP),
Moderate (dining)

From Route 16 north, take Route 113 west toward Tamworth. The inn is in the center of town, across from the Barnstormers Playhouse.

This multigabled hotel built in 1833 will easily take you back to yesteryear without denying you the amenities of today. Set in a petite hamlet, its tiny Main Street punctuated with a steepled church, old-fashioned theater, and this delightful village inn, the Tamworth strives to preserve its country heritage and succeeds. In the guest rooms, furnishings such as a bentwood rocker, iron-and-brass bed, patchwork quilt, eyelet canopy, or white wicker accents all add to the simple country feel. In the parlor, snuggle by the fireplace, with its Wedgwood blue hearth topped by a Federal-period dome mirror.

In the main restaurant, Lincrusta-style wall coverings, calico overlays and curtains, multipaned windows, and a spinning wheel add rustic panache. A wood stove warms the smaller dining room. Clam chowder, smoked trout, and provolone and pesto terrine whet your appetite for their specialties—classic beef Stroganoff, chicken with crabmeat stuffing, and shrimp and scallops topped with dill sauce. After dinner, take time for an old-fashioned "constitutional" down Main Street, just as couples did decades ago.

Snowville

Hotel/Bed and Breakfast Kissing

SNOWVILLAGE INN, Snowville   ◆◆◆
Stuart Mountain Road, (603) 447-2818, (800) 447-4345
Moderate to Expensive (B&B), Expensive (MAP)

Call for directions.

As the name implies, the best season at this picture-postcard farm is winter, when snow dusts the high-peaked gables of the rooster red farmhouse and cross-country ski trails emanate from the inn like rays from the sun. Or is it spring, when flowers splash a border of color along the grassy lawn? In summer, you can be refreshed in clear mountain streams. In autumn, the view from the inn's porch is mesmerizing, with forests resplendent in golds and crimsons and the magnificent Presidential mountain range filling the horizon. In the main section, the Robert Frost Room shares this view, visible from the comfort of your pillow, and you may be moved to poetry. Throughout the inn, a comfortable country feel prevails. In the Chimney House, each room is warmed by a fireplace. The lofty Carriage Barn, with a total of eight rooms, is Swiss-inspired, with plenty of knotty pine, bold stenciling, and beamed ceilings (two of these have absolutely no head room and feel somewhat cramped if you stand over five foot five).

The Swiss influence continues in the brightly hued, heart-motif stenciling in the dining room, heated by a wood stove. The Austrian innkeeper/chef is well known for her entrées, but only one is offered each evening. Favorites include veal piccata, pork Dijon, wiener schnitzel, and Viennese beef tenderloin. Dinner comes with soup, their famous homebaked breads, and desserts such as Mississippi mud pie and Schwarzwalder Kirschtorte. After dinner, or après ski, the parlor is a relaxing place for a quiet evening of old-fashioned pursuits, with its comfortable, overstuffed sofas by the hearth, rough-hewn beamed ceiling, window seat, and bookshelves. In the morning, a full country breakfast will keep you warm throughout the day, no matter what the season.

◆   **Romantic Note:** On certain weekends, the inn offers llama hikes to the top of the adjacent mountain. Gourmet picnic lunches are served on china with linen napkins and come complete with champagne and a spectacular view.

Outdoor Kissing

CRYSTAL LAKE, near Snowville
Route 153
From Conway, head south on Route 153. The lake is at the corner of Route 153 and the Snowville turnoff.

Pack a picnic lunch and take a drive through the country to reach this glorious New England scene. Picnic tables are tucked along one end of aptly named Crystal Lake. On the distant shore, a tiny white village complete with steepled church gleams in the sunshine, almost too precious to be real. This is the place to forget about the distractions of today and spend time simply with each other in the quiet outdoors.

White Mountains

North Conway

Hotel/Bed and Breakfast Kissing

STONEHURST MANOR, North Conway
Main Street (Route 16), (603) 356-3271, (800) 525-9100
Moderate to Expensive (MAP), Inexpensive to Moderate (EP)

Call for directions.

At the turn of the century, horses and carriages brought honored guests to this English-style country manor on a hill, where they were entertained in grand style befitting these stately surroundings. Today, the hotel retains its air of dignity, but one can't help noticing a wrinkle or two in the proud facade. The parlor is still resplendent, its rich oak paneling glowing with a light of its own. The intricate leaded windows and immense wood-burning hearth make it even more splendid. Upstairs, seven of the guest rooms have fireplaces. Your room might feature a king-size four-poster, Early American reproduction furnishings, and stained glass accent windows. Sadly, it may also have a tacky metal wardrobe or a torn rattan porch table. Overall, the feel is that of a grand old resort nestled in the midst of New Hampshire's beloved White Mountains.

Off the foyer, a series of dining rooms, each one different in decor and ambience, steps down like garden terraces. In one, light-colored bentwood chairs set the mood, while another is reminiscent of a formal garden. A brick patio forms the third dining room, and in the fourth and lowest room, a deep green carpet echoes the lush colors outside its two walls of windows. Wood-fired pizza is a specialty, and won't bust a budget. More formal entrées include chicken and cashew stir-fry, veal Oscar, and soft-shell crab. In winter, cross-country ski trails leave from the inn's door; in summer, the outdoor pool offers refreshing swims.

WYATT HOUSE COUNTRY INN, North Conway
Main Street (Route 16), (603) 356-7977, (800) 527-7978
Very Inexpensive to Inexpensive

On Route 16, north of the village center. One-half mile north of the traffic light and the Carroll Reed shop.

Flounces and frills occupy every room of this fine Victorian inn. You will be greeted with a sherry or cookies and tea in the afternoon. Settle by the corner hearth in the parlor, with its billowing lace curtains, balloon valances, floral sofa, and collection of old photos. On the mantel is a fine crocheted piece, one of many found throughout the inn. In the six bedchambers, piles of pillows, a ruffled balloon half-tester, floral flounces above headboards, dried flower arrangements, and select knickknacks—a peacock fan or an antique bridal book—add a soft, feminine flair. A faceted ceiling crowns the Rose Room, with its private balcony overlooking a splendid view of the Saco River and Saco Mountain. Breakfast is served by candlelight, using Wedgwood china and Irish lace.

Jackson

Untouched by Conway's outlet shopping bonanza, Jackson is a picture-postcard New England town. To reach it, drive across the covered bridge, known locally as the "kissing" bridge (when you see it, you'll know why). You'll come upon a small town centered around a spacious green with a splashing mountain river flowing by—a perfect scene whether it's blanketed in snow or verdant in spring.

Hotel/Bed and Breakfast Kissing

CHRISTMAS FARM INN, Jackson
Route 16B, (603) 383-4313, (800) HI-ELVES
Expensive to Very Expensive (MAP)

After crossing the covered bridge from Route 16 into Jackson Village, drive through the village and head uphill on Route 16B toward the Black Mountain ski area. The inn is on the right.

Not surprisingly, kids are invited here too, but with a spread of half a dozen buildings, you're sure to find a room right for you. The 1786 Main Inn harbors 10 guest rooms, named appropriately after Santa's reindeer. Half-poster beds, wing chairs, and Jacuzzis highlight the better rooms. Laura Ashley prints figure prominently in the adjacent 1777 Salt Box, where one room is appointed with a pencil-post bed and an immense whirlpool with dimmer lights above. A game room with bumper pool, foosball, Ping-Pong, and sauna invites relaxing in the Barn, and the rustic rooms upstairs are geared toward families. The Log Cabin is more private, with knotty pine paneling and a combination living room/bedroom. All accommodations are homespun and understated, places to put your feet up.

On cold winter nights, a fire blazes in the living room. You can add pieces to the jigsaw puzzle in the adjacent television room. In the large restaurant, high-backed booths provide the most privacy as you enjoy such dishes as scampi, broiled scallops Rockefeller, veal Dijon, and grilled pepper steak. Eat hearty. The snow awaits you in the morning. The now-famous Jackson Ski Touring Foundation was formed here some two decades ago. A special inn trail will connect you to the village and the 145-kilometer trail system.

INN AT JACKSON, Jackson
Thorn Hill Road, (603) 383-4321, (800) 289-8600
Inexpensive

After crossing the covered bridge from Route 16 into Jackson Village, drive one-quarter mile, then turn right onto Thorn Hill Road. The inn is immediately on the right, on the corner of Thorn Hill Road and Main Street.

This classic red-shingled, black-shuttered home offers large, gracious guest rooms and simple homespun decor. The one-lip rating is due to its popularity with families who enjoy this place, not to mention that the innkeepers have a young child. However, this is one of the few places you can experience the charm of a bed-and-breakfast inn even if you can't get a sitter for the weekend, because kids are welcome. After a day of skiing, thaw by the fire in the wood-paneled living room. Cheerful country details are found throughout: a ruffle-edged quilted bedspread, stenciled rocker with calico chairpad, silk flower bouquet. Rooms in the newer wing, all with four-poster beds and modern baths, rank highest in romance. In the morning, a full breakfast is served by the fire in the breakfast room, a warm start to even the coldest winter day.

THE INN AT THORN HILL, Jackson
Thorn Hill Road, (603) 383-4242, (800) 289-8990
Expensive to Very Expensive (MAP), Moderate to Expensive (B&B)

After crossing the covered bridge from Route 16 into Jackson Village, drive one-quarter mile, then turn right onto Thorn Hill Road. The inn is up the hill on the right.

The drawing room of this 1895 inn is like a museum period room depicting the Victorian era. A graceful soapstone wood stove sits at one end, a Steinway baby grand dominates the other. In between, two mannequins in beaded, lace-trimmed vintage dresses almost come to life amidst the red velvet settees and other fine antiques. The turn-of-the-century motif continues in the 10 upstairs guest rooms. Antique bureaus, canopy beds, Americana prints, fringed lamps, marble vanities, and cutwork accent pillows are some of the highlights, but the ambience is more relaxed than refined. The bedchambers aren't so precious that you're afraid to put your suitcase down.

A fire crackles and oil lamps flicker in the restaurant during dinner, glowing on the Currier and Ives-inspired china. Seasonal entrées include lobster pie, polenta lasagne, and salmon in a cornmeal crust with honey mustard and dill sauce. At breakfast, the spicy chicken hash will warm the chilliest dawn.

NESTLENOOK FARM, Jackson
Dinsmore Road, (603) 383-9443
Expensive to Unbelievably Expensive

Turn right onto Dinsmore Road immediately after crossing the covered bridge into Jackson Village. The inn is at the end of the lane.

A storybook picture comes to life at this extraordinary Victorian farm, hands down the best place to kiss in New Hampshire. Trundle down the lane and over a small knoll to find a magical stage set of resplendent Victoriana, complete with curving brick walkways, snow white bridges arching over a river, a stunning gingerbread-covered house, and an inspiring mountain backdrop. Enter from the wraparound veranda into perfection. Masterfully carved woodwork, shimmering stained glass, and even the vintage steam radiators are works of beauty, their intricate swirls and patterns meticulously painted to coordinate with each room's colors. The aroma of freshly baked cookies draws you into the guest kitchen, where you can choose complimentary juice or tea. In the early evening, wine, cheese, and fruit are presented in the parlor dating from the 1700s, near a fire blazing in the river rock hearth.

Each of the seven guest rooms feels intimate. Some contain hand-carved canopy beds, French doors opening onto a balcony overlooking the Currier and Ives scenery, and immense whirlpool tubs. Every detail adds to the rich, indulgent ambience, from an antique mantel clock to a stained glass lamp to an electrified wood stove that adds warmth. In the basement recreation room, you'll find a billiards table and a big-screen TV with video disk player, surround sound, and a variety of movies. As the sun begins a new day in this wonderland, you'll be pampered with a gourmet breakfast served in the firelit breakfast room on Royal Worcester china. Just how special is it? In the evening, a cover is placed over the graceful Victorian birdcage and its family of beautiful finches so that they can be uncovered at dawn to sing through your breakfast.

◆   **Romantic Note:** Horse-drawn sleigh and trolley rides, ice skating, a heated outdoor pool, massages, and trout fishing in the farm's own Emerald Lake are just a few amenities you can enjoy as a guest here.

Restaurant Kissing

WILDCAT INN and TAVERN, Jackson
Route 16A, (603) 383-4245
Expensive

In the center of Jackson Village, across the street from the ski touring center.

This inviting restaurant, considered the best in town by visitors and locals alike, serves top-notch meals in a low-key setting. In the summer, diners head to the candlelit, umbrella-topped tables in the back garden, with its brick walkways and bed of lilies. Crabmeat in artichoke hearts, shrimp in bacon, asparagus with prosciutto, and provolone wrapped in puff pastry and topped with marinara sauce are some of the seasonal appetizers. Eclectic entrées include quiche, lobster fettuccine, chicken martini, lasagne, Oriental duck stir-fry, and baked scallops. On chilly winter nights, round out your meal with a specialty coffee for that cold walk or drive home.

Outdoor Kissing

NESTLENOOK FARM SLEIGH RIDES
AND ICE SKATING, Jackson
Dinsmore Road, (603) 383-9443
Inexpensive

Turn right onto Dinsmore Road immediately after crossing the covered bridge into Jackson Village. The inn is at the end of the lane.

If you've ever dreamed of jumping into the perfect winter scene, this storybook farm will make your fantasy come true. Skaters glide along the river, beneath arched white bridges and around tiny islands, overlooked by a Victorian gingerbread house and ring of mountains. If you're cold, head for the Victorian gazebo and sip hot cocoa by the fireplace, or warm cold hands by the bonfire blazing on an island. Horse-drawn sleighs course merrily through the grounds, coasting over the bridges, through the woods, along the river, and past the imported deer, which you're invited to feed from your palm.

North Woodstock

Hotel/Bed and Breakfast Kissing

WOODSTOCK INN, North Woodstock   ◆◆◆
80 Main Street (Route 3), (603) 745-3951, (800) 321-3985
Very Inexpensive to Expensive (B&B), Moderate (dining)

In the village center, near the intersection of Routes 3 and 112.

Candles flicker on the tables, brushing the rosy cheeks of daytime skiers, now dressed in their evening finery, with a hint of gold as the snow falls silently in the night. The subtle scent of fresh flowers, a toast with green-stemmed glasses, a bounty of hanging plants, the morning glory china, and garden green table cloths—all add a welcome touch of romance after a day on the slopes. On this enclosed porch of a century-old Victorian home, a friendly wait staff begins your meal with artichoke dip, followed by such appetizers as frog legs, seviche, or wild mushrooms with smoked salmon and Havarti-dill cheese in puff pastry with red pepper coulis. Classic entrées include four versions of the inn's famous duckling, half a dozen veal specialties, beef Wellington, lobster diavolo, and more. Many dishes are flamed tableside. The sorbet is homemade; try the raspberry-peach flavor to cleanse your palate.

Upstairs, charmingly decorated guest rooms set the stage with antique brass or white iron beds. In the tradition of old-fashioned bed and breakfasts, all six rooms share baths (not romantic, but worth noting). More modern accommodations are available across the street in the Riverside building; these smaller, unpretentious rooms all have private baths, plus amenities such as a step-up, four-poster, or white wicker bed; sitting area with television; or a pile of pillows to sink into. Newly added whirlpools enhance the inn's best rooms, one with a fireplace. After skiing, the outdoor Jacuzzi reinvigorates tired muscles. In summer, a riverside deck is perfect for sunning. Breakfast, served in the dining room, is an extravaganza, with 15 types of omelets, half a dozen styles of pancake, crêpes, gourmet egg dishes, waffles, lox and bagels—just about any kind of breakfast food you can imagine.

◆ **Romantic Note:** The boisterous and cheerful lounge, tucked into the rear of the inn, is a fun place for a casual meal. Built as a train station in the late 1800s and particularly busy during the ski-train days of the '30s, it bustles with the hearty spirit of yesteryear. The 14-page menu offers Mexican specialties, sandwiches, salads, pastas, seafood, stir-fry, and an amazing array of potent potables, ice cream drinks, and coffees.

Franconia

Hotel/Bed and Breakfast Kissing

BUNGAY JAR, Franconia
Easton Valley Road (Route 116), (603) 823-7775
Very Inexpensive to Moderate

From Interstate 93, take Exit 38 and head south on Route 116 for five and a half miles. The inn is on the left, about 200 yards beyond Sugar Hill Road.

Shades of the 1960s survive in this hobbit of a six-room inn, which may feel a little confining until you look out the back windows to an eye-stretching view of the woodlands and mountains, particularly spectacular during fall. Peer through the telescope or watch the birds fit between the many feeders. Inside the converted 18th-century barn, the decor is country bordering on funky. Old farm tools hang from the barn-wood wall, shelves are crowded with books, and dried flowers dangle from the rafters in the parlor. Two rooms share a bath on the first floor. Two rooms on the second floor have their own private baths and details that include a pencil-post ruffled canopy bed, stained glass lamp, private balcony, pedestal sink, and patchwork quilts. Climb the hand-hewn stairs to the attic of a third floor, where skylights frame the stars above the bed in one room, above the shower in another. In the morning, after a breakfast with a view, you're welcome to explore the woodland paths near the inn.

FRANCONIA INN, Franconia
1300 Easton Valley Road (Route 116), (603) 823-5542
Inexpensive to Moderate (B&B), Very Inexpensive to Moderate (EP), Expensive (MAP)

From Interstate 93, take Exit 38 (Franconia/Sugar Hill) and turn left off the exit. Cross the road to Route 116. The inn is two miles up, on the right.

All year round, the Franconia Inn's focus is on activity. In the warmer months, gliders lift off for flights above the hills from the grassy landing strip across the street. Horseback riding, biking, tennis, swimming in the heated outdoor pool, fishing a trout stream, playing croquet, or just plain lazing about fills summer afternoons. In winter there's cross-country skiing, ice skating, sleigh rides, and sledding for the kids. Families find plenty to do here, but those seeking a getaway for two will find seclusion on the wooded trails and in the relaxing suites.

Built in 1934, the hotel can't hide its age, but face-lifts have brightened up all 35 guest rooms. Third-floor rooms offer down-to-earth warmth, with knotty pine paneling, more modern baths, and a few floral half-canopy beds. The spacious Inn Suite is their premier accommodation, with a wood stove, four-poster bed, unobtrusive kitchenette, and back porch overlooking the meadows and hills. In the dining room, white columns shoulder a faceted ceiling, while elegant candles, stemware, and linens add a refined touch. The continental menu includes crowd-pleasers such as veal cordon bleu, chicken Florentine, and steak Diane.

Outdoor Kissing

FRANCONIA NOTCH PARKWAY   ❂❂❮
Route 3 and Route 93, (603) 823-5563 (winter),
(603) 745-8391 (summer)

A scenic drive along Routes 3 and 93 between North Woodstock and Franconia.

Generations of native New Englanders and tourists have come in their carriages and automobiles to ogle this sylvan scenery. The **GREAT STONE FACE**, a natural profile of a man high on the crest of a mountain, was immortalized by Nathaniel Hawthorne and Daniel Webster, and is perhaps the best-known attraction on this drive. But more romantic diversions can be pursued while hiking along a wooded trail to a hidden stream or biking the paved path that winds through the forest. Lovers of adventure will enjoy **THE FLUME** ($6 fee charged, open May to October), reached by boardwalks and stairways clinging to the sides of an 800-foot-long, 20-foot-wide natural gorge. Rock walls tower eight stories above you; water thunders down falls and through the chasm below your feet. For an easy way up to a spectacular view, the **CANNON MOUNTAIN AERIAL TRAMWAY** ($8 fee charged, open Memorial Day through late October) ascends more than 2,022 vertical feet in five minutes, taking you to a place where eagles soar, where only your love for each other could take you before.

Sugar Hill

Hotel/Bed and Breakfast Kissing

FOXGLOVE, A COUNTRY INN, Sugar Hill
Route 117, at Lover's Lane, (603) 823-8840
Inexpensive to Moderate

From Interstate 93, take Exit 38 and travel about two and a half miles to Sugar Hill. From Interstate 91, take Exit 17 and head east on Route 302 to Route 117, where you will find the inn.

This newly opened inn is refreshingly cosmopolitan in decor, yet small enough to fall under the heading of quaint. A wood-burning fireplace warms the living room, with its swagged draperies, soft sea-green sofas, tapestry armchairs, and coffee table crafted from glass atop an Oriental urn. One guest room is right out of *Metropolitan Home*, with a leopard-look carpet, black-and-gray-striped wall coverings, and gold-trimmed black chair. The room serves as a sitting room by day, but the sofa converts to a bed at night. Other rooms are more traditional; the Paisley Room showcases a white lacquered Jenny Lind bed atop a sky blue floor. Special touches, such as a stack of feminine hat boxes tied with a satin ribbon, add panache. In the morning, guests gather around the glass table in the breakfast room for a repast of French toast, herbed eggs, locally smoked bacon, and other delectables. The meal is served under the apple tree in warmer months, inspiring couples to take a short stroll through the inn's backyard garden and woods.

MAINE

Maine Coast

York Harbor

After crossing the bridge from New Hampshire, stay on Interstate 95 North. (Note: This is a service road that leads to the Maine Turnpike.) Take Exit 4, "Yorks/Ogunquit," immediately *before* the York tollbooth. Bear right off the exit to the first set of lights, turn right onto Route 1 South, then left at the first set of lights onto York Street/Route 1A. Follow signs to York Harbor.

Hotel/Bed and Breakfast Kissing

YORK HARBOR INN, York Harbor
Route 1A, (207) 363-5119, (800) 343-3869
Moderate to Expensive

From the intersection of Route 1 and York Street/Route 1A, go exactly three miles (through York Village) to the inn, which is on the left, opposite the harbor.

A century ago this was a roadside café along the trolley line. Then it became a restaurant and tea room. Today, the 32-room York Harbor Inn is a gracious year-round haven for guests who want to sample southern Maine ambience or simply gaze at the boats in York Harbor. I like both options.

The heart of the inn is a fisherman's cabin built in 1637, now a cozy "gathering room" with a floor-to-ceiling fieldstone fireplace, hand-hewn beams, and comfy sofas for reading. The guest rooms vary in size and all but five have private bathrooms; two have working fireplaces. Reserve early if you want the popular and spacious Honeymoon Suite, complete with Jacuzzi.

There's a wonderful feeling at this authentic country inn, with its warren of rooms, small-paned windows, and irregular roof line. The bedrooms reflect a touch of Victoriana in the floral wallpaper, chenille bedspreads, marble-topped dressers, and dormer ceilings. Hearty dinners are elegantly served in five intimate dining rooms; all offer views of the ocean through lace curtains. The beat goes on each evening in the lower-level Wine Cellar Pub-cum-piano bar.

Mystery murder nights and cabaret sing-alongs throughout the year verify that there's more to Maine than an August sojourn. The York Harbor Inn is a great place to discover that, together.

Ogunquit

After crossing the Piscataqua River bridge from New Hampshire, stay on Interstate 95 North. (Note: This is a service road that leads to the Maine Turnpike.) Take Exit 4, "Yorks/Ogunquit," immediately *before* the York toll-booth. Bear right off the exit ramp to the first set of lights, turn left, and follow Route 1 North for six miles to the intersection of Shore Road, Beach Street, and Route 1. This is Ogunquit center.

Hotel/Bed and Breakfast Kissing

THE DUNES, Ogunquit   ◆◆
Route 1, (207) 646-2612
Inexpensive (Open mid-May through Columbus Day)

Drive north three-quarters of a mile from the intersection of Route 1, Shore Road, and Beach Street. The Dunes' driveway is on the right.

What could be more romantic than white clapboard cottages with green shutters and petunia-stocked window boxes, surrounded by picket fences and set on 12 grassy acres just yards from the Atlantic Ocean? I found nothing else like the Dunes in southern Maine.

Granted, it's not ostentatious, but neither are the prices. And the entrance driveway off Route 1 gives no clue to the appeal of this lovers' hideaway. For those who appreciate privacy, crisp sea breezes, and old-fashioned charm, these 19 housekeeping cottages are really quite special.

Most have screened-in porches with a million-dollar view of sand dunes and beach. Knotty pine paneling, brick fireplaces, and braided rugs dominate the simple decor. Cottage 17 is particularly alluring because of its scintillating view.

The village trolley stops hourly to whisk you around town; rowboats are available for exploring the tidal inlets along the Ogunquit River. There's also a pool, shuffleboard court, and croquet grounds.

Most of the Dunes' bookings come from returning guests. That alone should convince you that its rustic allure casts a magic spell.

HARTWELL HOUSE, Ogunquit
118 Shore Road, (207) 646-7210, (800) 235-8883
Moderate to Expensive

Turn right onto Shore Road from Route 1 North and go about three-quarters of a mile. The inn office is on the right.

This wonderful inn is guaranteed to fulfill your romantic requirements. The innkeepers spared no expense to furnish 16 luxurious rooms and suites in mellow fruitwoods, vibrant chintzes, and Florida-style pastels. It all positively glistens with cleanliness, from the sparkling Palladian windows in the spacious solarium to the antique harvest table in the dining room.

Special touches are *de rigueur*. Complimentary Gilcrist & Soames herbal soaps and lotions are furnished in the elegant private bathrooms. Afternoon tea is served every day at 4:30p.m. Secluded balconies and patios allow intimate chats. There's even a flower-banked backyard where the two of you can sun the afternoon away.

A full gourmet breakfast is served on the side porch in warm weather. Leave your diet at home and splurge on home-baked muffins, fruit crêpes, or shrimp in puff pastry.

Booking a room at the Hartwell House means you're near all the good stuff to discover in Ogunquit, such as antique shops, craft fairs, and windjammer cruises. Amazingly, even though the inn is situated on the busy road leading to Perkins Cove, that rush of traffic fades into oblivion once you cross the threshold. Blissfully, it's open year-round for amorous adventures.

THE TRELLIS HOUSE, Ogunquit
2 Beachmere Place, (207) 646-7909
Moderate

Turn right onto Shore Road from Route 1. Go four-tenths of a mile and turn left on Beachmere Place.

The art galleries and picturesque fishing boats of fabled Perkins Cove are just a few minutes' trolley ride away. The shops of Ogunquit Village wait right around the corner. But the cozy little Trellis House, tucked away on a peaceful side lane off Shore Road, offers overnighters more than convenient location.

Children are not allowed, which makes for uninterrupted tete-a-tetes on the ambling screened-in porch. Two private beaches are within easy strolling distance for sunrise dips. And none of the seven guest rooms has a phone or television to distract your romantic inclinations.

Each guest room has an immaculate private bath, a queen- or double-size bed, and enough decorative collectibles gracing the walls and maple dressers to keep you captivated for hours. The atmosphere here works like a charm, because the Trellis House doesn't advertise, yet reservations are a must year-round.

A light summer breakfast of muffins and fruit is served in the country kitchen. The innkeeper stokes up more caloric fare during the winter and invites guests to keep their champagne in the refrigerator.

This is a nice, private spot for a relaxing two-day getaway. But if you get the urge to mosey around a historic seaside village, it's all there right outside your door.

Restaurant Kissing

ARROWS, Ogunquit
Berwick Road, (207) 361-1100
Expensive (Open May through Thanksgiving)

Turn left off Route 1 North onto Berwick Road, one-tenth mile north of the Route 1, Shore Road, and Beach Street intersection. Drive two miles; the restaurant is on the right.

Tucked away on a side road two miles from clamorous Route 1, Arrows doesn't offer ocean views or tangy sea breezes, but nobody misses them. This is the premiere dining spot in southern Maine, one of very few to earn four lips, and, thank goodness, it's not the slightest bit stuffy or pretentious. Romantic gourmets have been known to motor all the way from Boston to celebrate their love and special anniversaries with a superb meal.

Lush flower gardens and brick walkways surround the 200-year-old clapboard farmhouse. The interior reflects its 18th-century pedigree with mellow, planked floorboards, ladder-back oak chairs, and a great walnut bar. An herb and vegetable plot sits out back, providing daily inspiration and fresher than fresh ingredients for the two chef-owners.

One of those chefs taps a knowledge of Oriental cuisine honed during several years spent traveling through Asia. His succulent wok-seared Atlantic salmon is divine. The menu runs the gamut from contemporary California to traditional New England, and it's deliciously imaginative.

Arrows will remind you of those wonderful *mere-et-pere* restaurants in the French countryside. But sorry, no afternoon delights here. It's open only for dinner, and although pricey, it's worth every tempting morsel.

BARNACLE BILLY'S, Ogunquit
Perkins Cove, (207) 646-5575
Inexpensive to Moderate (Open mid-April through mid-October)

Turn right off Route 1 North onto Shore Road. Go one mile, following signs to Perkins Cove. Billy's is on the right as you enter the cove.

There's nothing I'd rather do in Maine than eat boiled lobster on a geranium-banked deck overlooking a rocky cove dotted with fishing boats and a sleek yacht. That's why I'd like to book a permanent table for two at Barnacle Billy's.

Don't expect the Ritz. This is a self-service, paper-plate-and-plastic-cup style of restaurant that accommodates 400 diners, indoors and out. The simple blackboard menu features Down East staples such as lobster stew and steamed clams. There are cheaper eateries up the coast, but few can match Billy's view (be still, my heart!) or his consistently wonderful seafood. Another plus is the valet parking directly across the street, a bonus in car-crowded Perkins Cove. Billy's is also one of the cleanest lobster pounds you'll find in Maine. The wooden and slate tables are spotless; the floor is immaculate; the windows in the glass-enclosed indoor dining room are washed daily.

The best time to get immediate seating is around five o'clock. Otherwise, you'll wait, but it's not too onerous. And be sure to opt for the deck.

HURRICANE RESTAURANT, Ogunquit
Perkins Cove, (207) 646-6348
Moderate

Turn right off Route 1 North onto Shore Road. Go one mile, following signs to Perkins Cove. Park in the public lot and walk one block to the restaurant, on the north side of the cove.

You'll have a tough time deciding whether it's the splashy ocean view or the enticing menu that gives the Hurricane its romantic ambience. Both delight the senses and the heart. Watch waves splash against the rocky coast while feasting on lobster gazpacho and crab Rangoon. The chef's commitment to "the freshest and the best of everything" means the daily carte features numerous specials, delectable sauces, and the tastiest of meals. All this makes the Hurricane a busy spot year-round. Fortunately, the wait staff realizes that lovers' chats often flourish over Irish coffee, and you'll never feel rushed.

The tiny bar, with its brick fireplace, is popular with the locals and gets crowded during cocktail hours, even earlier on rainy days. Parking next door is impossible, but there's a public lot one block away. Settle in with a sinful concoction called a Cove Cool-Ade (Bacardi, peppermint schnapps, and cranberry-lemon mix) and watch a Down East sunset. This is just the beginning of an unforgettable evening.

Kennebunkport

From Boston, head north on Interstate 95, through New Hampshire and onto the Maine Turnpike (still Interstate 95). At Exit 3 (Kennebunk), follow Route 35 South for six miles to the intersection of Routes 35 and 9 at a traffic light. Go left on Route 9 into Dock Square, the heart of this Down East village.

From Ogunquit center, head north on Route 1 for seven miles; turn right onto Route 9 East and go four and a quarter miles to the traffic light at the intersection with Route 35. Go straight on Route 9 into Dock Square.

THE CAPE ARUNDEL INN, Kennebunkport
Ocean Avenue, (207) 967-2125
Moderate (Open mid-May through mid-October)

Turn right in Dock Square onto Ocean Avenue and drive one and three-quarters miles; the inn is on the left overlooking the ocean.

Nothing ignites passion like watching moonlight dappling the Atlantic or lying in bed and listening to the steady shush of waves rolling in. It's all here at the Cape Arundel Inn, where every room overlooks the irresistible Maine coast.

When the sun is shining, you'll want to claim one of the pillowed wicker rockers on the porch, which boasts the best view in town. If a cool fog rolls in, take afternoon tea by the fireplace in the cozy living room. You don't have to budge for dinner. The dining room here is excellent, especially for seafood lovers.

The decor is pure summer cottage: nothing fancy, yet undeniably charming. Seven spacious guest rooms in the main house are sun-washed and simple, with rattan chairs, antique chiffoniers, matchboard walls, ruffled white curtains, and private baths. You're sure to feel happier here than in the six-room motel-style annex.

Ocean Avenue traffic occasionally gets a bit thick with tourists who want to photograph this outermost point of Cape Arundel. Don't let that deter you from renewing your love in this breathtaking corner of Maine.

THE CAPTAIN JEFFERDS INN, Kennebunkport
Pearl Street, (207) 967-2311
Moderate to Expensive (Open April through December)

Call for directions.

A pristine Federal spool-and-finial fence surrounds this white clapboard storybook mansion. Brick walkways lead to an oversized door that opens into a veritable museum of period furniture, American folk art, and collections of maiolica (special porcelain ware), English Staffordshire pieces, and wicker.

You could spend hours admiring the eclectic decor, and even purchase some treasures in the owners' shop, but other temptations await.

A gourmet breakfast is the only meal served, and each day it's deliciously different. Two sittings ensure that all guests can sample wild Maine blueberry crêpes, frittata with sausage, or "flannel," a traditional New England dish of broiled corned beef hash and poached eggs. Sip afternoon tea on the flower-banked west terrace, or in the sunny solarium in cooler weather, and be sure to request the house pâté. After a dinner at a charming Kennebunkport restaurant, guests gather by the fireplace in the living room, where a Steinway grand piano often sparks a sing-along.

The 12 individually heated guest rooms, each with bath, vary in size from cozy to commodious. All feature Laura Ashley wall coverings and crocheted coverlets over colorful hand-sewn quilts. The innkeeper's commitment to romantic ambience is verified by the abundance of bird's-eye and tiger maple dressers, cherry and pine four-poster beds, and pillowed wicker chairs. Three adjoining Carriage House suites (the Moosehead, Key West, and Hamptons) are spiced with a sense of humor, and a dedication to comfort and privacy.

Captain Jefferds' 190-year-old home still looks like the affluent sea captain's mansion it once was, right down to the widow's walk and interior bridge stairwell. But you'll bless the owners for converting it into an elegant B&B.

THE CAPTAIN LORD MANSION, Kennebunkport
Pleasant Street, (207) 967-3141
Moderate to Expensive

Turn right from Dock Square onto Ocean Avenue. Go three-tenths of a mile and turn left onto Green Street. The inn is at the top of the village green.

When a guest told the innkeeper he wanted to propose marriage, he found a willing co-conspirator. That evening, in the spacious gathering room, an unsuspecting young lady opened a faux menu to find a headline reading "Catch of the Day" above a photo of her boyfriend.

For that same lovely purpose, the owner of the Captain Lord Mansion has arranged sleigh rides, hot-air balloon trips, even a plane flying over the domed cupola, trailing the message "Will you marry me?" So if you're looking for an amorous tryst or an unforgettable way to propose, this is the spot.

Set on a slope above the village green, this butter yellow three-story inn has an imposing facade. Inside, don't be disappointed by the reception area, with its worn wallpaper and brochure-laden sideboard. You're here for romance, and that starts upstairs in the sumptuous bedrooms.

Each of the 16 rooms is individually decorated and positively immaculate. It's worthwhile to go deluxe, because the match-ready wood-burning fireplaces, four-poster king-size beds, snuggly quilts, and nonalcoholic mini-bars are all amorous amenities you can appreciate. The bonus is that there's no phone or television to interrupt the *plaisir d'amour*.

Breakfast is served family-style in the country kitchen, and it's substantial. Return guests discover a plate of home-baked chocolate chip cookies in their rooms. Those special details have earned this year-round inn a reputation for leisurely sojourns any month of the year.

THE INN AT HARBOR HEAD, Kennebunkport
41 Pier Road, on Cape Porpoise Harbor, (207) 967-5564
Moderate to Expensive

Taking Route 9 East from Dock Square, drive two miles, past Bradbury Market, through the intersection to the head of the cove. From there, the inn is the eighth house on the right.

Without a doubt, this is one of the most phenomenal places I've ever been to. You could stay here forever and never grow tired of the sumptuous atmosphere and the kissing. The setting alone makes this exceptional bed and breakfast a premier Maine stay, especially if you're in the mood for love. The 100-year-old rambling, shingled farmhouse overlooks picturesque Cape Porpoise Harbor, a Down East icon complete with fishing boats and swooping sea gulls.

Snuggle into king-size rope hammocks and watch lobstermen haul their traps. Sit on the dock and splash your toes in clear ocean water. But remember, the Inn at Harbor Head isn't a great romantic hideaway just for its picture-postcard location. Inside and out, this is a multicarat gem.

Each of the five luscious rooms is entirely different and tastefully done. One has a private latticed deck facing the sea. Two feature Jacuzzis. All have luxurious private bathrooms with plush terry robes for lounging. The king- and queen-size canopied beds are smothered in plump down comforters that are turned down each evening by the attentive innkeepers.

If you appreciate classy details, such as sherry in a crystal decanter and hand-painted floral tiles in the bath shower, they're all here, right down to the lace place mats and silver napkin rings on the mahogany dining room table.

You can spend the day roaming through nearby art galleries to work off the Sinful Chocolate Toast or eggs El Greco at breakfast. Sip afternoon wine and nibble cheese and crackers in either of the two treasure-filled sitting rooms. The hard part will be packing your bags and leaving this pastel paradise. Make no mistake. A night or two at the Inn at Harbor Head is an exquisite experience, and worth every cent.

THE KENNEBUNKPORT INN, Kennebunkport ◆◆◆
1 Dock Square, (207) 967-2621, (800) 248-2621
Moderate to Expensive

To the left at the northwest end of Dock Square.

This century-old Victorian mansion hugs the northwest corner of Dock Square, Kennebunkport's bustling hub. It's only a quick step to shops, art galleries, and scenic ocean cruises, but the heart-of-town location denies this country inn curb appeal. Once you're sitting hearthside in the matching wing chairs near the 25-foot mahogany bar, or sinking into the plump cranberry-hued sofas in the intimate upstairs parlor, or sharing chilled pinot grigio in the pillowed wicker rockers on the wraparound front porch, you realize this is a treasure designed for romance.

Love in the afternoon, and evening, is preferable in the 14 commodious guest rooms the main inn building. However, the 20 smaller bedrooms in the River House annex are equally comfortable and enticingly decorated in chintz and florals, with antique chests, armoires, and Queen Anne writing desks.

The personable, hands-on innkeepers have all bases covered. One is a justice of the peace who can tap an instant group of witnesses and attendants from the kitchen. The other is a Paris-trained chef whose prize-winning bouillabaisse and mustard-coated rack of lamb compel dining reservations.

This year, despite 14 straight years of almost constant "No Vacancy" signs, the inn did a mini-makeover. The result? A new menu featuring healthier, lighter, and innovative versions of traditional New England dishes (especially recommended is the native swordfish served with roasted pepper and tomato vinaigrette, and arugula and walnut pesto). But the ambience hasn't changed. Candles and fresh-cut wildflowers still enhance each table.

THE WHITE BARN INN, Kennebunkport ◆◆◆◆
37 Beach Street, (207) 967-2321
Expensive

At the intersection of Routes 35 and 9, continue straight on Route 35, which becomes Beach Street. The inn is a quarter mile from the traffic light, on the right.

Thick terry robes, a hand-written welcome note, and a fresh fruit basket with mineral water on a mahogany bedside table immediately reveal the elegant hospitality and romantic personality of this Relais & Chateaux inn, one of a handful in the entire New England area. (Relais & Chateaux is an exclusive inn association that holds the highest standards imaginable for the places included in their directory.) Creature comforts abound, from the twice-daily maid service to complimentary afternoon tea to evening brandy in the antique-appointed garnet sitting room.

The White Barn Inn, set on two and a half wooded acres, is only a six-minute walk to the beach. Its suites are the sweetest in town. King-size four-poster beds, fireplace logs awaiting the strike of a match, and huge marble whirlpools rejuvenate weary travelers who opt for the seven Carriage House suites. The four Gatehouse suites and other inn rooms are smaller, but no less sumptuous or comfortable. You're Down East, but it's upscale all the way.

The two spectacular dining rooms are both restored New England barns with exposed rafters, planked floorboards, and seasoned wood walls. White tables draped in white linens hold crystal goblets, Villeroy & Boch china, and floral sprays. A pianist plays softly through dinner. And what a dinner!

Country restaurants with their own vegetable garden out back indicate a kitchen's dedication to freshness and quality. And that's true of the savory cuisine presented with finesse at this inn. The menu changes weekly, capitalizing on seasonal produce and the Atlantic's freshest catch. Splurge on the sausage of salmon, scallops, and lobster in a vegetable vinaigrette, or sample the steamed lobster served over fresh fettuccine. Work off the hearty continental breakfast by exploring this seacoast village on bikes available to guests.

◆ **Romantic Warning:** The only yellow light at the White Barn is that reservations for both lodging and dinner are at a premium. Book early, because you'll have no trouble staying late.

Freeport

It all started with a tiny L.L. Bean, a mail-order company selling gear and essentials for the rugged outdoorsman. From the Bean grew a stalk that even Jack would be proud of, sprouting more than 100 outlet and retail stores. L.L. Bean itself has bloomed into a huge retail store, complete with a stocked trout pond, that is open 24 hours a day, 365 days a year. You may think, then, that Freeport is a tacky conglomeration of bargain basements, but miraculously it has retained its small-town charm, with storefronts carefully designed to retain their historic integrity. Even the McDonald's, recognizable only by an unobtrusive (yes, I said unobtrusive) sign, is housed in a restored Colonial, with swagged drapes, gilt-framed antique prints, and classy wooden furnishings. South Freeport, a short drive away, is completely different, with a working harbor, rustic lobster pound, and some of the freshest seafood around. From the deck, you can watch the catch of the day being hauled in.

Hotel/Bed and Breakfast Kissing

HARRASEEKET INN, Freeport
162 Main Street, (207) 865-9377, (800) 342-6423
Moderate to Very Expensive

On Interstate 95, take Exit 20, turn left off the ramp, and continue for 500 yards.

Something old becomes something new and turns into something magical at the Harraseeket Inn. Two vintage buildings, one built in 1798, the other in 1850, have been refurbished and expanded to encompass Freeport's most indulgent inn. Although the inn retains its charming old New England facade, inside you'll discover spacious guest rooms, modern baths with steam showers and jetted tubs, and wood-burning fireplaces. One fire casts a golden glow on the rich mahogany in the expansive parlor, elegantly decorated with just the right blend of antiques, comfortable sofas, and tufted accent chairs. Afternoon tea is served here with all the accoutrements, including six kinds of cookies. Another fire lights the Broad Arrow Tavern, on the lower floor. This hunting lodge-style room is punctuated with an immense moose head and an antique birchbark canoe filled with furs.

Trompe l'oeil reproductions of Early American antiques add to the elegant decor of the commodious guest rooms. Rich fabrics, some highlighted with woven gold, rise above the headboards—enough to make any colonial feel like royalty. Deluxe rooms and suites feature wet bars, jetted tubs, and fireplaces; some overlook the inn's inner courtyards of green lawns and colorful flower beds.

The Maine Dining Room is Freeport's most elegant restaurant. Candles sparkle inside etched glass on each table, as you begin your evening with oysters, crab cakes, or foie gras. Entrées include lamb or pheasant prepared tableside, lobster, duckling, salmon, and other delicacies. Your love is sure to warm up with a flambéed dessert, including Jamaican bananas with ice cream, rum, and coffee liqueur, or fresh berry crêpes.

THE KENDALL TAVERN BED AND BREAKFAST, Freeport ◆◆
213 Main Street, (207) 865-1338
Moderate

About a half mile north of Freeport center.

Gaze into the crystal ball on the parlor table and you may see that your future holds many happy days together. You'll know that you've got a good start at this unassuming, cozy inn. Soak away any past worries in the spa/sun room, lined with potted trees to bring a sense of the outdoors in. Afterwards, warm your hearts and thoughts by a glowing fire in one of the parlors, furnished with antique wing chairs, sofa, and upright piano. Guest rooms are smallish, but individualized with a pencil-post bed in one, a daybed sitting area in another. All have private baths and a bright country feeling. Fresh flowers and brass chandeliers in the breakfast room highlight a hearty start on your way to a bright future.

◆ **Romantic Alternative:** Just down the street, **181 MAIN STREET,** 181 Main Street, Freeport, (207) 865-1226, (Moderate), is similarly charming in a country style. This restored 1840 Greek Revival is home to two parlors (one with television) and seven cozy guest rooms, some with four-poster beds and patchwork quilts, all with private bath. An added bonus is the large outdoor swimming pool, a welcome sight on a sultry summer day.

Restaurant Kissing

FIDDLEHEAD FARM RESTAURANT, Freeport
15 Independence Drive, (207) 865-0466
Moderate to Expensive

From Interstate 95, take Exit 19 (Desert Road). Go north one mile to a traffic light. Turn left at the light; the restaurant is nearby.

Toast your everlasting love in this intimate restaurant, housed in an 1853 farmhouse. Former parlors have been transformed into dining rooms, each with just a handful of tables elegantly laid out with white linen, silver, gold-trimmed china, candles, and fresh flowers. Seasonal menus focus on fresh ingredients; you may begin with a smoked Maine trout appetizer, followed by lobster strudel served with wild mushroom and cognac cream, Long Island duckling with raspberry sauce, or linguine with scallops. For more casual fare, the adjoining Country Café and Bakery serves reasonably priced sandwiches that can be enjoyed at one of the light pine tables or booths, or taken out for a picnic. Terra-cotta floor tiles and the high peaked pine ceiling add polish to this delightful lunch spot.

JAMESON TAVERN, Freeport
115 Main Street, (207) 865-4196
Moderate

On Route 1, just off Highway 295.

Waitresses pour water from pewter pitchers in this historic 1779 tavern. Records show that commissioners met here in 1820 to sign the final papers separating Maine from the Commonwealth of Massachusetts. Today, classical music, white linens, swagged drapes, and bronzed candelabras add finesse without overpowering the simple Colonial feel of the tavern. The service is more earthy than elegant, and the menu is traditional, featuring shrimp cocktail, lobster stew, steaks, and local seafood dishes.

Outdoor Kissing

WOLFE'S NECK WOODS STATE PARK, Freeport
Wolfe's Neck Road, (207) 865-4465, (800) 322-1501
From Freeport center, follow Bow Street out of town for several miles. Turn right onto Wolfe's Neck Road.

This may be the most perfect place for a picnic on the Maine coast. Tables face an open lawn just right for sunning and playing, but each is ringed by trees offering privacy and seclusion. Paths radiate toward the water, where a trail winds along the top of a forested hill, trees coquettishly masking the water beyond. Along the way, displays point out natural features—trees once used for masts, an osprey's nest—to enhance your appreciation of the natural beauty around you. At one point, the trail leads down to the rocky shore, where tiny seashells are tossed like confetti from the sea, gathering in wells between the boulders. Visit at low tide and you can scramble along the shore to a secluded kissing spot as unblemished as your love for each other.

◆ **Romantic Note:** Follow your intrepid spirit and drive farther down the road past the entrance to the park. **STONE HOUSE** will reveal itself to you, an unexpected castle in the woods. The gardens are small but sensual, with bright perennials in spring and summer, lavender and pink heathers in fall. Several picnic tables are set on the lawn.

Brunswick

Hotel/Bed and Breakfast Kissing

CAPTAIN DANIEL STONE INN, Brunswick
10 Water Street, (207) 725-9898
Moderate to Expensive

From Route 1 North, exit right at Route 24 (South Maine Street). Go right onto Maine Street. Turn immediately left at the light onto Mason Street, go one block, and turn left onto Water Street. The inn is on the right.

At this cross between a country inn and a cosmopolitan hotel, you can enjoy polished charm without feeling obligated to hobnob with the innkeeper or fellow guests. The guest rooms in the original 1819 home are architecturally interesting, and decorated with Early American, Ethan Allen-style dark wood highboys and occasional tables blended with comfortable contemporary couches and chairs. The new wing has a more modern appeal. Suites are especially commodious, but even "standard" rooms are invitingly decorated, with a brass bed blanketed with a white woven spread or a heavy four-poster bed so high off the ground a stepping stool is provided. Tufted velveteen chairs, brass floor and table lamps, and richly colored floral wallpapers complete the look. In many you can bubble away your cares in a deep oval jetted tub, with tubside phone just in case you want to gloat.

◆ **Romantic Warning:** Wedding receptions complete with buffet and band are popular here, although the manager assured me the honeymoon must start by 8 p.m. Also, some of the rooms look over the highway.

Bath

Hotel/Bed and Breakfast Kissing

FAIRHAVEN INN, Bath   ◆◆
Rural Route 2, North Bath Road, (207) 443-4391
Very Inexpensive to Inexpensive

Call for directions.

A ramble down the back roads of industrial Bath will reveal a new perspective on coastal Maine, far removed in spirit from lobster pounds and lighthouses, yet just a short drive away. Surrounded by 27 acres of rolling meadows and woods, this 1790 Colonial is a truly rural getaway. The only reason tourists come this way is to stay at this inn. Creaky floors harmonize with classical music to set the tone for old-fashioned country charm. Antique headboards, patchwork quilts, white woven spreads, and semiprivate baths make the inn feel as warm as a hand-knit glove. A full breakfast of oatmeal or Maltex, fruit, a baked entrée, and breakfast meats will give you a hearty start for a day of hiking. In the winter, you can ski practically from the door and return, rosy-cheeked, to warm frosty fingers by the wood stove in the parlor.

Restaurant Kissing

KRISTINA'S, Bath   ◆◆◆
160 Centre Street, (207) 442-8577
Moderate

From Route 1 North, exit onto Route 209. Turn left at the top of the exit onto High Street. Look for the restaurant on the right, at the corner of High and Centre Street.

Subscribing to the adage "Life is short; eat dessert first," Kristina's greets you with a glass display case brimming with caloric wonders as you enter this home turned café. More than a dozen gourmet cakes will tempt you, along with muffins, cinnamon rolls, cookies, and dessert bars. If you have the will power to save the sweets for after dinner, ask for a table in the cozy downstairs dining room to the left. Its white and pink linens, bud vases, Windsor chairs, and swagged valances above sheer curtains make it much more charming than the plain-Jane lunch room with its mismatched chairs or the upstairs tavern. The creative seasonal menu highlights such favorites as baked chèvre in a pistachio-peppercorn crust; mussels steamed in lemongrass, chile pepper, and garlic; macadamia chicken in champagne-Dijon sauce; and fresh fish specials. Perhaps that adage should read "Life is short; enjoy dessert, too, and kiss as much as you can."

Georgetown

Hotel/Bed and Breakfast Kissing

GRAY HAVENS INN, Georgetown   ◆◆◖
Seguinland Road, (207) 371-2616
Moderate to Expensive (Open Memorial Day through Columbus Day)

Call for directions.

Conjure a vision of a grand old hotel on a stunning slice of Maine seacoast. Give it a wraparound veranda, partially screened to fend off flies. Twin turrets crowned in witches' hats holding court on each corner. Gabled windows punctuating the roof line and Adirondack chairs dotting the lawn that rolls to the seaside cliff. A ladder leading down to the dock, where rowboats challenge gentlemen to prove their prowess to the ladies and lobster traps set an imaginary course. This vision is Gray Havens Inn, believed to be the last of the classic shingle-style hotels operating on the Maine coast.

Be sure to get a room with a view of the water. It is spectacular, a silky blue ocean studded with jade islands. In the turret rooms, the scene wraps around you as you lie on your antique iron bed, cuddling beneath a down quilt. Wood paneling throughout the inn lends a down-to-earth rusticity to the comfortable antiques. The dining room, open from Tuesday through Saturday in the summer, is simply furnished and offers a choice of three or four entrées. When you order lobster, be assured it's fresh. The crustaceans are pulled from the waters outside an hour before dinner.

Robinhood

Restaurant Kissing

THE OSPREY, Robinhood
Robinhood Marine Center, off Route 127, (207) 371-2530
Expensive (Closed January 1 through March 1)

Call for directions.

"Is this it?" will most likely be your comment when you first see the funky entrance—which looks more like a marine warehouse than a restaurant—but locals drive from miles around to dine at this bright waterside café. Inside, it holds delights for the eye and the palate. A glassed-in balcony overlooks a splendid view of a quiet harbor, sailing yachts bobbing at their moorings. Though a low partition separates this area from the inner dining room, a skylight invites the sunshine (or moonshine) in as well. White linens, fine china and silver, fresh flowers in pottery vases, and lovely pottery-based candleholders create a fresh, artistic atmosphere. The menu is creatively abundant. On any given day, the more than 30 entrées might include pan-blackened lamb chops, Szechwan swordfish, wiener schnitzel Viennoise, scallops Nicoise, or pecan-encrusted halibut. For dessert, "Obsession in Three Chocolates" proves that, for chocoholics, love isn't the only thing that can be obsessive.

Wiscasset

Hotel/Bed and Breakfast Kissing

THE SQUIRE TARBOX INN, Wiscasset ◆◆◆
Route 144, Box 620, (207) 882-7693
Expensive to Very Expensive (MAP), Very Inexpensive to Expensive (B&B)
(Open mid-May through October)

From Route 1, take Route 144 toward Westport Island. The inn is eight and a half miles from Route 1.

Centuries-old farmhouses converted to inns and restaurants are not uncommon in New England, but this one is unique. It is a charming inn, a first-class restaurant, and a working farm reserved strictly for adults. Come here to relax a while, about as far off the beaten path as you can get on the Maine coast. Ramble down a forest path to the serene salt marsh, where a rowboat invites you to explore the secluded waters. Binoculars entice bird-watchers into the screened porch, where proposals of all kinds have been made and accepted. In the evening, take a ride on the adult-size swing hanging from the rafters of the massive barn or watch the goats being milked. You can sample the farm-fresh results at cocktail hour, when seven types of goat cheese are served, but save room for dinner. In the 1763 dining room, its beams taken from ancient vessels, four memorable courses are served by the light of candles and the flames dancing within an immense copper-hooded hearth. In keeping with the farmhouse spirit, several guest rooms are carved out of the old barn, corralled around a whimsical playroom with exposed barn boards where you can throw darts.

Restaurant Kissing

LE GARAGE, Wiscasset
Water Street, (207) 882-5409
Moderate

From Route 1 North, turn right onto Water Street just south of the Wiscasset bridge.

Dining here can foment dreams of mighty sailing ships in mightier seas, adventuring to faraway lands to discover new trade routes, and of dashing captains and their dedicated ladies. How can you help it? A wall of windows in this welcoming restaurant overlooks a scene that evokes Maine's shipbuilding heyday: the decaying yet picturesque hulks of two massive schooners, one with three of its four original masts still pointing heavenward as though grasping for wind. Today, they are marooned on the muddy shores of the Sheepscot River. Though the panorama is best at lunch, when you can enjoy traditional sandwiches, filled crêpes, and generous salads, dinner is equally inviting on the enclosed patio, lit solely by candles. The Down East menu features charbroiled steaks, pork and lamb, local shrimp and seafood, and, of course, boiled lobster, for the salty New England seafarer in all of us.

Boothbay

Hotel/Bed and Breakfast Kissing

KENNISTON HILL INN, Boothbay
Route 27, (207) 633-2159,
Very Inexpensive to Moderate

From Route 1, turn onto Route 27 South. The inn is about 10 miles down on the left.

Master shipbuilders strive to create vessels that are not only practical and steadfast, but also evoke a sense of majesty and grace. These are the qualities that prominent shipbuilder David Kenniston bestowed upon his stately 1796 Colonial home, which now crests a hill above busy Route 27. Fireplaces warm the parlor and dining room, as well as four of the 10 guest rooms, which are decorated in down-home fashion. Antiques mix with older furnishings to create a comfortable atmosphere with a touch of charm. On a summer afternoon, the nicely landscaped lawn and garden invite you to sit and dream of yesteryear.

Boothbay Harbor

Hotel/Bed and Breakfast Kissing

SPRUCE POINT INN, Boothbay Harbor
(207) 633-4152, (800) 553-0289
Very Expensive to Unbelievably Expensive (MAP)

Call for directions.

As most couples know, sometimes you just have to dive in head-first to brave the waters of romance. At Spruce Point Inn, you can test the waters in several senses. The inn has a saltwater pool set so close to the shore, it's nearly a finger of the ocean, but it's guaranteed to be much more congenial than the frigid Atlantic. Even on cooler days, sunbathers can find heartwarming spots in this heart-stopping seaside location. The sprawling resort, the epitome of "grand old," first opened in 1906. Its white gabled buildings are set along a private shore. Recent renovations have spruced up the guest rooms, but the heavy wood furnishings and motel-shaped spaces in many of them still feel a tad outdated. A pianist or big-band combo is often on hand to entertain you during the four-course dinners. Before sunset, ask for a table for two by the window. The view and each other are all the entertainment you'll need.

Restaurant Kissing

RUSSELL HOUSE, Boothbay Harbor
Route 27, (207) 633-6656
Moderate

From Route 1, turn right onto Route 27 South. The restaurant is about 12 miles down on the right.

The ambience at the Russell House is pure country: bright and cheery, rather than sedate, with pine chairs gathered around cozy tables topped by floral cloths and candles flickering in faceted glass holders. The cuisine, however, is anything but ordinary. The appetizers include spicy sesame noodles, pot stickers, jalapeño-cheese nuggets, salmon cakes, spanikopita, and scallion pancakes, to name a few. Fifteen styles of pasta will further tempt you, along with such seafood specialties as lobster chardonnay and lobster stir-fry. The meat dishes are creative; try the veal Marengo or Moroccan chicken.

◆   **Romantic Note:** On the second floor, five spacious, simply decorated, reasonably priced rooms, with television and private bath, are available for lodging.

East Boothbay

Hotel/Bed and Breakfast Kissing

FIVE GABLES INN, East Boothbay   ◆◆◆
Murray Hill Road, (207) 633-4551, (800) 451-5048
Inexpensive to Expensive (Open mid-May through mid-November)

From Route 1, take Route 27 South toward Boothbay. At the light, turn left onto Route 96. Drive about four miles to East Boothbay and turn right at the blinking light on Murray Hill Road. The inn is a half mile down on the right.

From your window, you can watch a watercolor come-to-life: a quintessential Maine coastal community, complete with a tiny settlement of Colonial and Victorian buildings nestled in the lap of a forest-lined inlet harboring an assortment of boats. As darkness overcomes the scene, you can light the candles on the mantel, then the log in the hearth, and snuggle into a cozy New England night for two.

Five Gables Inn was built 125 years ago, and little has changed in town since then. The inn's recent restoration is just short of miraculous. Its architecture remains true, with a wraparound veranda crowned by five high-peaked gables. Inside, the decor is as fresh as a sea breeze, as delightfully detailed as a wildflower garden. On a chilly night, you can embrace by the fire in the parlor and sip sherry. Pencil-post beds, posies of dried flowers, designer fabrics, and the occasional curio lend the guest rooms a cozy, welcoming feel. In the most commodious room, you may be torn between watching the fire or the splendid view. On the third floor, a rocking chair invites lingering at one gabled window; a bed is tucked underneath a skylight in another room. In the morning, the distant call of gulls and the aroma of muffins greet you in the sunny breakfast room, where windows frame that watercolor once again coming to life.

West Boothbay Harbor

Restaurant Kissing

THE LAWNMEER INN RESTAURANT,
West Boothbay Harbor
Route 27, (207) 633-2544, (800) 633-7645
Moderate

From West Boothbay Harbor, continue for two and a half miles south on Route 27. The inn is on the right; follow the signs.

Come to the Lawnmeer before sunset and you may be tempted to postpone dinner. Adirondack chairs invite lingering on the lawn, which slopes down to a small but serene cove. A wall of windows fronting the dining room of this timeworn, century-old lodge brings this splendid view inside. Window tables are placed at oblique angles so couples can enjoy the view and each other, and nearly forget that others are dining behind them. As darkness falls, the flickering oil lamps, burgundy cloths, warm pine paneling, beamed ceiling, new-age music, and glowing fireplace create a romantic, yet unstuffy, ambience. Classically prepared seafood is prominent on the menu, along with chicken fettuccine, filet mignon, and seasonal lamb and pork specials. After dinner, when all is quiet and dark, you might not be able to resist sneaking out to a lawn chair for a late-night embrace.

Newcastle

Hotel/Bed and Breakfast Kissing

NEWCASTLE INN, Newcastle
River Road, (207) 563-5685, (800) 832-8669
Expensive (MAP), Inexpensive to Moderate (B&B)

From Route 1, bear right on River Road (look for the Newcastle Inn sign). Go a half mile to the inn, on the right.

"To love and be loved is the greatest joy on earth" is the needlepointed adage on display in most of the rooms. Share in the joy at this enchanting inn, which serves some of the most exquisite dinners on the Maine coast.

The guest rooms, more charming than posh, will whet your appetite for a night that will surely satisfy it. Each room has special touches, such as a pencil-post bed crowned with a crocheted canopy, a cozy sitting area tucked beneath the eaves, a private balcony, or a floral half-tester. Walls are painted in soothing hues highlighted by lovely embroideries and coordinating borders. A brick hearth warms the parlor's contemporary sofas and select antiques. A second public room, the Stencil Room, takes its name from the beautiful stenciled floor, a mellow yellow set off with soft reds and greens in a leaf and flower pattern. Accent chairs and hand-hooked rugs complement it perfectly.

As the day winds to a close, a cocktail party begins in the bright sun porch, with its white wicker sofa and rocking chairs, and ice cream parlor tables and chairs overlooking the back lawn and the Damariscotta River beyond. Waitresses come by with delicate edibles on silver trays as guests warm to each other. Dinner is, in a word, masterful. The five full courses may include leek, bacon, and goat cheese polenta or a Vidalia onion tart, followed by a cold spiced plum soup, then a green salad with some of the best cream biscuits you'll ever taste. The entrée may be rack of lamb, stuffed tenderloin of beef, or a salmon dish that would transform any landlubber into a seafood fanatic. Dessert, the *pièce de résistance*, could be anything from chocolate truffle cake to raspberries in puff pastry with caramel sauce. Breakfast is equally generous and scrumptious. Guests have been after the innkeeper's recipes for so long, she's recently come out with a new cookbook, a culinary souvenir of your joyful stay.

◆ **Romantic Note:** Like a perfect host, the innkeeper acts as a bit of a matchmaker, joining two couples with similar interests at a table for four. If you prefer to dine only with each other, request this in advance.

Damariscotta Mills

Hotel/Bed and Breakfast Kissing

MILL POND INN, Damariscotta Mills 💋
Route 215, (207) 563-8014
Very Inexpensive

Call for directions.

For those who long for the era of "free love," at least for a weekend, this commune of an inn promises a put-your-feet-up type of hospitality. No pretension here, just a quiet setting in a residential neighborhood and pleasant rooms with private bath (some down the hall). Fresh flowers year-round accent the pleasant country decor. Relax in the bentwood rocker or stretch out on the plaid sofa by the parlor's wood-burning hearth on a blustery winter afternoon.

On a sunny summer morning, lounge on the patio overlooking the placid mill pond just beyond the back lawn. Guests are invited to paddle the well-used canoes upriver to glistening Damariscotta Lake, where bald eagles soar as high as your love for each other.

New Harbor

Hotel/Bed and Breakfast Kissing

BRADLEY INN, New Harbor
361 Pemaquid Point (Route 130), (207) 677-2105
Moderate

From Coastal Route 1, take Business Route 1 into Newcastle/Damariscotta. Follow signs to Routes 129-130 toward Pemaquid. The inn is on the right, shortly before Pemaquid Point.

Most romantics are in a hurry to reach Pemaquid Point before sundown, but it would be a mistake to bypass the Bradley Inn. Like a mythical siren, the rambling turn-of-the-century inn calls you to stop and stay awhile. The newly renovated guest rooms are as fresh and clean as the sea breezes whispering from the bays that hug the inn on either side. Simply decorated in soothing hues with high-peaked, knotty pine ceilings, elegant reproduction highboys, plush wing chairs, and lace curtains, the rooms enjoy views that extend over the spacious lawns and delightful flower beds, past the trees, to the water. In the attractive new bathrooms, brass faucets, glasses placed on doilies, seashell-shaped soaps, and massage-style showers illustrate the innkeepers' attention to pampering details. A fire warms the parlor, where you can relax with a magazine or enjoy the grand pianist who plays here on summer weekends. Outside, a summer afternoon could be well spent kissing in the gazebo, enjoying an old-fashioned game of croquet, or cuddling in the wood swing.

◆   **Romantic Note:** After breakfast, enjoy a short loop walk down a quiet back road along a splendid shoreline to Pemaquid Point. Along the way, nibble on wild berries and watch an artist capture the scene as a sailboat glides by. What could be more Maine?

Restaurant Kissing

SHIPS, New Harbor   ◆◆◀
361 Pemaquid Point (Route 130), at the Bradley Inn, (207) 677-2105
Moderate

Call for directions.

I hesitate to call this restaurant "nautical," for that sometimes conjures up images of fishing nets dangling from musty paneling, plastic lobsters, and initials carved into rough wood tables. The museum-quality collection of sea-inspired memorabilia showcased here, however, is what nautical should be. Intricately detailed model ships, paintings and carvings, and framed antique maps offer a fascinating look into man's love and respect for the ocean. Traditional seafood dishes include lobster stew and lobster ravioli, grilled swordfish, baked haddock, and poached salmon. Landlubbers will enjoy chicken Sonoma (a western twist on chicken Kiev), lamb, and filet mignon. If you think of lobster as lovers' food, but the mess is a turnoff, lazy lobster (served out of the shell) does the work for you. After all, where else can you be lazy if not at this serene spot on the Maine coast?

Outdoor Kissing

PEMAQUID POINT LIGHTHOUSE

From Coastal Route 1, take Business Route 1 into Newcastle/Damariscotta. Follow signs to Routes 129-130 toward Pemaquid. Continue on Route 130 all the way to the water.

If you're lucky, a full moon will cast its light like diamonds upon the water the night you visit Pemaquid Point. Hug each other close in the brisk ocean breeze as the flash from the lighthouse reaches out to dance with the moonbeams. Waves crash on the rocks below, pounding in a ritual as immortal as love. In the morning, return to witness the impossibly picturesque white lighthouse guarding Maine's rugged coast. Pack a lunch to enjoy together at one of the picnic tables perched on the cliff, then scramble over the boulders that are piled high on the shore, rounded smooth by hundreds of seaswept years. You may choose to spend an afternoon here, searching for treasures among the rocks and watching the sailboats and an occasional windjammer glide past.

◆ **Romantic Alternative:** Nearby, our colonial forefathers chose a peaceful site on a knoll overlooking a natural harbor hemmed by forest for one of the first settlements on the Maine coast. Abandoned long ago, the **COLONIAL PEMAQUID STATE HISTORIC SITE** is now an archaeological area with signposts marking ancient foundations. It is also a little-known picnic area, with tables overlooking the quiet cove and its kaleidoscope of colorful lobster pots. To get there, follow the signs off Route 130 to **PEMAQUID BEACH** and **FORT WILLIAM HENRY** (two more kissing spots) and turn right on the dirt road after the beach entrance.

Round Pond

Hotel/Bed and Breakfast Kissing

BRIAR ROSE, Round Pond
Route 32, (207) 529-5478
Very Inexpensive (Open by reservation only after Columbus Day through April)

Call for directions.

Are you ready to stop and smell the roses? Then come to the Briar Rose. Like its namesake, this inn is pretty without being cultivated and seems perfectly at home on a quiet country back road. Just three guest rooms bloom here. The two that share one bath are charmingly decorated with delicate floral wall coverings with coordinating borders, and tassel-trimmed curtains. Upstairs, a spacious third-floor suite features a four-poster in the bedroom and a comfortable sitting room brimming with fascinating antique curios. Antiques also adorn the inn's parlor, which turns into a gift shop in summer and is heated by a wood stove in winter. Another cozy, clean, and bright sitting room is upstairs. Round Pond's harbor and its lobster pounds, the town's main attractions, are just a block away. Here, you can pick up a ready-to-eat picnic lobster for a few dollars from a local fisherman. This is the place to stop and smell the roses.

Rockland

Restaurant Kissing

JESSICA'S BISTRO, Rockland
2 South Main Street (Route 73), (207) 596-0770
Moderate

On Route 73, one mile south of the center of Rockland, on the west side of the street.

As lusty and unassuming as a Parisian chanteuse, Jessica's promises a European-style evening to those who voyage off the beaten path to dine here. Set in a vintage Victorian, the dining rooms are intimate, with no more than four or five small tables in each. Framed black-and-white prints by eminent photographers capture scenes of the earthy Paris of 50 years ago: a couple kissing in a bistro, another couple hugging as they stroll down the street; a young boy grinning with pride as he totes home two bottles of burgundy. Bud vases with fresh blooms, oil lamps, and bargello-striped place mats spice the room with unpretentious flair. The food, classic French bistro with a twist, is some of the best in Maine, from the lobster ravioli and *buendnerfleish* (dried beef) appetizers to homemade soups to such entrées as roasted pork with tomatoes, mushrooms, pancetta, garlic, and herbs; lamb Provencale; paella; and cassoulet. The chefs are Swiss, so the desserts are, *naturellement*, indulgent.

Rockport

Hotel/Bed and Breakfast Kissing

SAMOSET RESORT, Rockport
1 Bay Point Drive, (207) 594-2511, (800) 341-1650
Very Expensive

From Route 1 North, turn right onto Waldo Avenue. Drive about a third of a mile. You will see the Samoset sign.

If a rousing round of racquetball followed by a sauna and swim is more your cup of tea than cookies and company in a frilly parlor, Samoset will fill your afternoon with delight. The only full-service resort in the area, this sprawling complex is splendidly located on a quiet Atlantic shore, surrounded by a rolling 18-hole golf course. Indoor and outdoor pools and tennis courts, racquetball courts, volleyball, whirlpools, tanning salons, aerobics classes, exercise equipment, even horseshoes, croquet, shuffleboard, and basketball will challenge the fitness-minded. Masseuses are on hand to pamper tired or achy muscles. Guest rooms are spacious, anonymous, and pleasantly decorated in quality hotel style. Most have private balconies overlooking a splendid water view.

◆ **Romantic Warning:** Like many resorts, Samoset attracts conventions, but the complex is large and varied enough that you usually won't feel as though you're the only ones who aren't here to sell cars or compare software.

Restaurant Kissing

MARCEL'S, Rockport
1 Bay Point Drive, at the Samoset Resort, (207) 594-0774
Expensive

From Route 1 North, turn right onto Waldo Avenue. Drive about a third of a mile. You will see the Samoset sign.

Sometimes we just can't resist a restaurant where dishes are flambéed tableside. It spices the evening with a special (albeit a bit pretentious) panache, a private show presented just for two. Flambé is the specialty of this posh dining establishment, one of the few in Maine that requires a jacket, something most tourists forget to bring. Rack of lamb, chateaubriand, and, occasionally, sautéed lobster receive a fiery finish before your eyes, while such continental entrées as filet mignon, chicken Gorgonzola, and turkey breast sautéed with sweet-potato butter, cranberries, and pine nuts please less flashy appetites. Seasonal flambéed desserts for two ensure that your hearts are not all that's afire at the end of your meal.

Outdoor Kissing

ROCKPORT HARBOR, Rockport
Beauchamp Avenue

From Camden center, head out of town on Bayview Street past the Waterfront Restaurant and Camden Harbour Inn. Turn left onto Chestnut. When you see the belted Galloway cows, turn left onto Calderwood Lane. Drive through the golf course and bear right onto Beauchamp Avenue, a dirt road. As the road winds along the wooded shore, you'll come to a turnoff where you can park your car along the side of the road.

Less than three miles from bustling Camden, but a world away, is a completely secluded, wonderfully scenic spot on the rocky shore of tiny Rockport Harbor. Sailboats bob at their moorings. Sea gulls soar overhead. Kayakers glide past. A lighthouse guards the channel on the horizon, seemingly holding at bay the tide of tourism. Bring along a picnic to enjoy on the rocks and you'll be reminded what "getaway" truly means.

Camden

Camden is like a schooner at full sail, racing with the wind of prosperity, floating on a high tide of tourism, yet it also remains securely anchored by its proud heritage and small-town charm. Downtown brims with boutiques, selling finely crafted wood items, pottery, jewelry, dolls, and more. Mealtime choices include a French bistro specializing in casseroles, gourmet sandwiches served harborside, or upper-crust cuisine in an Edwardian home. This small, bustling town harbors a surprising number of country inns, from plain to princely. Unfortunately, many inns are set along busy Route 1, but the road quiets down at night and in many the charming decor amply compensates for this distraction. Graceful windjammers ply the harbor waters, carrying parties of romantics on day trips and overnight sails back into an era when wind was king.

Hotel/Bed and Breakfast Kissing

A LITTLE DREAM, Camden
66 High Street, (207) 236-8742
Moderate to Expensive

*From Camden, proceed for a quarter mile on Route 1 past the harbor and historic
district. The inn is on the left, across from Nurembega.*

Dreams of delight can begin with a chocolate kiss, shared by the fire in the
parlor, as you read passages from a collection of the world's greatest love letters,
one of many extraordinary books piled high on floral chairs and sofas. Wander
into the conservatory, an indoor Eden of ivy-draped windows, white wicker
furnishings, embroidered and white-on-white pillows, exquisite garden books,
and posies of dried flowers all around. Upstairs, angelic bedchambers await,
each so delightful it is difficult to choose a favorite.

As soothing as the sea, the muted blue walls in the Blue Turret Room
shimmer in the light of the corner hearth. Lace floats like angel wings above
the carved headboard and around the windows of the turret, accenting the
white wicker rockers, soaring mirrored armoire, and marble-topped dresser.
Upstairs, a life-size unicorn invites the playful into a world of whimsy where
antique teddy bears have their tea and would-be Peter Pans can relive youthful
fantasies. In the Master Suite, sink into the pillows below a canopy intertwined
with pussywillows and pansies. Every detail is dreamy, with ribbons and flowers
everywhere, and enchanting clothing, toys, and dolls waiting to delight you in
every niche.

Breakfast too is a masterpiece for the eye, and the appetite. A sprig of mint,
a pansy, a daisy, and a delicate heart of watermelon topped our fresh fruit. The
ricotta-lemon pancakes with raspberry sauce were as light as the bacon was
crisp. Gourmet jams enhanced the date, pear, and walnut muffins. Even the
sugar was unusual—peach-flavored for the peach spice tea.

BLUE HARBOR HOUSE, Camden
67 Elm Street (Route 1), (207) 236-3196, (800) 248-3196
Inexpensive to Moderate

*On Route 1 (Elm Street), three blocks from the village center. The inn is on the left,
as you head North.*

This inviting 1835 New England inn serves one of the most intimate
dinners in Maine, open only to guests staying in one of its 10 rooms. Off-season
you may have the place all to yourselves. The reasonably priced cuisine is
remarkably good. Homemade soup, a garden salad, freshly baked raspberry-

honey-oatmeal bread, roast rack of lamb, red potatoes with rosemary and basil, and a banana brûlée for dessert rounded out one menu. Poached salmon is another favorite. You're welcome to bring your own wine. Breakfasts are equally heartwarming.

The guest rooms are delightful; stenciling, pencil-post beds, patchwork quilts, ruffled valances, and velvet wing chairs add up to country-fresh charm throughout. In the private Carriage House suites, you can luxuriate in a jetted tub or rent an old love story to watch together on the VCR.

◆ **Romantic Alternative:** Just a few doors closer to town, the HARTSTONE INN, 41 Elm Street (Route 1), Camden, (207) 236-4259, (Moderate), is equally charming, with stenciling, a fireplace in the parlor, four-poster Shaker beds, and antique accent pieces. Dinner is served only to guests.

CAMDEN HARBOUR INN, Camden
83 Bayview Street, (207) 236-4200
Expensive to Very Expensive

Heading north on Route 1, turn right onto Bayview Street. Head out of town for two long blocks past Wilson Street. The inn is on the right, across from Laite Memorial Beach Park.

Like a Victorian grande dame, this 1874 inn is refined and elegantly appointed, but also a bit reticent, at least until you're comfortable with each other. The decor is stalwart rather than dainty, with deep rich shades of plum, burgundy, and forest green, and solid wood furnishings built to last. Nine of the 22 rooms have fireplaces. Several rooms are grandly commodious and have partial harbor views; all are uniquely decorated. You may find a bed with a regally massive carved headboard or a canopy arching above trimmed with an ivory ruffle. Contemporary sofas ensure comfort as you sit by the fire and dream of an era forgotten in the bustle of city life.

EDGECOMBE-COLES HOUSE, Camden
64 High Street, (207) 236-2336
Moderate to Expensive

Going north on Route 1, the inn is seven-tenths of a mile past Camden center.

In this homespun hostelry, family photos crowd parlor tabletops and furnishings are more an eclectic collection of antiques than a determined decorating motif. Built as a summer residence in 1891, its slumping floors and dark Victorian furnishings feel their age but evoke the home's original personality. The inn's collections of Blue Willow china, stuffed animals, cross-stitch samplers, and antique toys are sure conversation-starters. In addition, a television, VCR, and paperbacks are available in the cozy firelit reading room and a grand piano invites maestros in the parlor. Because the building is set back from the Route 1, it is somewhat spared the traffic noise. You will barely notice the road as you gaze out at the water from the front-facing guest rooms.

HAWTHORN INN, Camden
9 High Street (Route 1), (207) 236-8842
Moderate to Expensive

Heading north on Route 1, go through the center of town and bear right. The inn is four houses past the library on the right.

You may feel a little like Romeo and Juliet as you lounge on the window seats in the turreted parlor of this 1894 Victorian. Outside, beyond the expansive lawn overlooking a partial harbor view, a secluded trail leads through a park, your secret pathway to romance. Inside, tapers enclosed in hurricane globes crown the mantel of the wood-burning fireplace. Vases of fresh flowers, Victorian love seats, accent pieces, and high-backed chairs fill the parlors and dining rooms, but an uncluttered, bright country feel reigns. If Romeo prefers old-fashioned charm in the bedchamber, the guest rooms of the main inn, with their white iron or four-poster canopy beds, patchwork quilts, and the occasional clawfoot tub (one is placed teasingly at the foot of the bed) will please him. If Juliet longs for more contemporary digs, choose the Carriage House. Broughman is especially spacious, with a deep oval jetted tub tucked beneath a skylight and a deck with a splendid harbor view where you can pledge your immortal love to each other.

INN AT SUNRISE POINT, Camden
Off Route 1, (207) 236-7716, (800) 23-SUNRISE
Very Expensive to Unbelievably Expensive (Open mid-May through October)

Drive four miles north of Camden center into Lincolnville on Route 1. Turn right at the Fire Road #9 sign (FR-9) and drive two-tenths of a mile down to the water.

Evenings bring moonbeams dancing on the waves and the glow of firelight from the hearth at this contemporary country inn, but daybreak is the big event here. Golden dawns rise over the slate blue ocean to bless the new day with rosy-cheeked warmt[h]. Even if you're not a morning person, the sunrise here is too precious to miss, especially since you only need turn your head on the pillow to drink in this unparalleled beauty.

One of Camden's newest places to stay, the Inn at Sunrise Point has the best location in the area, far removed from busy Route 1 on a secluded stretch of rocky shore. All public and guest rooms take full advantage of the location. Morning sun pours in through the wall of windows that front the spacious, firelit living room, which opens to the airy breakfast room, which, in turn, is crowned by a glass-domed conservatory. Just outside is the veranda and a lawn leading to the stony beach below the ridge. The library, where gourmet appetizers are served each evening, is sedate and gentlemanly, and especially cozy when the fire is lit after a brisk Maine afternoon.

Three guest rooms in the main inn are decorated in soothing shades of periwinkle, lavender, or sunny gold, with coordinating hearths, large modern baths, high cathedral ceilings, and comfortable sitting areas by the picture windows. Light pine cabinets hide the television and VCR, for which a selection of movies—romances and musicals—are provided. If you prefer absolute seclusion, two outlying cottages near the water ensure complete privacy (there are two new cottages that couldn't be reviewed before press time, but because they are farther away from the ocean, they're probably not as preferrable). One perches on the edge of the short cliff above the water; its beds are arranged so you can look at the sea, as well as the hearth, as you lie in each other's arms. The other is nested in the trees above the water, with a deck that's custom-made for lingering. Both cottages have deep oval Jacuzzis for a heartwarming soak when the sea grows cold. After an inspirational breakfast, yet another small pleasure awaits. As you get in your car, you'll find your windshield cleaned to perfection so you can fully enjoy the splendid scenery around you. It's the inn's way of bidding you bon voyage.

LODGE AT CAMDEN HILLS, Camden
Route 1, (207) 236-8478, (800) 832-7058
Moderate to Expensive

One mile north of Camden center.

If you're concerned that country inns are filled with too many frilly, precious amenities, this complex of Cape Cod-style shingled buildings is a refreshingly modern respite. Like a motor inn, each room has a private entrance, contemporary decor, television, small refrigerator, and instant hot water for morning coffee (packets provided). Suites are warmed by wood-burning fireplaces and boast kitchenettes where the restaurant-weary can create their own romantic dinner for two. Each unit also has a private back porch. Alas, the partial water view is across Route 1 and traffic noise precludes lingering, and there are no common rooms or breakfast to help you focus solely on each other.

MANSARD MANOR, Camden
5 High Street (Route 1), (207) 236-3291
Very Inexpensive to Moderate

A two-minute walk from the village, in the historic High Street District.

Not long ago, bed-and-breakfast inns were simple affairs, providing unpretentious hospitality, comfortable lodging, and decor just quaint enough to be a departure from home but homey, too. This graceful 1875 Victorian is as simply old-fashioned as the spinning wheel, skirted plaid sofa, and collection of Dedham pottery in its parlor. Guest rooms are cozy. You may find yourself peeking through eyelet curtains at the dawn in one or sleeping late in the brass and iron bed in another, with cheerful wall coverings lending a modest charm throughout. All rooms have private baths, although one is across the hall and others are squeezed into closets.

NUREMBEGA, Camden
61 High Street, (207) 236-4646
Expensive to Unbelievably Expensive

On Route 1, a half mile north of Camden center.

In 1886, a wealthy Maine inventor named Stearns toured the castles of Europe. From each, he chose a favorite feature—a turret here, an archway there—and combined them to create his own stone castle by the sea: Nurembega. This is Camden's Queen Mother, its grandest, most elegant palace. In the public rooms, rich, glowing woods are reminders of the days when local master craftsmen created the finest wooden ships in the world. Basket-weave marquetry highlights the parlor, while a magnificent carved hearth frames the immense ceramic tile fireplace in the dining room. Breakfasts and afternoon wine, cheese, and crudités are served here, though many guests retire to the grand patio on a warm afternoon to relish the magnificent bay view. Everything is on a grand scale, from the piano to the bountiful bouquets of flowers to the upstairs guest rooms, many with a heart-stopping view. High ceiling, a cozy window seat, candles topping a white-manteled wood-burning fireplace, a white-on-white embroidered comforter warming a white wicker king-size bed, sea blue carpet, a sitting area tucked into a box window, a clawfoot tub: all this is just one room. Kissing here is downright regal.

Restaurant Kissing

THE BELMONT, Camden
6 Belmont Avenue, (207) 236-8053, (800) 238-8053
Expensive

From Elm Street (which is Route 1 as it enters Camden from the south), turn onto School Street. After one block, this turns into Belmont Street. The restaurant is on your left after one more block.

This is one restaurant where you may enjoy waiting for a table. The parlor of this historic Edwardian, small but inviting, done up in an understated Victorian way, is where you can relax on a love seat with an aperitif or two. The dining rooms themselves, though architecturally intriguing, could use some panache and attention to detail in their decor. On the otherwise inviting enclosed porch, the potted geraniums on each table were gangly and had no blooms, and the massive kitchen doors in an inner room were all too intrusive. The creative cuisine, however, is impeccable. Even the pineapple chutney served with the tender Cornish game hen and delectable cornbread-raisin stuffing can make you sigh with appreciative delight.

CAMDEN DELI, Camden
37 Main Street, (207) 236-8343
Inexpensive

On Route 1 in town.

For a casual lunch with one of the best views in town, this unassuming but tremendously popular deli is a surprising find. More than 30 kinds of sandwiches will satisfy any appetite. Old-style counter service, the black-and-white tile floor, and a wall of wines add to the nostalgic air of this eatery. Enjoy your goodies on the bright, glassed-in porch cantilevered over the waterfall where the river plunges into the harbor, or, if crowds cram the deli, take out your picnic to the pleasant park around the corner, which has plenty of benches and an expansive lawn overlooking the harbor.

CASSOULET, Camden
31 Elm Street (Route 1), (207) 236-6304
Moderate

On Route 1 in town.

Unquestionably romantic, the Garden Room at this tiny bistro is open only in the growing season. Enjoy while you can the glassed-in greenhouse encompassing small candlelit tables set with soft rose cloths and muted green napkins beneath a ceiling of hanging plants and softly blowing fans. Happily the cozy inner dining room is open year-round. A French country ambience flows throughout, as diners tackle the lusty French cuisine. Cassoulet, a hearty casserole of beans, lamb, pork, and homemade garlic sausage, is their trademark dish, but you also can savor the broiled salmon en croûte, cannelloni verdi, and bouillabaisse. Desserts are homemade and equally luscious.

WATERFRONT RESTAURANT, Camden
Bayview Street, (207) 236-3747
Moderate

Right on the waterfront.

Lunch at this harborside restaurant is akin to dining on your own private yacht, tied up in scenic Camden Harbor. The patio cantilevered over the water is literally dockside: diners seated on one side of the wooden planking, boats tied up to the other. Reasonably priced, creative sandwiches (the grilled vegetable grinder and the smoked turkey with asparagus on six-grain bread were our favorites) come with a zesty gazpacho, cucumber salad, or fries. In the evening, old ship lanterns lend a refined nautical tone that sets off the hand-hewn beams and rough wood walls in the main dining room. Local seafood is the specialty, with steak and chicken for landlubbers. On most days, especially when the summer sun glints on the great wooden masts of the windjammers harbored here, the view will make your hearts set sail.

Outdoor Kissing

MOUNT MEGUNTICOOK
Camden Hills State Park

Head north out of Camden center on Route 1. The entrance to the park is on your left shortly after the Lodge at Camden Hills. The trail to the summit starts past the pay station (where you can pick up a trail map) and continues through the campground.

Bring sturdy hiking boots and a hardy spirit for this climb through forests, past streams, and over boulders. You may wonder if it's worth it, especially on a hot, humid summer day. It is. The view from the bald table of rock at the crest of the trail is spectacular on a clear day. From here, you get a true sense of the rugged Maine coast, with Camden nestled like a toy village in the palm of a natural, tree-lined harbor. Beyond, the Atlantic stretches dreamily to the horizon. You'll likely be alone up here, or you can easily find a secluded kissing spot amongst the boulders for that top-of-the-world feeling you can experience only with each other.

◆ **Romantic Alternative:** Driving to the summit of **MOUNT BATTIE** is the easy way up. Although the view is not as spectacular as the one from Mount Megunticook, you'd only know this if you did the climb. It's still splendid. Not surprisingly, it's also crowded.

Lincolnville

Restaurant Kissing

THE YOUNGTOWN INN, Lincolnville
Route 52 (Youngtown Road), (207) 763-4290
Moderate

Just north of Camden's main business district, turn left off Route 1 onto Mountain Road (Route 52) and drive four miles to Youngtown Road.

For more than seven generations, this classic New England farmhouse was home to a poultry and dairy farming family. Without a doubt, its kitchen had a heritage of fresh, wholesome cooking. It's only fitting that it now houses a restaurant, albeit one with a French accent. The decor is unfussy but refined, with white linens, brass oil lamps, and flowers on the tables. A wood stove provides the heat in the main dining room, a fireplace warms a more intimate space, while an enclosed patio offers a pleasant respite on a summer evening. A blend of local delicacies and French specialties fills the menu, from crab cakes to boeuf bourguignon en croûte. The cocoa soufflé is a sweet ending to your French interlude.

◆ **Romantic Note:** You'll find bright, uncluttered rooms upstairs, ranging from spacious to small, highlighted by stenciled borders, brass beds, and braided rugs on hardwood floors. The six rooms share three baths and include a full French breakfast.

Castine

Casting for charm and tranquillity? Castine is a prize catch. This quiet hamlet has just the right bounty of natural beauty, architectural charm, interesting handicraft boutiques, and welcoming inns. Amble down to the harbor and you may find a windjammer calling in port or the 13,300-ton *State of Maine*, a cruise ship turned Korean War troop transport turned teaching vessel for the Maine Maritime Academy. Castine is a place for quiet strolling, window shopping, and simply relaxing.

Hotel/Bed and Breakfast Kissing

CASTINE COTTAGES, Castine
P.O. Box 224, (207) 326-8003
$400 per week

Overlooking the water on Route 166, a couple of miles from downtown Castine.

These six storybook cottages form their own little neighborhood, with a new group of couples, families, and their dogs each week. Nothing fancy here: a tiny kitchen, a knotty pine-paneled living room with wood stove, comfortable, well-used furnishings, and two bedrooms, one with twins, are all you'll find. So why do couples return every year for a romantic getaway? Location. The cabins are set back from the road, perched high on a ridge with an angel's viewpoint of the saltwater cove far below. Pour two tall lemonades and while away an afternoon together on the screened-in porch and you'll feel you've found your own piece of heaven.

CASTINE INN, Castine
Main Street, (207) 326-4365
Inexpensive to Moderate (inn), Moderate (dining)
(Open May through October)

Call for directions.

Dinner here is akin to leaping, Mary Poppins-style, into a painting of the quintessential Maine coastal village. All around you are trompe l'oeil murals of an ideal town of steepled churches and orderly Colonial homes shaded by birches and oaks. The town is Castine, and you may well see the real-life models when you enjoy an evening constitutional after dinner. The traditional flavors of Maine will titillate your taste buds as well, with lobster, crab cakes, and seafood classics supplemented by such specialties as prime rib, New England boiled dinner, and pork loin with barbecue sauce. Desserts, from the caramelized apple tart to the chocolate bread pudding to the rhubarb crisp, are all in keeping with the spirit of the setting.

Upstairs, the inn, really a small hotel, has been welcoming overnight guests since 1898. Guest rooms are tidy and comfortably furnished, with a smattering of antiques, beds dressed in white woven spreads, and some water views, especially from the third floor. The fireplace-warmed parlor and cozy Colonial tavern invite late-night snuggling, but, of course, are also open to patrons of the inn's popular restaurant. At your leisure, head outside to the colorful garden and just sit and relax for a spell, breathing in the salty Maine air and your love for each other.

THE PENTAGOET INN, Castine
Main Street, (207) 326-8616, (800) 845-1701
Expensive (MAP only) (Open May through October)

On the corner of Main and Perkins streets.

Chamber music plays in the parlor as guests gather for the innkeeper's reception. Some enjoy the carrot pâté, crudités, and crackers, others sip a cocktail or glass of wine, as the soothing melodies fill this stylish Victorian home with a pastel tranquillity. More than a night's lodging and a four-course gourmet dinner, the Pantagoet offers an experience you'll long remember, whether you find yourself enjoying a pianist, wine tasting, storyteller, or murder mystery. The decor alone is heartwarming, enhancing an uncluttered, airy feel throughout. Lace curtains filter the sunlight streaming into the turret of one guest room; a huge brass bed promises nostalgic moments in another. Basins set in antique cabinets make in-room sinks a pleasure rather than an inconvenience, and a collection of beautiful pastel hand-hooked rugs adds a special flair to guest and common rooms.

In the evenings, the entertainment is just the appetizer for an intimate, candlelit dinner. Your meal may start with a chanterelle tart, followed by your choice of such entrées as boiled lobster, pork with pear puree, or Maine scallops with ginger and scallions. Next, European-style, a creative salad is served, then such luscious desserts as cappuccino layer cake or homemade vanilla ice cream with raspberry puree and Cassis. Breakfasts are equally indulgent, with your choice of cooked entrées. Standard muffins are banished, replaced with specials like warm blueberry cinnamon rolls.

Deer Isle

Hotel/Bed and Breakfast Kissing

PILGRIM'S INN, Deer Isle
Main Street, (207) 348-6615
Expensive (MAP), Expensive (restaurant)
(Open mid-May through mid-October)

Follow Route 15 South from Blue Hill into the town of Deer Isle.

As a fire blazes in the immense, eight-foot-wide brick hearth in the tavern downstairs, you can well imagine early "Americans" discussing their new nation over a mug of ale. Built in 1793, this rambling Colonial evokes that historic era as well as any inn in the state of Maine. Oddly angled rooms, antique beds, exposed timbers and beams, and sloping floors lend a nostalgic ambience, though the inn feels fresh and sprightly rather than weary after two centuries.

In the evening, after cocktails and hors d'oeuvres in the common room, a gourmet dining experience beckons you into the barn turned restaurant. A capacious wood stove warms the room. Straw mats blanket the floor. Rough, barn-wood walls are decorated with antique farm equipment. On the tables, stoneware pitchers clutch posies of wildflowers and brass lanterns flicker. Each night, a multicourse dinner is served, featuring such main dishes as marinated salmon, grilled lamb, catch of the day, and mixed grill, prepared with fresh vegetables and herbs, some grown out back. Beyond, a lawn slopes down to the mill pond, a scene—like the tiny town of Deer Isle—of timeless serenity where the pursuit of happiness is all but ensured.

Blue Hill

If you're questing for an unspoiled coastal Maine village but enjoy gourmet dinners, classic country inn lodgings, and first-class handicraft galleries, look no further than Blue Hill. This sleepy hamlet is perfect for dreaming of the past while you stroll by the more than 70 structures listed on the National Registry of Historic Buildings. Visit the small harborfront park for a picnic or a sunset kiss. At low tide, you can climb the ladder down to the beach and walk out to an egg-shaped rock for a secluded smooch, but be sure not to linger too long. At high tide, the rock becomes an island.

Hotel/Bed and Breakfast Kissing

BLUE HILL INN, Blue Hill   ❂❂❰
Route 177 (Union Street), (207) 374-2844
Moderate to Expensive

Follow Route 15 South toward Blue Hill and watch for the Blue Hill Inn sign. Follow the signs, which will take you to Route 177 East, where you will find the inn.

Welcoming guests since 1840, this stately, Federal-style Colonial evokes a timeless hospitality. In the evening, guests gather in the firelit parlor for wine and appetizers. The intimate dining room, lit only by candles, has a quintessential romantic glow throughout. The service was downright royal as we enjoyed a meal fit for a king, feasting on lobster bisque, caviar with tagliatelle, a grapefruit-Campari ice to clean the palate, lamb with a delectable wild mushroom fricassee, a tabouli salad, and a luscious pear tart with cinnamon whipped cream.

Guest rooms are modestly decorated with a select collection of vintage furnishings on original, wide-plank, pumpkin pine floors. Several are warmed by fireplaces, all have a private bath, but there's nary a television or telephone to be found. Instead, entertain yourselves with a swing in the hammock built for two, strung between apple trees in the inn's lovely garden, or go for a moonlit constitutional (the innkeeper provides flashlights) through the sleepy town to the beach to hear the water lap at the shore as it has, and will, for eternity.

Restaurant Kissing

FIREPOND RESTAURANT, Blue Hill
Main Street, (207) 374-2135
Expensive (Open May through October)

Call for directions.

The mill stream seems to gurgle with delight as it dances by, hemmed with a steep bank of wildflowers on one side and this enchanting restaurant on the other. In the evening, couples dine by candlelight on the enclosed patio, cantilevered over the happy waters. Candles set in brass holders flicker indoors as well, topping wood tables dressed with burgundy runners, glowing on the hardwood floors and exposed timbers and beams. In a third intimate dining area, a brick hearth chases away the Atlantic chill. Escargot, lobster ravioli, and baked Brie whet your appetite for such entrées as lamb with wild mushrooms, tournedos of beef, and lobster in a Boursin cream sauce served over pasta. The Firepond provides a fresh twist to romance down by the old mill stream.

JONATHAN'S RESTAURANT, Blue Hill
Main Street, (207) 374-5226
Moderate to Expensive

On Route 172 in the village of Blue Hill.

Maine meets the Mediterranean in this fresh, uncluttered restaurant known for its creative cookery. Perhaps you'll start with an antipasto of local foods, created especially for two. Or try the Greek spanakopita, or the baked salt cod with ouzo-soaked raisins, garlic, tomatoes, Calamata olives, and pine nuts. Sea-inspired specialties include ouzo-flamed shrimp over linguine, jambalaya, and seafood stew accented with Key lime juice, dark rum, sweet potatoes, hot and sweet peppers, and more. The wine list consistently wins top awards. The surroundings are as simple as the menu is seasoned. In the front room, overlooking Main Street, blue tablecloths, red napkins, and serene watercolors of boats add a refined nautical touch. In the back room, the emphasis is on light wood, from the candlelit tables to the Windsor chairs to the cathedral ceiling. For more than a memory, bring home the chef's cookbook, *Saltwater Seasonings*, to recreate your Mediterranean Maine interlude.

Bar Harbor

Hotel/Bed and Breakfast Kissing

BALANCE ROCK, Bar Harbor
21 Albert Meadow, (207) 288-9900, (800) 753-0494
Very Expensive to Unbelievably Expensive (Open May through October)

From Main Street, turn toward the water on Albert Meadow. The inn is at the end of the street on the right.

Wedgwood and sterling are *de rigueur* at the gourmet breakfast here, but that's just the splendid denouement to your indulgent stay in this 1903 mansion built by a railroad tycoon. Recently refurbished, this majestic "cottage" has been outfitted from head to toe with elegant furnishings and modern luxuries. You may find yourself bubbling away your cares in your jetted tub overlooking the ocean, warming up to each other in your private sauna, climbing up to your personal rooftop deck, or simply cuddling on the canopy bed or by the hearth. Each room's amenities are different, but all are lavish. Perhaps best of all, the splendid Shoreline Path, where couples have been strolling hand-in-hand in the moonlight for nearly a century, is just past the outdoor pool and across the rolling lawn.

BAR HARBOR INN, Bar Harbor
Newport Drive, (800) 248-3351
Moderate to Very Expensive (inn), Expensive (Reading Room),
Moderate (Terrace Grill)

From Main Street, head towards the water. The inn is on the right-hand side. Between Cottage and West streets.

Embrace on the private balcony of your room and you, too, will feel as though you have set sail. It's that close to the water (and to the public Shoreline Path). Recent refurbishments have created a comfortable, small luxury hotel ambience throughout. In the main inn, spacious deluxe rooms are replete with canopy beds and rich antique-reproduction furnishings with cabriole legs. In the aptly named Ocean Front, contemporary hotel decor is a pleasant departure from homey bed and breakfasts. A continental breakfast is included, served in the bright Ocean Front Lounge overlooking the bay. And if all that water looks inviting on a hot summer day, but its temperature is fit only for polar bears, indulge in a splash for two in the large outdoor swimming pool.

Perched above the harbor, the Reading Room restaurant enjoys a splendid view, unmatched by any other Down East dining establishment. Ruffled valances trim the tops of the windows that gracefully encircle the dining room, offering a more-than-180-degree panorama. Crystal chandeliers, sterling oil lamps, deep plum cloths offset by pink napkins, and fine china add elegance to the traditional continental menu of seafood and steaks. For a less formal feast, the outdoor Terrace Grill, just below the restaurant, is a delightful spot on a warm afternoon. Enjoy sandwiches, steak, or a full Maine lobster bake beneath its cheerful table umbrellas, while watching a four-masted schooner set sail from the adjoining dock.

BREAKWATER, Bar Harbor
45 Hancock Street, (207) 288-2313, (800) 238-6309
Expensive to Unbelievably Expensive (Closed Christmas week)

From Main Street, turn onto Hancock Street toward the water. Bear right at the fork to find the Breakwater.

As you stroll along the Shoreline Path, you will gasp with disbelief when you behold this overwhelmingly opulent mansion overlooking the bay. Surely a billionaire must live there, with a bevy of servants just to wash the plethora of multipaned windows. But the two of you can be Gatsby and Daisy for a night when you stay at this sprawling English Tudor. A remnant of Bar Harbor's old money (its creator was a ridiculously wealthy descendant of John Jacob Astor, no less), Breakwater is one of the last surviving Mount Desert "cottages" from the early 1900s, and was recently refurbished by modern-day millionaires.

In the afternoon, nibble "magical goodies" on the grand brick veranda. In the evening, toast your toes by the hearth in one of the six grand guest rooms. Mrs. Kane's Room (named after one of the original owners) is cavernous; an immense canopy bed is dwarfed in this bedchamber, which has spectacular ocean views. The walk-in closet alone encompasses six full-size closets. Feeling mischievous at midnight? In Mr. Kane's Room, you can sneak down a private secret staircase to the billiards room. Like the other common rooms, this masculine den is anything but common. You will be mesmerized by the unparalleled ocean view from the elegant parlor, with its box window seat and engraved tin ceiling. Or perhaps you'd care to sip tea in the majestic great room, with its 1918 Steinway. As you ascend the stone staircase, you'll pass the mezzanine where musicians played for the Kanes' grand balls. On the second floor, yet another parlor, with a gas fireplace, beckons. Outside, a kiss on the spacious patio, as dusk sends its rosy glow over the water and three-masted schooners sail past, is a golden moment you will treasure forever.

CASTLEMAINE INN, Bar Harbor
39 Holland Avenue, (207) 288-4563
Moderate to Expensive

In downtown Bar Harbor, between Mount Desert and West streets.

Like an old-fashioned rolltop desk, this rambling 1886 inn opens to reveal an eclectic array of odd-sized compartments, held together by polished, modest decor. A fireplace warms the homey parlor, while morning sun blazes into the breakfast room, although the view and noise of the downtown side street it overlooks are not conducive to lingering over the buffet of coffee cakes, breads, fruit, and scones. In the guest accommodations, four-poster and canopy beds invite nostalgic romance, while modern baths and televisions add contemporary comfort. In several rooms, including the long, narrow Honeymoon Suite, fireplaces thaw even the chilliest Maine evenings. If you prefer to awaken to the morning sun, choose a room on the upper floors, as the ground floor is at basement level and somewhat dark.

CLEFTSTONE MANOR, Bar Harbor
92 Eden Street (Route 3), (207) 288-4951, (800) 962-9762
Moderate to Expensive
Open May through October

Heading north on Route 3 from the village of Bar Harbor, look for the inn on the left, just outside of the downtown area.

Festive afternoon gatherings at this congenial inn soften an otherwise formal but unfussy British air. If you arrive in the late afternoon, you can hardly resist the company and cookies on the sunny porch, with its white wicker furnishings and lace curtains. In the evening, the cozy parlor, with its wood stove and tapestry settee, invites more intimate snuggling while you tip a glass or nibble on cheeses neatly laid out. When you retire to your bedchamber, you may find yourself inspired to poetry in the commodious Romeo and Juliet Suite, where a full lace canopy flows to each corner of your bed, casting passionate shadows by the light of the brick hearth. Sun lovers will bask in the Hampton Court Room, with its sunken sitting room framed in glass. The breakfast buffet, served in the dining room, its crystal chandeliers and baronial table flanked by high-backed royal chairs, ensures a grand start to a day by the seashore.

◆ **Romantic Warning:** Although the Cleftstone cleaves to a steep hillside above Route 3, traffic noise, especially during the day, distracts from the otherwise relaxing ambience.

GRAYCOTE INN, Bar Harbor
40 Holland Avenue, (207) 288-3044, (800) 472-2683
Inexpensive to Expensive

Take Route 3 into Bar Harbor. Turn left on Cottage Street, go two blocks to Holland Avenue, and turn right. The inn is on the left.

Perhaps you'll enjoy the evenings best at the Graycote Inn, when you can relax on the tapestried love seat in the refined but welcoming parlor, watching the firelight glow golden on the inn's fine collection of cranberry glass, Lladro porcelain, and Hummel figurines. Or mornings may win you over, when scrumptious breakfasts are served on the sun-soaked porch with its tables set for two. Every detail adds to the inn's elegant ambience, from the pink cloths and fresh flowers on the breakfast tables to the crystal chandelier in the dining room to the upright piano in the parlor. You'll be sleeping beneath a cloud of lace and cutwork canopy in eight of the 10 guest rooms. Several boast fireplaces and sun porches. While I found rooms in the main inn more charming, the two-bedroom Carriage House in back is serenely secluded, with a private entrance; the bed is tucked beneath a unique trellis canopy intertwined with silk ivy—your personal garden of Eden.

HEARTHSIDE, Bar Harbor
7 High Street, (207) 288-4533
Inexpensive to Moderate

Between Mount Desert and Cottage streets.

Sink into the ocean blue sofa and warm each other hearthside at this turn-of-the-century home turned country inn. A fireplace sends out a welcoming warmth in the pretty parlor, but you can also chase away the Atlantic chill in several of the nine guest rooms. Others, though heartless, are heartwarming in decor. In the Romeo and Juliet Suite, a tasseled canopy floats above the brass and white iron bed, its head- and footboards encompassing you with a graceful heart design. Rooms on the third floor are smaller, with eave ceilings, but charmingly cozy. Refreshments, from cookies in the afternoon to a full breakfast served in the dining room, are sure to invigorate you for making the most of your time Down East.

HEATHWOOD INN, Bar Harbor
Route 3, (207) 288-5591, (800) 582-3681
Inexpensive to Expensive

About six miles north of downtown Bar Harbor on Route 3.

As the last rays of daylight dance through the stained glass windows, it's time to light the candles, pour the champagne, and sink into the bubbly world of your Jacuzzi built for two. This is your private heaven, nestled in a cloud of white. Through lace-curtained French doors, the bridal chamber awaits. A crown canopy of peach satin rises above your pillow. From it flows a river of white lace, like an epic bridal train, enveloping the bed in a snowy embrace.

Create your own cloud as your temperatures rise in the steam showers built for two in each guest room (except for the whirlpooled Honeymoon Suite). You'll find a private sauna in one room, a corner hearth and private balcony in another, and cheerful decor, from music boxes to dolls to splendid plaster-work, throughout. Once an out-of-the-way farmhouse, this inn now boasts modern renovations and indulgences that would delight any weary farmer, or tourist, while retaining its simple charm.

MANOR HOUSE INN, Bar Harbor   ❖❖❖❨
106 West Street, (207) 288-3759, (800) 437-0088
Inexpensive to Expensive (Closed mid-November through mid-April)

Call for directions.

More than just the period antiques and architecture of this beautifully restored 1887 mansion preserves the Victorian era at its finest. At the Manor House Inn, you can easily experience the time when wealthy New Englanders flocked to Bar Harbor for the ultimate romantic getaway by the sea. Robust paisley and floral wall coverings, vintage furnishings, soaring ceilings, a grand piano, Oriental rugs on polished hardwood floors, and fringed lamps set the scene in the common rooms. Fireplaces warm the foyer and both parlors. Yet the inn is more welcoming than overwhelming, with regally carved wooden beds harbored in cheerful, cozy guest rooms. The Chauffeur's Cottage, set back from the inn, offers the utmost in privacy, and the Honeymoon Suite, with its skylighted, sloping ceiling, wood stove in the living room, and private balcony in the treetops, is the perfect place to contemplate nearby Acadia's timeless riches.

MIRA MONTE INN, Bar Harbor   ❖❖
69 Mount Desert Street, (207) 288-4263, (800) 553-5109
Inexpensive to Expensive (Open May through October)

Route 3 turns into Mount Desert Street at a stop sign in Bar Harbor. Turn left there; the inn is on the left.

During the warmer months, the flowers in the side yard of the Mira Monte burst with such color, vibrancy, and abundance that they can't help but find their way into vases in almost all the inn's rooms. In some rooms, you may be inspired to embrace on your private, wrought-iron balcony overlooking the garden below.

Built in 1864, the inn combines homespun character and Victorian flair, although televisions and telephones have invaded the guest rooms. Wood stoves in some guest rooms inspire more old-fashioned entertainment.

◆ **Romantic Warning:** Several inns line both sides of Mount Desert Street, plus traffic is busy on this small town's main route, especially during the day.

Restaurant Kissing

THE CARRYING PLACE, Bar Harbor   ◆◆◀
130 Cottage Street, (207) 288-8905
Moderate

Near the intersection of Route 3 and Cottage Street.

Sometimes food, like love, is best when it's simple, creative, and happily self-indulgent. This is the philosophy of the Carrying Place, a cozy home converted into two intimate dining rooms. Although the menu boasts such well-bred specialties as crabmeat bisque, lobster with curried cream sauce in puff pastry, beef Wellington, and sweetbreads bagaduce, the decor is refreshingly unpretentious. Cheerful, veggie-motif watercolors painted by the owner set the mood, along with light wood chairs and tables, blueberry-patterned china, fresh flowers, and votive candles in frosted glass bowls. For dessert, try the tira misu—"lift me up"—cake and you will certainly rise to a happy ending.

THE FIN BACK, Bar Harbor   ◆◆
78 West Street, (207) 288-4193
Expensive

Call for directions.

Sculpted neon lights swirl like modernistic waves on the ceiling of this tiny, cosmopolitan bistro where jazz sets the tone at tables for two with bright, rosy floral cloths and white wooden chairs. Local ingredients and creativity are the hallmarks of the menu, with such specialties as Maine crab quesadillas, lamb with curry sauce and Maine blueberry chutney, and lobster served over tangy peppercorn pasta. Wild mushroom raviolis, pork medallions with mango-shallot sauce, and chicken with tarragon-pecan pesto will delight those searching for exotica in traditional Maine.

GEORGE'S, Bar Harbor   ◆◆◆
7 Stephens Lane, (207) 288-4505
Expensive (Open mid-June through October)

Call for directions.

Fine restaurants, like romance, can be elegant without being overblown, pampering without being pretentious. George's satisfies your appetite for exceptional cuisine in a refined, yet comfortable, atmosphere. Set in a charming older home, the intimate dining rooms are simply decorated with wooden chairs, pink linens, votive candles in fluted glass holders, and fresh blooms in bud vases. In season, and on busier nights out of season, you'll woo each other to live piano music while enjoying such specialties as shrimp ravioli, lobster strudel, paella, and a different lamb dish each night. Luscious desserts, such as their Mississippi mud cake and macadamia-and-chocolate ice cream bombe, prove that fine dining, like romance, can be deliciously indulgent.

MAMA DI MATTEO'S, Bar Harbor
34 Kennebec Street, (207) 288-3666
Moderate

At the corner of Kennebec and Rodick streets.

As fun and festive as a glass of Chianti, this cozy bistro is a slice of old-world Italy, where passion and laughter are celebrated, not censored. Lacquered wooden booths are topped with al fresco-style umbrellas advertising wine, as though a street in Rome had been transported inside. Hanging plants add to the feeling, while oil lamps flickering in etched glass globes lend a touch of class. The meals are casual and delicious, beginning with a variety of breads served with pesto butter and a tomato-onion relish. Entrées such as pesto and crab pasta, baked sausage and peppers, and grilled shrimp and prosciutto are supplemented with fresh seafood dishes. For a surprising departure from the ordinary, try the best apple-smoked baby back ribs on the Maine coast. *Buon apetito!*

THE PORCUPINE GRILL, Bar Harbor
123 Cottage Street, (207) 288-3884
Expensive

Near the intersection of Route 3 and Cottage Street.

Intimate dining rooms are joined like pearls on a necklace in this converted home. Downstairs, the front room looks onto Cottage Street, while an inner room is divided into private areas by leaded glass partitions. Upstairs, rooms are so intimate that each encircles just a single table, as though reserved for your private party for two. Muted neutral tones, wood tables, candles, and fresh flowers create an understated elegance throughout. You may want to begin your dinner with a warm Camembert and lobster salad appetizer made for two. Seasonal specialties could include lamb chops with black olive-cabernet sauce, salmon with a dill vinaigrette, or lobster with a crabmeat and tarragon stuffing.

NATALIE TODD, Bar Harbor   ◆◆◆
Sails from the Bar Harbor Inn pier, (207) 288-4585 (summer),
(207) 546-2927 (winter)
$17.50 per person

Call for directions.

We hauled the red sails high into the blue sky. With the breeze's caress and
a salt-sprayed kiss, we were off for an afternoon of romance on the sapphire sea.
Grand sailing ships restored to their original luster still ply the waters of
Frenchman's Bay, and the grandest of the day sailers is the *Natalie Todd*. With
three towering masts and six billowing sails, this wooden schooner stretches
more than 100 feet. Even with a full complement of passengers aboard, you'll
still find plenty of room to walk about or to find your own niche for two. Bring
along a picnic, if you like, for your two-hour cruise, or just enjoy the view of
the rugged Acadian coast from the open water and keep an eye out for seals and
porpoises. Remember, this is a sailing vessel, subject to the whims of the
weather. Bring along warm clothing and sunblock.

◆   **Romantic Alternative:** Several sailing ships offer two-hour cruises
along the Maine coast, especially out of Bar Harbor and Camden, ranging from
comparatively small six-passenger Friendship sloops to two-masted schooners.
Most have tables set up at the harbors for making reservations.

Outdoor Kissing

SHORELINE PATH, Bar Harbor

Begins at the Bar Harbor Inn and heads away from downtown.

As dusk casts its rosy mist across the sky and the full moon rises for its nightly
waltz on the waters, you can almost hear the sea breezes whisper of bygone
couples strolling hand-in-hand along its shore, once upon a time in bustled
skirts and top hats, today in slacks and wool sweaters. Since the turn of the
century, the residents of homes set back from this path have realized that the
beauty of this shoreline should be shared by all and have sacrificed (willingly
and unwillingly) a bit of their privacy for the lovers and friends who find
serenity here. By daylight or moonglow, a stroll overlooking the waves lapping
at the rocky coast, the wooded Porcupine Islands, and the vast blueness beyond
will remind you why the Maine coast holds a timeless romance.

Mount Desert Island

Restaurant Kissing

JORDAN POND HOUSE
Acadia National Park, (207) 276-3316
Moderate

Call for directions.

In the 1880s, couples came to the Jordan Pond House to linger over a cup of tea, stroll along the shore of the pond, and, perhaps, to be inspired to poetry by the serenity that surrounded them. Today, the splendid setting is the same, only you may be the one composing odes to your love. Sturdy wooden tables and chairs are set on the expansive lawn that flows downward to the shore. Beyond the sapphire pond rise the sensuously rounded twin summits of the "Bubbles." For $5 each, you can enjoy tea and popovers. Those with a hearty hiker's appetite can enjoy crabmeat quiche, curried chicken salad, or steamed lobster. Tall windows bring the outside into the contemporary restaurant, with its pale wood tables, Windsor chairs, fieldstone hearth, and framed art displayed, gallery-style, on the light-hued walls.

◆ **Romantic Note:** Even if you don't come for tea, come for the scenery. Just settle on the lawn for some old-fashioned courting.

Outdoor Kissing

ACADIA NATIONAL PARK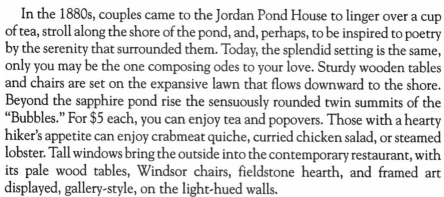
Mount Desert Island, (207) 288-3338
The Visitors Center is located on Route 3, three miles north of Bar Harbor.

It is a joining of sea with mountain, sun with fog, man with nature, lovers with romance. This is Acadia, not a land of grandeur and spectacle, but a place of rugged yet serene beauty. The natural attributes of this splendid preserve are the primary attraction of Maine's Down East coast. Carriage trails, created by John D. Rockefeller between 1915 and 1933, wind through the forest, offering some 50 miles of hiking and mountain biking, but many of Acadia's most romantic sites are easily accessible by automobile.

The one-way **PARK LOOP ROAD** along Acadia's Atlantic shore is one of Maine's most inspiring drives, especially when sunset paints the sky in roses and golds, silhouetting points of pine forest jutting into the water. Pause at the **ACADIA WILD GARDEN** and stroll through a microcosm of Mount

Desert's botanical diversity. Every month of the growing season showcases a unique bouquet of blooms. South of Southwest Harbor, in another section of the park, picnic tables are perched along the water and sheltered in shoreline forest at the **SEAWALL**. Just beyond, the **SHIP HARBOR NATURE TRAIL** is a delightful, easy stroll that passes through woodland carpeted with wildflowers, across brushy meadow, and along the rocky shore.

On a clear day, the summit of **CADILLAC MOUNTAIN** seems on a parallel with heaven, overlooking the vast panorama of Maine's rugged coast, with a bevy of green islands set like emeralds in the deep blue velvet of the Atlantic far below. The horizon stretches as far and as deep and as wide as your love for each other as you share this magical moment.

Northeast Harbor

Hotel/Bed and Breakfast Kissing

ASTICOU INN, Northeast Harbor
Route 198, (207) 276-3344
Very Expensive to Unbelievably Expensive, Very Inexpensive to Moderate (B&B only off-season), (Open April 1 through January 1)

On Route 198, near its intersection with Route 3.

"Same time, next year" may well be the motto of the Asticou, whose well-heeled patrons feel no need to look elsewhere for their annual sojourns on Mount Desert Island. Established in 1883, the Asticou is a grand old dame, stately and refined but somewhat tired. The array of accommodations ranges from standard rooms in the main inn to apartment-size suites in adjacent inn-style buildings to rounded "Topsider" cabins. All share a splendid location, overlooking picturesque Northeast Harbor and its bevy of boats. You can warm your toes by the hearths in the lobby and the reading room, or bask in the sun on the deck overlooking the outdoor pool and horseshoe-shaped harbor. Sadly, the fireplaces in several guest rooms no longer work.

Anchored in tradition, the main dining room is one of the few places on the coast to require a jacket and tie. A proper continental dinner is served by the glow of brass chandeliers on golden walls decorated with Oriental-motif murals, a touch of class in an otherwise worn setting.

HARBOURSIDE INN, Northeast Harbor
Route 198, (207) 276-3272
Inexpensive to Expensive (Open mid-June through mid-September)

On Route 198, before entering the town of Northeast Harbor.

We sat by the blazing fire in the cool Atlantic evening, sinking into the wing chairs, one for each of us, placed toe-toastingly close to the hearth, and settled in for a quiet night together, reading, talking, and simply enjoying the peace. A vase of prize-winning purple cosmos sat on the table, another filled with white carnations and daises topped the bureau, while a fountain of evergreen branches decorated the mantel—all in one guest room. As the fire dimmed, it flickered on the intricate brass and iron bed, setting a warm stage for a soothing slumber.

We weren't the first couple to be reminded that old-fashioned pleasures are sometimes the best (nor will we be the last). Since 1888, the Harbourside Inn has been providing guests with solitude. You won't find flouncy inn decor here, but you will find working fireplaces in all first- and second-floor rooms (except one), spacious suites with wonderful enclosed porches in the treetops, and select antiques such as a birchbark log holder made by local Indians or a Wallace Nutting canopy bed. You won't find a television or telephone anywhere. The original bathrooms with their grand marble sinks and unique century-old stoppers are still in working order. In the morning, fresh-baked blueberry muffins and tea provide a warm start to an invigorating day of exploring Acadia. Hiking trails begin just behind the inn.

THE MAISON SUISSE INN, Northeast Harbor
Main Street, (207) 276-5223, (800) MAISON-8
Moderate to Expensive (Open May through October)

Call for directions.

A delightful informal garden beckons you to follow its path from Main Street to the front porch of this late-19th-century Shingle-style home. It is a legacy of the original owner, who hoped to transplant a little of the beauty of his Swiss homeland. Inside, a gracious home awaits. The decor is charming but unfussy, with white ruffled canopy beds, wicker chairs, grand armoires, and the occasional private porch. A corner hearth warms one two-bedroom suite, and fireplaces flicker in the living room and den. You may even want to tickle the ivories of the upright, or simply sit together on the porch to enjoy a quiet summer evening while watching Main Street slumber. Breakfast is included with the room, but is ordered from the menu and served at the diner across the street.

◆ **Romantic Note:** Babies stay free at Maison Suisse—a benefit for those who can't get a sitter but still need a romantic getaway, but not so welcome for others.

◆ **Romantic Suggestion:** Try **REDFIELD'S,** Main Street, Northeast Harbor, (207) 276-5283, (Moderate to Expensive), for superb cuisine in a casually elegant, upbeat atmosphere. The clam chowder, filled with a variety of fresh herbs, is extremely popular; and creative entrées like fillet of salmon with a horseradish-raspberry chantilly, and loin of lamb with a hazelnut crust, illustrate the efforts made at this new restaurant. Try the orange sambuca sorbet for a light but satisfying dessert. Be forewarned, this place is very popular; at times, reservations need to be made up to a month in advance!

Outdoor Kissing

THUYA GARDEN, Northeast Harbor
Asticou Terraces, (207) 276-5130

Park in the small lot just north of the Asticou Inn along Route 198. Cross the road and climb the terraces up the hillside to the formal gardens.

Stepping through the garden gates here is like crossing over the rainbow. Suddenly, a kaleidoscope of color greets you, a startling contrast to Maine's forest greens, stone grays, and ocean blues. Bridal white lilies, colorful cosmos, and other bright annuals and perennials nearly burst from beds that hem the velvety green lawns. Benches and stones beckon you to linger together in the beauty, sharing a sweet-scented moment that, like a flower, can bloom in your memory for years to come.

◆ **Romantic Alternative:** The **ASTICOU AZALEA GARDEN** is just down the road. Walk or drive past the Asticou Inn, turn right on Route 3, and turn immediately right into the parking lot. It's particularly stunning during the June azalea season, but other seasons have their own colorful glory as well. A Japanese atmosphere prevails: stroll down the sandy path, crossing streams and skirting a reflecting pond, or pause to contemplate the soothing design of the dry garden, with patterns raked into fine gravel.

Southwest Harbor

Hotel/Bed and Breakfast Kissing

THE KINGSLEIGH INN, Southwest Harbor
100 Main Street, (207) 244-5302
Moderate to Expensive

From Route 3, take Route 102 to Southwest Harbor. The inn is just past the center of town, to the left.

Just as ancient mariners found their way by the stars, you can search the night sky for your destiny together if you share a special occasion in this inn's third-floor suite. A telescope in the Victorian turret sitting area gives you a captain's-eye view of the celestial canopy, as well as a peek at ancient-looking mariners chugging into the working harbor below with their daily catch. Daydreamers may prefer the cozy second-floor guest room, where your pillow affords a harbor view. Brass and iron beds, balloon valances over lace curtains, a wood-burning fireplace in the parlor, and a wraparound veranda all lend charm to this homey hostelry. The inn is just a lobster's crawl from the small town center and lobster pound, which makes it convenient but subject to traffic noise. Also, views from many of the inn's windows are obstructed by a cluster of homes.

"... then I did the simplest thing in the world. I leaned down ... and kissed him. And the world cracked open."

Agnes de Mille

INDEX